1,000,000 Delinquents

1,000,000 DELINQUENTS

BY BENJAMIN FINE

EDUCATION EDITOR, *The New York Times*

CLEVELAND AND NEW YORK

THE WORLD PUBLISHING COMPANY

Library of Congress Catalog Card Number: 55-5282

FIRST EDITION

H C 355

TO MY WIFE

Lillian

WITH EVER-INCREASING
AFFECTION AND ADMIRATION

FOREWORD

When President Dwight D. Eisenhower, in his message to Congress on January 17, 1955, called for $3,000,000 with which to attack the problem of juvenile delinquency, he focused attention on this major American problem. This was by all odds the most important recognition of the delinquency menace that has ever been made in the United States. The 1954 budget, in contrast, contained the item of $75,000 for reviewing the question of juvenile delinquency. Here, indeed, is dramatic evidence that finally the people of this country have awakened to the need for a concerted campaign to help our troubled boys and girls.

On Independence Day in the year 1953, some twelve thousand teachers assembled in the civic auditorium of Miami Beach to discuss major educational problems. This was the annual convention of the National Education Association, and the teachers, coming from all parts of the country, represented the more than one million educators of the land.

As a newspaper correspondent I listened with that half-ear that one assumes after hearing addresses at similar assemblies year after year without end. But suddenly the United States Attorney General, Herbert Brownell, Jr., said something that made all of us in the large hall sit up in haste. Within the coming year, he predicted, one million boys and girls would get into trouble serious enough to be picked up by the police.

That was the start of a year-long study that took me into many byways and away from charted paths. It was incredible to think that this country, great and prosperous, at its peak in power, at its height in world fame and prestige, at its greatest in fulfilling the democratic traditions, could have failed its youth in this way. I had hoped, frankly, that the Attorney General had used the speaker's prerogative to shock his audience through exaggeration. But even half a million delinquents would be bad enough, I thought, as I began my research into this field.

I found that Mr. Brownell did not go out on a limb. Indeed, he did not go far enough. Because in the year 1955 we will have more than one million juvenile delinquents. All the evidence suggests that we are on a tragic upswing. Informed authorities predict that by 1960—less than five years away—the juvenile delinquency rate will go to two million.

There are two ways to get the material for any report or survey. You can send out a questionnaire, and then tabulate the results; or you can do an on-the-spot, firsthand study of the situation itself. I did both. I sent out several hundred questionnaires to school superintendents, college officials, psychologists, psychiatrists, social workers, judges, and government officials interested in this field. That gave me a detailed view of the general problem of delinquency.

But that was just the beginning, a prelude, as it were, to the question of juvenile delinquency itself. I found soon enough that to get to the bottom of the problem, I would need more than cold figures or data. Unfortunately, a boy or girl in trouble is not a statistic but an individual. I visited with school people; I went to the training schools to see the "bad" boys and girls at work and play; I interviewed crime commissioners, youth boards, school authorities, parole workers, and children's court judges.

I was "judge" for a day at the children's court in Brooklyn where I sat with Judge Nathaniel Kaplan, who was on the bench. I listened to him as he talked to fifty or more delinquents, their parents, their relatives, and their case workers. It was a heartbreaking experience, but one that brought me more insight and understanding than a carload of questionnaires ever could.

I talked to juvenile delinquents in public and private training schools, in the courtrooms, and in their own backyards. In each case, I found that these young boys and girls had a story to tell. Each had a reason for his or her own falling-out with society. That is when I found that there is no delinquent boy—only an emotionally disturbed child . . . there is no "bad" girl—only an unhappy one.

This book is the product of this firsthand experience with boys and girls that society calls delinquent. I have included many of their stories, written or spoken to me over the course of the past year. I found that the boys and girls were eager to talk, were ready to put down on paper what was uppermost in their minds. What I found was startling. For, from these troubled children came the most enlightening insight into delinquency that I found anywhere.

In addition, I read the more significant pamphlets, studies, reports, surveys, and documents that have been written about delinquency in recent years. The various state reports, the report of the Senate Subcommittee to Investigate Juvenile Delinquency, headed by former Senator Robert C. Hendrickson of New Jersey, and the endless stream of newspaper stories—all helped to give me a broad picture of juvenile delinquency in the United States at mid-twentieth century.

I have tried, as a reporter, to get the facts, and then to present them in as unbiased and honest a fashion as is humanly possible. I have tried, also, to interpret these facts.

Throughout I have had but one thought—to be both constructive and frank. I believe, as so many of the boys and girls in training schools or awaiting trial in sordid detention rooms told me, that these youngsters want to be helped. I do not believe that they are bad or vicious or dangerous or thrill-killers because they want to be that way. They are usually caught in a web of circumstances, beyond their control. Many have already shown that they can be helped. They need the help and guidance that we have the power to give them.

The community, working together, can slow down the rate of delinquency, and thus eliminate the tragedies that go with one million disturbed, troubled, police-recorded boys and girls.

I have confidence in our democratic way of life. Working within our democratic traditions and principles, we can provide a decent childhood and a sound background for *all* of our children.

I believe that it can be done.

Benjamin Fine

February 1, 1955
New York, N. Y.

ACKNOWLEDGMENTS

I wish to acknowledge my indebtedness to the many individuals and organizations whose assistance and advice I have received in learning the story of the one million delinquent boys and girls. Unfortunately, it is impossible to list all of them, but I would especially like to thank the following for their co-operation:

The Senate Judiciary Subcommitte to Investigate Juvenile Delinquency.

Herschel Alt, Executive Director, Jewish Board of Guardians, New York City.

Bertram M. Beck, Director, Special Juvenile Delinquency Project, Children's Bureau, Department of Health, Education and Welfare.

Dr. George C. Boone, Assistant Superintendent of Schools and Director of the Passaic Children's Bureau, Passaic, New Jersey.

A. Alfred Cohen, Superintendent, New York State Training School for Boys, Warwick, New York.

Frederic A. Fitch, Superintendent, New York State Home for Boys, Jamesburg, New Jersey.

Herman D. Hillman, Director, New York Field Office, Public Housing Administration, New York City.

Judge Nathaniel Kaplan, Chairman, New York City Youth Board, and members of the Youth Board staff.

Anna M. Kross, Commissioner, Department of Correction, New York City.

Dr. Bernard Lander, Director, Graduate School, Yeshiva University, New York City.

Judge Samuel S. Leibowitz, Kings County Court, New York.

Douglas H. MacNeil, Chief, Bureau of Community Services, Department of Institutions and Agencies, State of New Jersey.

Abraham G. Novick, Superintendent, New York State Training School for Girls, Hudson, New York.

Dr. Joseph F. Phelan, Jr., Administrator, Children's Village, Dobbs Ferry-on-Hudson, New York.

Charles Plotkin, Assistant to the Director, New York Field Office, Public Housing Administration, New York City.

Mark C. Roser, Gary Public Schools, Gary, Indiana.

Charles E. Slusser, Commissioner, Public Housing Administration, Washington, D. C.

Floyd Starr, Founder and President, Starr Commonwealth for Boys, Albion, Michigan.

Judge Fred G. Stickel, Commissioner, Housing Authority, City of Newark, New Jersey.

Robert C. Taber, Director, Division of Pupil Personnel and Counseling, Board of Public Education, Philadelphia.

Allen M. Thomas, Executive Director, Graham School, Hastings-on-Hudson, New York.

Dr. William W. Wattenberg, Professor of Educational Psychology, Wayne University, Detroit, Michigan.

I would also like to thank the following authors and publishers:

Columbia University Press, for permission to quote from *A Court for Children* by Alfred J. Kahn, copyright 1953; and from *An Experiment in the Prevention of Delinquency* by Edwin Powers and Helen Witmer, copyright 1951.

Harcourt, Brace and Company, Inc., for permission to quote from *The Cocktail Party* by T. S. Eliot, copyright 1954.

Harvard University Press, for permission to quote from *Unraveling Juvenile Delinquency* by Sheldon and Eleanor Glueck, copyright 1950 by The Commonwealth Fund.

Alfred A. Knopf, Inc., for permission to quote from *The Juvenile in Delinquent Society* by Milton L. Barron, copyright 1954.

McGraw-Hill Book Company, Inc., for permission to quote from *Social Treatment in Probation and Delinquency* (2nd ed.) by Pauline V. Young, copyright 1952.

Meredith Publishing Company, for permission to quote Dr. James C. Moloney from "Is Your Wife Too Civilized?" by Walter Adams, in *Better Homes & Gardens* (November, 1949), copyright 1949.

National Education Association of the United States, Research Division, for permission to quote from the *Research Bulletin* (October, 1953), copyright 1953.

New York City Youth Board, for permission to quote from *Reaching Teen-Agers* (Monograph No. 1), copyright 1954; and from *Reaching the Unreached* edited by Sylvan S. Furman, copyright 1952.

The Public Affairs Committee, Incorporated, for permission to quote from *Children in Court* (Public Affairs Pamphlet No. 207) by Helen W. Puner, copyright 1954.

Syracuse University, for permission to quote from "Juvenile Delinquency" by John Edgar Hoover, in *The Syracuse Law Review* (Spring, 1953), copyright 1953.

Yale University Press, for permission to quote from *New Light on Delinquency and Its Treatment* by William Healy and Augusta Bronner, copyright 1936; and from *The Criminal and His Victim* by Hans von Hentig, copyright 1948.

I am sorry it is not possible for me to acknowledge specifically all the printed material, from organizations and public agencies, to which I referred, for without this material I could not have obtained a comprehensive knowledge of the juvenile delinquency problem.

I wish to thank Dr. Morris Goodman of the New York City public schools, who read copy and helped edit the manuscript, and Kendall Smith for aid in research.

For valuable insight and judgment in gathering and the preparation of material, I accord special acknowledgment to Maxine and Hubert Davis.

I also want to express appreciation to my wife, Lillian, for the devotion and understanding that contributed so much to the completion of this book.

Contents

1,000,000 Delinquents

1. Headlines and Facts

*"Last night was a supreme
adventure for me."*

Kill for Thrills, Whipped Girls, the headlines said.

Two Teen Thrill Killings Climax City Park Orgies.

Another headline screamed:

DA Hunts More Victims of 'Kill-for-Thrill' Gang.

Still another headline shouted: Brutal Slaying by Three Youths Baffles Everyone Involved.

And yet another New York City paper put on its front page this headline, Teen-Aged Killers Pose a Mystery. Why Did They Do It? Police Wonder. And the story followed: "A baffled district attorney asked for and received yesterday ten days in which to study the habits and home lives of four Brooklyn teen-agers in his search for some reason for their apparently senseless rampage of beatings and murder."

The four boys, between the ages of fifteen and eighteen, themselves appeared unmoved, almost indifferent. Police and prosecutors could recall no case to match the wanton brutality described by the four youths themselves. Their parents were shocked and disbelieving at the picture of the four stalking their victims in the shadow of the Williamsburg Bridge connecting Brooklyn with Manhattan, whipping, beating, kicking, and murdering in the park after dark.

The story: Four teen-agers went through a Brooklyn park seeking persons to torture and murder. As the eighteen-year-old leader said, "I have an abstract hatred and distaste for bums and vagrants."

This youth had an exceptionally high IQ. He had been a bank clerk for some time, but at the same time, he bossed the beatings and killings. The boy told the police, "Last night was a supreme adventure for me."

19

He pointed out that he and the other three members of his gang had found a young man on the park bench, beaten him up, burned his feet, tortured him in other ways, and then walked him, half dazed, to the East River and tossed him in. His body was found several days later.

One of the other boys, a seventeen-year-old, referring to his part in the beatings of unfortunates found in the park, said, "I used them for punching bags, to see how hard I could punch. I did this for sheer enjoyment."

Everyone in the community was stunned. The four families suddenly found themselves personally and tragically enmeshed in the question: Why are more and more young Americans becoming delinquent? One of the mothers cried, "What did I do wrong?"

The psychiatrists aired their views about the killers: some said these boys were insane, others that they were abnormal but not actually insane. The usual battle to discover motives began. Yet the fact remained that the boys had killed for thrills. They had brutally, sadistically, without rhyme or reason, murdered and killed as a form of amusement.

An editorial in the New York *Herald Tribune* summed it up this way: "One point is incontrovertibly clear about the four Brooklyn boys. They were on the surface completely normal. 'Good boys,' their parents called them. Their intelligence, so far as this quality can be measured, was above average or better. The same can be said for environment, which was certainly respectable. Their home life may or may not have been perfect; other parents may wonder why lads of fifteen, seventeen, eighteen, were allowed to roam the streets at all hours of the night. But it is evident that the conventional concomitants of crime and delinquency such as slums, dope and degradation, play no part."

In Kings County, home of the four Brooklyn "thrill-seekers," Judge Samuel S. Leibowitz ordered the grand jury to begin an investigation of the operations of the children's court after the thrill-killers were arrested. He warned that we are losing the battle against juvenile delinquency and that the court is "not curing" but "encouraging young hoodlums."

Investigations into the lives of the young "hoods" have revealed little more than the ordinary experiences of any youngster from the home of a middle-class family. Newspaper editorials during the trial expressed surprise at the fact that while there was a pronounced religious element in the home life of all four, it had had little actual effect on the attitudes and choice of activities of these boys. A schoolteacher said that she had recommended one of the boys for psychiatric treatment, years before the actual murders, because of his behavior in school. There must be psychiatric action and guidance as soon as such tendencies are discovered; in this case the time lag was tragic.

In these times, even the discovery of symptoms of a pre-disposition toward delinquency by parents or teachers, and an attempt to nip them in the bud, is not enough in the face of the growing defiance of recognized authority, including uniformed police.

Not long ago, eight young men attacked two patrolmen in Brooklyn. One member of the group initiated the struggle by shouting, "There's only two. Let's get them!" It was only after the officers drew their guns and threatened to fire that the group was brought under control. Recently a sixteen-year-old Bronx youth attacked a patrolman with a three-foot club after the officer warned him and his girl to leave a bar because they were underage. In order to protect himself, the officer had to shoot the boy. A little later a patrolman was attacked by ten men in the heart of New York City. They required hospital treatment when the battle was over. On the same night only a few blocks away, a detective suffered hand and body injuries while helping a patrolman disperse some disorderly youths. Later that night, in the same neighborhood, a patrolman was badly cut as he attempted to question four youths sitting in a parked car. Contempt for the law is part of the underworld pattern of thinking. To be known as a "cop hater" is a badge of courage and belonging—to the gang or to other hoodlums or delinquents. This behavior pattern has been emphasized strongly in motion pictures and in other media like fiction and comic books.

Let's look at a few more headlines and stories. They provide an introduction to the subject of juvenile delinquency in blunt and terrible language.

YOUTH CONFESSES OHIO GIRL KILLING. The story: A gaunt seventeen-year-old youth has admitted he raped and stabbed a girl, also seventeen, whose nearly nude body was found in a lonely woods in Toledo, Ohio.

After the *fait accompli,* one can do little more than wonder where the parents and officers of the law were; one needs an entire background before real judgment can be passed. Yet the reports of the incidents of violence go on and on.

Here are two cases of criminal conduct of a most brutal nature.

YOUTH HELD IN RAPE. "A husky six-foot youth confessed that he and a burly accomplice burned his girl-friend with lighted cigarettes and that each raped her in a jealous rage touched off by his suspicions that she had dated another teen-ager.

"The girl, a beautiful seventeen-year-old brunette, tried under hours of questioning to shield the identity of her assailants but finally broke down and provided names to the district attorney."

SEVEN YOUTHS ARRESTED IN CONEY KNIFING headed this story: "Seven members of the 'Little Count' gang, from the best residential section of Brooklyn, were arrested early today, charged with stabbing two men at Coney Island. Police said the trouble started yesterday when one of the Little Counts started to change from street clothes to a bathing suit beneath the boardwalk."

Senseless, brutal fighting. We hear about it over and over again. The headlines shout it at us day after day. Why? One of the most powerful elements in the creation of the juvenile delinquent is the gang. When good parental influence is lacking, the child frequently turns to the gang for approval, or he might be taken into a gang simply because the leaders don't want any one who is *different* in the neighborhood. The seeking of superior status is a tremendous factor in the gang activities, both within the organization and outside it in demonstrations with rival gangs.

Here are the headlines and stories of other incidents.

22 JUVENILES NABBED IN GANG WAR. "A junior order of eighteen Bronx youths, armed with a Molotov cocktail and thirteen garrison belts used for inflicting battle scars, was seized last night at 169th Street and Clay Avenue, The Bronx, before any action took place.

"The hoodlums, eight of them fifteen years old and the rest ranging from sixteen to twenty-two, confessed that they were organizing to do battle with members of a near-by gang they accused of insulting one of their friends Thursday night at Paramount Park. The police then picked up four sixteen-year-old youths at their homes and booked them at the station on charges of assault and robbery against the gang members."

HELD IN SCHOOL PILLAGE. "The police yesterday picked up three boys ranging from eight to eleven years old, who, they said, had spent two days systematically wrecking the interior of P.S. 45 in Jamaica, Queens.

"Nearly half the windows of the school were broken. Eight door panes were smashed, furniture was overturned, and books, paper and other supplies were strewn about. Damage was estimated at $1,000. Three radio cars were sent to the scene in the early evening after a call from a near-by resident. Police of the Jamaica station surrounded the three-story building. The boys were found perched on a first-floor window sill twenty feet above the ground."

Boys from eight to eleven years old, already turning toward delinquency, already filled with hatred and spite against a society that censures, but does not help, them.

TEEN-AGE MOB RIPS UP BMT [subway] TRAIN. "The transit authorities today were adding up their loss in ripped-up seats and broken windows and electric bulbs, the work of some thirty teen-age vandals of a BMT Sea Beach express train in Brooklyn. Police said the boys piled into the last car of a train at the Stillwell Avenue terminal from Coney Island last night and immediately began their depredation. The action forced some twenty adult passengers to seek safety in another car."

This conduct was not merely the enthusiasm which follows a school football game victory, which was the excuse the youngsters gave. It is the outward sign of an attitude of reckless defiance of the law and lack of respect for public property.

Even more serious is the growing lack of respect for the human body. In Camden, New Jersey, little John Delow, nine, and his brother Joseph, seven, were walking home from school. An unknown teen-age bully pulled them into an alley and demanded money. When they said they had none, he struck them again and again. He knocked them down, stripped them of their jackets, shoes, and socks. These he threw over a near-by wall. Seven-year-old Joseph was knocked down several times and kicked in the face. Then the bully began to torture him. He stabbed the child about two hundred times with a lead pencil, puncturing much of the upper portion of the body. Later the two boys stumbled out of the alley and slumped to the curb. Bleeding and partially disrobed, they were picked up by a passing salesman who rushed them to a hospital. Police described the attack as one of the worst cases of cruelty they had ever seen.

The mother of one of the four thrill-killers cried, "What did I do wrong?" In the following case, a father did everything he knew and co-operated with the law; yet he failed to prevent the criminal actions of his son. He just failed.

From Baltimore: FATHER BARS LENIENCY FOR HIS SON AS BURGLAR. A sixteen-year-old was "brought before Magistrate Howard L. Allen yesterday and charged with burglary of $6.50, a novelty machine, and a clock radio from a grocery. The magistrate offered to release the boy in the custody of his father, but the father refused custody and said the boy belonged in jail.

"'I can't handle him,' he told the magistrate. 'The only time I ever see him is on Friday night, when he comes in for his allowance.'"

The youth then was sent to the city jail.

Joy riding in stolen cars has been a major type of crime. The result in the case reported next was death. Yet such accidents do not seem to curb this thrill-seeking activity.

BOY DEAD, FOUR HURT IN STOLEN CAR CHASE. "One youth was dead today and four others injured as a result of an off-duty policeman's chase of nine teen-agers in stolen cars. One of the autos crashed on the Harlem River speedway, killing a sixteen-year-old boy and injuring four others.

"Police said that one of the cars was stolen from Jackson Heights and the other from Flushing by five youths who piled in one of the autos, four in the other. They began racing. The stolen cars sideswiped near 172nd Street. The one containing five youths crashed into a concrete railing, the other just a short distance away. Three youths escaped on foot. The driver was caught."

Unfortunately, the prestige accorded offenders by their gang or neighborhood negates the deterrent effect that the catching of one delinquent might have had.

From Washington, D.C.: CONGRESSMAN STONED, COPS HUNT TEEN GANG. "Police today combed the Capitol Hill area and questioned hundreds of youths as they cracked down on teen-aged hoodlums. About two hundred adults and juveniles were questioned in connection with the attack on Representative Thomas B. Curtis, Republican, of Missouri. Police said purse-snatching, robberies and other criminal acts have been carried out by teen-aged gangs here for many months. But after Mr. Curtis made a speech on the floor of the House yesterday about an attack on him and a visitor from Toledo, Ohio, there was a sudden flurry of activity. Mr. Curtis said that when he first spoke with police on Tuesday night about the attack on himself and the Toledo visitor, he was told by two patrolmen that 'there is not much we can do about this—it goes on all the time.'"

These headlines and stories shocked and disturbed the people of this country in the year 1954. These headlines brought a constant parade of killers, of armed robbers, of delinquent boys before the eyes of the public. These headlines spoke of the young boys and the increasing number of girls who are becoming or who already are, dangerous criminals.

The papers don't make delinquency. The papers report what happens. Many people feel that juvenile delinquency is not as large a problem as one would suppose from reading them. But this theory is the easy way out—and is destroyed once we look at the facts behind the headlines.

In an address to the National Education Association in July, 1953, Attorney General Herbert Brownell, Jr., said that if one million youngsters showed the first symptoms of cholera during the year 1954, the nation would be aghast. People everywhere would be galvanized into effective action; they would take every conceivable step to prevent the disease from taking hold and spreading. And he went on to say that, in effect, this is what we are facing, that there was every sign that in 1954 more than one million children would be in trouble serious enough to cause their arrest. One million delinquents, and we know that for every person picked up by the police, three, four, and sometimes five, are not apprehended. One million delinquents, plus.

There is good reason to think of delinquency as a national epidemic, a serious epidemic. Between 1948 and 1954, the crime rate in the United States jumped about 50 per cent. The incidence of all crime is outstripping the increase in population by a ratio of 4 to 1. Our population has increased 5 per cent since 1950, while the number of crimes committed has jumped 20 per cent in those years. Late in 1954, the FBI reported that major crimes had reached a record figure of 2,159,080. An FBI survey of two hundred cities showed a rise in the crime rate of adults in 1953 of 1.9 per cent as compared with an increase of 7.9 per cent in the crime rate of boys and girls under eighteen.

There is every reason for parents to be disturbed at the rate of juvenile delinquency in America. Here are more figures: In 1952, approximately 400,000 children were referred to the juvenile courts on delinquency charges. The average increase in juvenile delinquency cases was 45 per cent between the years 1948 and 1953. In 1953 more children came before the children's courts than in any other previous year.

By 1960 this country will have a further enlarged population of the ten-to-seventeen age group. If the rate of juvenile delinquency continues to mount at the rate experienced during the past five years, the number of boys and girls going through the juvenile courts will skyrocket to 750,000 a year by that date. And if we take into account the number of delinquents that are not brought to court, within five years we may reach the fantastic annual number of 2,250,000 delinquents.

As Fillmore H. Sanford, executive secretary of the American Psychological Association, pointed out to the Senate Judiciary Subcommittee to Investigate Juvenile Delinquency, "For every juvenile who actually engages in delinquent behavior—or who is caught in delinquent behavior—there are hundreds or thousands who may

have delinquent tendencies or who fail in subtle and socially harmless, but still dreadfully crippling ways, to make a full and creative
adjustment to life."

Ex-Senator Robert C. Hendrickson, former chairman of the subcommittee (which included Senator William Langer, Senator Estes
Kefauver, and Senator Thomas C. Hennings, Jr.), reported to the
Senate in 1954. He said, "I am not an alarmist, nor is my distinguished colleague [one of the subcommittee members]. We do
not subscribe to the gloomy prophecy that American youth is
deteriorating beyond redemption, but we are disturbed by the results
of our investigation.

"The evidence received conclusively establishes juvenile delinquency as a problem of sharply increasing severity. Annually since
1948 both its volume and rate have mounted. Younger children
in larger numbers are becoming involved in serious crime; although individual communities may be excepted, we find that all
sections of our country have experienced aggravated juvenile delinquency problems. *Measured in terms of volume we are waging a
losing battle against juvenile delinquency* [my italics]."

This, then, is the problem with which we are now confronted.
It is a nationwide problem. It is not peculiar only to the slums of
New York, Los Angeles, Boston, and Chicago. Unfortunately, many
of the nation's smaller communities and city suburbs now find that
they also must cope with juvenile delinquency. The courts serving
communities of less than 100,000 persons show a case increase of
more than 40 per cent. Juvenile cases in many small courts have increased more than 100 per cent in the last two years.

A police official in a small city in the state of Washington recently reported, "Gang warfare reared its ugly head in our community, and already reports have reached our ears of a number of
beatings having taken place. Numerous weapons, including zips
made from car battery cables and car fan belts, along with a large
collection of assorted knives and a homemade .22 pistol or two,
have been seized from juveniles."

Thus, the statistics show not only an increase in the over-all rate
of delinquency but also its spread. Unless this cancer is checked
early enough, it can go on spreading and contaminate many good

cells in our society. As Bertram M. Beck, the director of a special delinquency project of the Children's Bureau of the Department of Health, Education and Welfare, points out, juvenile delinquency is already creeping from the wrong side of the tracks to the right side. He adds that "the spread of delinquency through economic levels of our community is a danger signal that must not be ignored." The four Brooklyn boys, for example, came from middle-class neighborhoods.

The problem becomes even more grave when we consider the nature of the offenses. These have become more serious, more destructive, as the headlines so dramatically state. From 1948 on, for example, more children under eighteen have been involved in such offenses as burglaries, robberies, and automobile thefts. The FBI found that 50 per cent of those arrested in 1953 for burglary were under eighteen years of age. One out of three was not yet sixteen. Over half the arrests for car thefts were of juveniles, and 29 per cent were not even old enough to qualify for a driver's permit. Seventeen per cent of the country's known drug addicts are less than twenty-one. Fifteen per cent of all cases of rape and assault are committed by adolescents under eighteen, and 15 per cent of the country's homicides are committed by those under twenty-one.

Vandalism, of course, has always been a favorite expression of juvenile rebellion. According to the Board of Education in New York City, vandals smash 265,000 panes of glass in the city's schools each year, at a cost to the city of three to five hundred thousand dollars. The breakage rate is rising. (Some authorities believe that school vandalism provides a yardstick by which juvenile delinquency can be measured.) In 1953, 85,000 more panes were broken than in 1948. These panes do not represent an equal number of carelessly thrown baseballs. In many cases, groups of teen-agers have deliberately set out to raid the schools. Vandalism is becoming organized destruction. In New York City teen-age mobs have done thousands of dollars worth of property damage to subway trains in 1954.

These figures support another statement made by Mr. Beck that delinquency has as its basic characteristic a sense of hating, an urge to injure and destroy. And, as we have seen, this urge extends to people as well as to property.

Something has gone wrong. The headlines tell us this, and the figures bear it out. Something has gone wrong either in the life of the child or in the life of the community, or probably in both. Have we as a society been deficient in developing laws to protect children from the delinquency disease? Have we been cheating our children?

Many communities and many states now recognize the problem of the delinquent boy and girl. They realize that it is a complex problem, a problem that requires more than superficial attention. We know that the fight against juvenile delinquency is necessary for the preservation of the American way of life; we know that the future of our nation depends upon the courage, the ideals, the character, the initiative, the strength, and the stability of our children and of their children. We must recognize that juvenile delinquency is not a passing phenomenon—it is not a flying saucer observed by a few—but a dark and all too real facet of our modern way of life, distressing to all of us.

We cannot sit back with a smug let-George-do-it attitude. We must not wait for the police to catch the thrill-killer and then send him up for life or electrocute him. This is a problem bigger than the headlines. We must look beyond the front-page news, now shouting daily from every state in the nation, and ask ourselves one all-embracing question: *Why did they do it?* And then these questions: Where shall we place the blame? How shall we find the solutions? How shall we put them into effect?

It is easy to raise questions, not so easy to answer them. But they are being answered now. During the past year much attention and great effort have been made to look behind the headlines. Although the rate of juvenile delinquency continues to increase, there has come an awareness of the problem in many areas of our society. The United States Senate has been studying the question of delinquency since 1953, focusing attention on the basic issues. Various municipalities are conducting research in their own. As ties. States have held conferences, are planning to h recently as January 3, 1955, New York State Attorney General Jacob K. Javits proposed a state-wide conference on children and youth as a move against juvenile delinquency.

This is all to the good. Only as we see the problem of juvenile delinquency in its broad perspective will we be able ultimately to find the solutions. By going behind the headlines we will be able to see the numerous implications, the tremendous ramifications, of this growing problem.

2. What Does Delinquency Mean?

". . . I couldn't stand it anymore."

Many different definitions of the term "juvenile delinquency" have been offered. Probably the one most commonly accepted is the legal definition that juvenile delinquency constitutes any act which, if committed by an adult, would be crime. That means a child who has violated any law of his community, state, or nation would be a delinquent. Various other definitions have also been offered.

A psychiatrist suggests: "Juvenile delinquency is a pattern of behavior manifested by a youth below the age of eighteen that is ntrary to the laws of the land, and the accepted mores, and al in character. This may be brought about by en- eprivation, conflict within the domestic situation or iculties in the youth or child."

ndent of schools in a southern state notes: "Juvenile s a serious type of deviation contrary to law. An puth to me is a delinquent."

tion was given by a Midwestern educator: "Juvenile night be defined as antisocial behavior, outside of the prmal misbehavior, which is so extreme as to endanger he delinquent."

definition that was made by another psychiatrist: linquency can be briefly defined as hostile defiance iority—whether it be vested in the policeman, the he parent. Generally the child in question is striking the world for reasons which become apparent as he is hiatrically.

ents may be overstrict or utterly unabl

the child in dealing with him on vital issues. At any rate, he is usually trying to prove himself, and makes a great show of bravado to cover up his feelings of inadequacy and fearfulness."

What does delinquency mean? News accounts and figures tell us that delinquency means burglary, murder, drug addiction, vandalism, sexual promiscuity, and rape. These are all frightening manifestations of the antisocial behavior defined above. But the most vivid picture of delinquency is presented by the children themselves; their stories define delinquency in a way that is frightening and clarifying at the same time—and, moreover, in a way that is very, very real.

When I first saw Rose, at an institution for delinquent girls, she appeared dreamy, tense, and withdrawn. She was small for fifteen years. Her speech was hesitant. She answered in a superficially evasive manner. Occasionally she smiled automatically, and occasionally her gaze seemed fixed and unseeing.

"Tell me about yourself, Rose," I said.

She relaxed a little. "I lived with my mother and my five brothers and five sisters," she said. "My father died two years ago. For the last year I've been a truant from school, and ran away from home twice. I just didn't want to go to school. The other children didn't like me. I ran away from home, lived with a girl for three days at ———. I don't know why, it seems I can't get used to the idea of living in the house now. My father isn't there, and I don't know if my mother really wants me around. Yeah, sure I've been out with boys. Bill the cop told about my having intercourse with several men and of finding me half undressed in a car with a man and a boy. But he said that just because he didn't like me. Then he said that I got mixed up with another girl."

"And did you, Rose?"

"Well, maybe I did, but . . ." She stopped. "I want to be a nurse, I want to go out and help people."

While I was talking to her, she displayed a shallowness of emotion and a marked tendency to disclaim responsibility for her

Suddenly Rose looked up and smiled an almost angelic smile. "The voice of the Lord once spoke to me," she said, "and Jesus said if you want to receive me as your Lord you should not say bad things, and I told the Lord I will try to be good and not say that word any more."

"What word?"

"I can't. It's terrible."

"Can you spell it?" I asked.

And she did: "G-O-D-D-A-M."

"And what happened?"

"Well, since the Lord talked to me the first time I feel a complete change inside me. I feel I'm not a sinner any more."

"Did you sin against the Lord, before?" I asked.

"Yes, I smoked, and I swore and I went to beer gardens. You know I had sexual intercourse."

"When?"

Rose said, "I was in a car, and a boy of eighteen and one of seventeen, a friend of his, were with me. The older boy twisted my arm and held me down while the other boy . . ." Again she stopped.

"What do you plan to do?" I asked.

"Well," she said, "I think that when I come out of here I will be good. I don't want to be bad, really I don't."

Unwanted. Heard voices. There is so much in what the girl says that indicates crying needs, personal for her own happiness, psychiatric for her unconscious needs. The conflicts in this story make a demand on society for earlier recognition of the fact that there must be places where such girls can go and people who will understand and help them.

This is Teressa talking. Teressa was in a girl's training school (as reform schools are now called) because of her record of sexual promiscuity.

"I was born in Brooklyn seventeen years ago. I remember a lot about my mother, not so much about my father. I lived in so many places. My mother tried to do all the best for us nine kids. There are four over and four under me. Mother sent all of us to high school but only one graduated. Some of the boys got in trouble with the truant officer. He said they were in gangs. Some of them were sent away.

"But I never got into any trouble until my mother died two years ago," she told me. "I lived with my father when my mother died, then I was sent to the detention home."

"How do you feel about your father?" I asked.

"He was not good to any of us, not to my mother either. I rarely saw him that he wasn't drunk. He used to beat my mother and argued a lot, and once when I was ten he pushed her to the stove while she was cooking a chicken and the frying pan fell over and the grease fell on her feet. She was burned very badly and couldn't walk for two weeks. One foot was so swollen she couldn't wear her shoe and couldn't go to work.

"When dad was drunk," Teressa went on, "he used to yell and holler at us kids, but when he was not drunk he would beat us up for the least little thing. You couldn't talk to him, he would always sit and mumble but the minute we would ask him something he would get all upset."

"And what about yourself?"

"Oh, I never had any difficulties at school. I stayed home when my mother was sick. When my sister had arguments with class-mates I brought them together and straightened them out. After my mother's death I stayed away from school and took care of the kids. We went to live with cousins because my father couldn't sup-port us."

The record shows that Teressa did not attend school for about six months. Then they found her to be pregnant. The child was later placed for adoption.

"How did you get along at home?" I asked.

"Mother used to fuss with me a few times when I didn't come straight home from school. I never had serious arguments with my brothers and sisters. Never had any arguments or trouble with the neighbors' children either."

"Why did you come here?"

"When I was living with my cousin I didn't want to go to

school. I tried to get work in five places, and gave the wrong age each time. They all fired me within two or three weeks because they said I was too slow. They also found out that I lied about my age. I met a nice boy, two years ago. I have loved him since, and Albert and I will get married when the proper time comes."

At another institution, I talked to a tall, well-set, good-looking lad of sixteen. His name was Dick. "I was in the tenth grade before coming here, but they put me in the eighth here," he said. "I never had trouble with teachers."

"You didn't?" I asked.

"No. The trouble is, though, I never did go to school. I came in the morning, checked in, and then at the end of the first class I just walked out. Didn't show up the rest of the day. I'd go down to the candy store to play pinball or play cards with the boys. I work for my uncle on Saturdays. I get five dollars for it. I just didn't like to sit around in classes. I live with my mother and grandmother. My father died when I was seven months old. Mother works as a secretary. Grandmother takes care of the house. She is the one I see most of the time. My mother was pretty strict, she didn't let me go no place."

It was hard to believe the facts recorded about this young lad on the record before me. The police called him a bully, called him sadistic because of the many tortures he had inflicted on others. Here are a few of the highlights of his police record, begun when he was twelve:

11/12/50: vandalism . . . and from then on: malicious mischief, incorrigible, truant, vandalism; vandalism; breaking railway signal light; breaking lights near the bridge; vandalism near house; broke windows; mother paid $150 damages; malicious mischief on railroad tracks; throwing stones at train signal lights; malicious mischief; malicious mischief; malicious mischief; twisted girl's arm and broke it . . .

I checked further. Now a sixteen-year-old boy, overgrown, husky, average intelligence, Dick had a police record of eighteen offenses.

The report runs the gauntlet from homosexual and heterosexual misconduct to brutal assaults. Fairly neat in appearance, he was a good-looking lad. In his face you discerned an air of perplexity under his slightly indifferent attitude. He kept up a stream of talk. At times he was inclined to be evasive; mostly he seemed indifferent. He seemed to listen to my questions—although he said to me with a smile, "I guess my trouble is that I don't listen. I don't listen to nobody, my mother or the judge. They have given me repeated chances but I didn't listen."

There was a charge of assault and battery in his record. It's a vicious story. As I sat before him, Dick repeated it to me. This is what he said:

"I was walking around the tracks," said Dick, "with a friend of mine. We saw a young boy. I don't hardly know him. I don't think he ever saw me. But I said to myself, let's go have some fun. I turned to the boy. 'Where you come from?' I says. He crossed the track and acted kind of scared. I said, 'Do you know me?' 'No,' he said, 'I don't.' 'That's good,' I said. I punched him in the face. I punched him again, his face became bruised.

"I said, 'Are you going to tell anybody what I did?' He didn't answer. 'If you do,' I said, 'I'm going to kill you.' He looked kind of scared. 'What'd you do with my dog,' I said. 'I never saw a dog,' he answered. Probably because I never had one.

"So then I started to punch him, picked up a rock, held it in my fist, and I hit the boy with it. My friend tried to stop the fight, but I wouldn't let him. He dragged me away; asked me to stop hitting the boy and held my arms and the little boy ran away.

"Yes, I guess he went to tell his mother and father because the next day I got a court notice. The lady asked me do I know the boy. I said I never saw him before. Well, they let me go, but I guess I was pretty roughneck. I got into all kinds of mischief. I don't know why, I just did, that's all. I wanted something to do.

"One time," Dick continued, "four or five of us boys went to an apartment just being built, took a whole wall of cement down. We took a chisel and knocked down hundreds of cinder blocks, just mischievous. We went to old houses, broke windows. We wore gloves so we wouldn't leave any fingermarks. In one house we found a big victrola. We threw it down the stairs, we pushed down the bannister, we broke the chandelier. We didn't steal anything, just broke things. Oh, just with the boys, I had to do it so they wouldn't call me chicken.

"I broke the windows of an apartment that was just built. The cops were waiting for us. We walked away, then ran. I jumped between two cars. The cop said, 'Halt or I'll shoot.' He got me.

" 'Who broke the window?'

" 'I don't know,' I said.

"Then the next day they brought me before some kind of court, I guess.

" 'I didn't do it,' I said.

" 'Who was with you?'

" 'I don't know. I can't tell you.'

"And the cop asked, 'Do you know these two boys?'

"I said, 'No, sir.'

" 'Are you sure you don't know them?'

" 'Never saw them before.'

"The cop said, 'You know Dick?'

" 'Sure,' they said.

" 'Well, you did it,' said the cop. 'Your fingerprints are on the rock.'

"I laughed to myself. I knew they were lying. I wore gloves. I said, 'Can I send the boy out to get candy?'

" 'Stop being a wise guy,' said the cop.

"My mother picked me up, took me home. She asked me was I with the boys. She said, 'Don't start stealing, if you need money ask me for it. I'll give you my last penny, but I don't want you to steal.'

"That made me feel bad. So I went out with the boys and we broke up a lot more windows."

Later he said, "I laid a couple of girls. One was thirteen. I laid her in her house. Her sister found out. She said she was going to tell my probation officer. When he picked me up he had me down for truancy.

"I said, 'I didn't bother with the girl.'

" 'You're not lying?' the judge asked.

" 'No, I'm not,' I told the judge.

" 'O.K., suspended sentence.'

"A week later the girl admitted it. The judge said, 'Better go to the State House for Boys for eighteen months.'

"I would have gotten out of there in eleven months but I was escorting some kids. Three ran away. I knew they were going to. Fact is, I helped them. I didn't want them to come back. My mother wants me to finish high school, to go to night school. I want to join the marines. When I was small I was pretty clumsy. I started to smoke when I was nine."

I looked at this lad who was talking to me just as you might talk to me about the weather on a rainy Sunday evening.

"Two girls—guess they were high school kids—baby-sat for me when I was about seven," he said. "They told me to take off my clothes, they made me get on top of them. They played with me. I guess that's when I first started going bad. I like to have lots of fun. I used to like to prove to the boys that I wasn't chicken. The boys said, 'I bet you can't beat up that boy.' Well, I always been big [he's 6 feet, weighs 170 pounds]. I guess I wanted to be bad although my mother always tried to help me. I always wanted to go out and have fun. I don't blame nobody for what I've done. I started going with the gang—there are five or six of us—we'd get together to have some fun. One day we bought a deck of cards, started out with pennies, ended up playing with quarters."

Dick continued: "Let me tell you about the strip poker game I got into," he said. "Three boys and three girls were sitting around playing."

"Strip poker?" I asked.

"Yes," he said. "You know, where you have the wrong card or something you have to take off your clothes. By the time the evening was over—we were in one of the girl's houses—we were all just about naked. We had a lot of fun that night, too. I've been having a lot of fun with a couple of steady girls I was going out with. You know, get laid whenever I feel like it. Guess that's what I miss more than anything here. I'd just like to get a pass and get laid again."

Another sixteen-year-old boy wrote down his story. In this and the other stories throughout the book, spelling and punctuation have not been changed. The way these children express themselves, the way they write and spell, is peculiarly their own. (Names and places have been disguised, however, in order to protect the privacy of individuals.)

"I live in ———. It's a small city with about forty thousand people. It's nothing compared to the city of N.Y. but you can get into just as much trouble as I found out. The first thing I ever did wrong was when me and two other boys broke into a garage and took large boxes of cigarettes in cartons. We didn't want the cigarettes so we brought some to school every day and sold them. After we ran out of cigarettes and money we decided to break in to more places.

"We gathered about 13 guys together and started a crime wave. Every night you would read in the paper about two or three jobs. We had the cops going crazy. One night one of the guys decided to make guns. We got car aerials and made some home mades or zip guns. One night we were up at Crestvue Park firing the guns when the cop came over. We threw the guns in the hedges and started to walk on. The cop hollered to stop and we stopped. I thought he saw the guns but he didn't. He came over to us and said Don't you know it's against the law to fire off fire crackers in New York State. We said no and he let us go. After that we left there and went to a little place called Eddie's Pool Room. We played cards in the back room the rest of the night and then went home.

"About a week later a guy came up to me and asked me if I wanted to buy a .38 revolver for 10 bucks. I said yea and bought it. Now my problem was getting shells. I couldn't buy them because I didn't have no draft card [to prove he was of age] so I had to steal them. That night 6 of us broke into a Sporting good store. We took six rifles semi-automatic 2 30-30 and a .22 winchester. Then we took 5 boxes of 32 and 38 shells and about 20 boxes of 22 and 30 shell. The next day we had a good time on the outskirts of town shooting at everything we seen.

"School was a good place to have fun. None of the teachers knew what was going on, but they had an idea. We used to get excused from class and walk around the hall waiting for some girls to get excused. We'd take them downstairs in the gym locker room. We felt them up down there, but we never copped off them until that night when we arranged to meet them some place. We would go to this used car lot and borrow a car and then we'd go to a place where there was nothing but wrecked cars and get a different license plate. Then we go over to this candie store and pick the girls up. After we pick them up we would go out in the country some place and cop off them. This was okay until one night the guy found out about the cars and took all the batteries out.

"Another thing we used to do was go up this kid's house when he wasn't home and go in his father's room and take money out of the small safe next to his bed. He was sick and mostly always left the safe open. But one night the lady up stairs snaged us going into the apartment—She called the cops. They brought us down the station but we denied everything and they had no proof that we went in there to rob anything or that we didn't go in there to call the kid that lived there so they let us go.

"About a month after that the gang started to develop and then gang wars. Gangs weren't so big only about 15–20 guys but that was enough to start trouble. We used to make our own brass knuckles and clubs. Brass knuckles we made in metal shop and clubs we made in wood shop at school. I was in only one war and it wasn't to bad because a lady called the cop and it broke up. Two guys were caught but were let go—

"After that two of my friends ran away from home and got caught in New Jersey with a loaded 32. It was about 6:30 P.M. and I was eating when the cops came up my house and got me. They told me how my two friends got caught and the one that ratted on me. I was down the station from 6:30 to 1:00 and they let me go home but after I got home and went to sleep the cops were up my house again. They took me back down the station and said to me that I hadn't told them everything which I hadn't and still haven't. I told them I didn't know what they were talking about and they brought me into this room where another one of the guys were held that got ratted on by the same guy. He sat there and told the cops everything and even squealed on a couple of more guys. It was like a rat race. They just kept on coming and squealing on each other.

"About two weeks after that we went to court for our hearing. The court room was loaded with parents and kids. We all were dismissed until our final trial. But during that time we got into more trouble. Some kid's father worked for the City collecting money from the parking meters when he got sick and went to New York for an operation. While he was there we got his son to get his keys to the meters and then we started to rob meters until two kids got caught and squealed on me and another guy. They brought us down the station and brought me in the back room and started beating the . . . out of me. They called me all kinds of names like you little lying. . . . You nothing but a . . . crook. I ought to kick your teeth down your throat After that I was brought to court and again was to wait for my final trial.

"I didn't get into no trouble till the day of my trial, ———, and I was sentenced to [the public training school] for an indefint time. After being here for 3 weeks and 3 days I decides it was time to leave and I breezed or as you would call it ran away. I was out two weeks before I got caught. Now I'm back waiting to make my visit home so I can get the guy that squealed on me."

And listen to Mike, whose court appearances include car theft, threatening a student with physical harm, with another boy forcibly entering a local public school and destroying public property valued at two hundred dollars, and finally armed robbery.

"My grammar school life was a good one. I was always getting into trouble by fooling around and things like that, but nothing serious. But then when I got to the sixth grade I started to come worse maybe it was because my mother died when I was about eight or nine years old. But anyway I started to get worse. I would fight and curse the teachers and always play with the girls that I guess is natural. I had my first sex experience at about twelve years old anyway that was the first one I enjoyed. It came about when I heard a rumor about a girl in the eighth grade so I made it my business to talk with her and that led to sexual intercourse ever since then I have been going strong. The fellers I hang out with always did say and still do say if anybody can make a girl it is sure Mike that is my nick name. They are always asking me for the line I hand them and I always tell them but it just doesn't work for them. All I tell them is to promise everything to them tell them your madly in love with them and before long you have them eating out of your hand why I even remember promising a couple of girls the moon.

"When I was about thirteen I got into my first bad trouble. About five guys were going down to take a warehouse and I was with them. The first night we cased the place to see what it was going to be worth we sent a couple of guys in to see and they marked everything down. When they came out we looked at the items. Mixmasters, deepfryers, refrigerators, gas ranges, etc. So the next night we got a truck where they got it from I don't know but one of the boys drove it down about an hour after we went inside. Two boys stood outside to watch for the night watchman. Well during that day we had already sold quite a lot of merchandise. Totaling about fifteen hundred dollars. Well we have every thing ready by the rear loading platform when the truck backed up. We had about half of the stough loaded when detectives and cops jumped up all over and told us to lay down. Well two of the boys made it. They started running then we heard the shots and found one got away the other one was hit and in pretty bad condition. Well we went up to the station to get booked. They found out my real age, I had told them I was almost sixteen. But on that they called up my father and he came down and took me home. The owner did not press charges. So I beat the rap easy.

"After that I quieted down for awhile. But when I was about fifteen I got mixed up with a gang called the hotrods and then after that I went and stole a car, me and another boy. We cut class out of the high school wich I was going to wich is ———. When we happen to pass this beautiful buick with skirts and all different ornaments all over it and it court my eye. When I noticed the keys in the ignection, I said Chuck the keys are in that

Buick back their lets take it comon he looked at me and said lets go. I looked around and noticed a cop standing on the next corner but the car was facing down on the right side so I knew I didn't have to pass him we didn't see anybody around. The car was parked outside Harry's Auto Parts. So I jumped in behind the wheel and he got in along side of me. I started the car and shot it in first and pulled out. When I came to the next corner I was doing about fifty when I went to make the turn I found out I had no breaks so I just made a fast turn then I went down to Jamacka Ave. When I got to the corner the light turned red and a cop was standing on the corner so I put it in second and clutch it but I stopped to late. I was already past the light the cop came over and asked me, Hay bud wots amatter with red lights, they only for trucks? I told him I didn't see it. Then he asked me for my licensed and registration. I asked if it was "all C" [all right] if I could pull over to the side. He said go ahead your blocking traffic. I started the car again and let it warm a little then I put it in first and started to move toward the curb slowly when I let up on the clutch and down on the gas and we was off. I went to blocks and then made a turn just about on two wheels I went up a couple of blocks when I come to another red light and when the guy in front of me stopped I pulled out to avoid hitting the cab and I side swipe a ford and then went threw the light and made another left turn and the next corner when Chuck said "Hay" Mike, the taxicab is following us so I didn't pay it any mind. But then he pulled up along side of me and tried to force me over. I was going over when I was coming straight for a parked car so I took the weel and turned to the right ripping off the cabs rear fender then I went two blocks and turned right one block and turned left parked the car and ran.

"By this time there were cops all over the place. We climed a fence and hid in one of the back yards. When a couple of squad cars pulled into the block so I told Chuck to walk out with me like nothing was a matter we started out of the yard down the driveway and walked right passed two cops and in between the two squad cars when the cab pulled up and the driver jumped out and said their they are.

"Enstantly all the guns came out and we froze. We were taken to the station house and booked and then to [a detention home]. We were there two weeks and went to court and then went home.

"I was doing pretty good then but I was not going to school. Then I was finally sixteen and I quit school. The next thing I knew I wanted drink more and more. I was getting so that every doller I had went to Liquor. But we sure used to have some good times.

"My farther took me fishing a lot and hunting a lot and I enjoy those sports. I remember last deer season when I went hunting I was trailing a bear when I spotted a deer he stood about fifty yeards from me and I had a twenty guage shotgun. I took my bead on him and squeezed the trigger. He jumped and then ran off so I continued following the bear tracks and they took me up just about up were the deer was standing and past the way he had run. When I noticed a spot of blood well I started to follow the blood on the snow it was pretty easy. Well, I guess I followed it for about a half mile and came upon my eight point buck and now his head is in my living room.

"Well everything went "all C" after that until I thought I needed more money so I was going to get it the easy way so I went with another boy called Johnny. We pulled twenty two Liquore store hold ups playing it always the same way. I would go in and stick the place up and Johnny would stand outside and keep chic [stand guard]. Because he didn't have the hart to take the gun and do the stickup. In one place I had a bit of trouble the store-keeper went behind the chashere to get something when I shouted to him and he moved faster so I shot him in the sholdr and he drop a 38 stub nose. Well the rest was easy. All together we got about fourteen and a half grand we bourt a new buick and other things, went to all the famous night clubs in New York.

"Then about a month after we had stopped pulling the jobs we got busted on a rap at breaking into Public School ——— and went to jail. When we got back to court we found out that some-one had ratted about the holdups. Johnny was sent to [the reforma-tory]. But my probation officer because he still had charge of me got me into [the public training school]. I was admitted into the instatution in Febuary. Then in March I tried to run away with a boy named Cal but got court. I was doing all "C" up here when I became seventeen. Then in July after I had been here about six moanth without a commitee I went to talk to my sponsor and I asked him when it was to come about and what did he think they would give me. He said about four months so I ran away again and this time I made it to the city with a boy named Mitchell. It was tough going but we made it.

"The following Wensday I went home to borrow some money and then my farther talked to me and I decided to come back to the institution and come home the right way so I could live with my family and start a decent life. Yes my wild life is over and believe me it doesn't pay take it from me I should know. Well I am back up here now and doing fine. I hope to go home in October and then start a good clean living life with a Job and I will then live a respectable life."

Will society help him? He cannot succeed alone.

Fifteen-year-old Tom wrote:

"I started playing hookey about four year's ago when I met a boy that I thought was a big shot and I looked up to him because he always had a lot of money and he dressed nice. He would tell the boys in the class how he held up a store and how the police chased him and he escaped so I started hanging out with him and his friends. People told my grandmother that I was hanging out with a rough group and she talked to me about it. I told her that I would stop hanging out with him and for the next week or so I didn't. I stayed around the block and played stick ball. In my mind that was a baby game but there was just something that attracted me to him so I started hanging around with him again and I knew it was breaking my grandmother's heart.

"When he got sent away I started doing right. But then I tryed to pull my first job robbing a radio store but I got caught in the act. The policeman took me home and told my grandmother that it was just something that all children want to do sometime, and

I got away with it. So I thought I could always get away with things of that nature and I tryed it again and got away with it.

"At that time my father [actually his uncle] was doing very well with two businesses and he sent me down south to live with my aunt. I stayed there for eight months and when I came home for Christmas I wanted to stay and I did. By now I was old enough to live with girls and I did. Then I met another boy who was older that I am but was a nice guy. I went to the movies with him and robbed stores with him and met some nice girls with him. Now I was in the eighth grade but still I had never been to court. And so this day he beat up a boy and I was with him. Three days later, on a Friday night, two detectives came to my house and got me out of bed. They took him and I to the station house. About eleven o'clock they took us to the [detention home]. Monday I went to court and from there home.

"I kept my nose clean for two-and-a-half-years, then I stopped going to school and wrote notes saying I was sick. Then I joined the gang. I would have to join some gang or get shot, and by joining one gang I was subject to get shot by another club or one of its members. That was how I mixed up with clubs. And when it was time to report to my probation officer I was with the gang and then he sent for me to come to court. They told me if I would go to school he would dismiss my case but I could not do it. When I came back to court he committed me to the state training school for boys.

"When I was on my way to [the detention home], I thought about it and wished I had went to school and listened to my mother. But then it was too late and all I could do was cry cry cry.

"After I was in the training school for three months I made my first visit home and every one thought I was a big shot because I was in reform school. But I didn't think I was very smart I thought I was pretty dumb.

"When I came back to the school I missed the city and I wanted to go back. So I ran away. I didn't know then that I had everything to lose and nothing to gain by running away. I been here seven month's and its almost time for me to go home. But there's only one thing I wish I could tell every boy in the world: You can't get away with it and I hope they will learn that before it's too late."

That was Tom, aged fifteen.

Bud, a sixteen-year-old boy at a state training school, is over 6 feet tall and weighs almost 190 pounds. He has always been sensitive about his size. He constantly strove to keep up with older boys. Here is his story as he wrote it:

"I was born on a small and dirty block in Down town Manhattan on the East Side. I can still remember when I was a boy of seven when all the boys used to run around breaking windows and robbing appels and pears off the corner fruit store. They weren't much older than I and I always wanted to stay out at night with them and go under the Johnny pump. But my mother wouldn't let me so I use to sit on the window and watch them and all so waiting for my farther to come home. You see my mother was disable and she hasn't been out of the house for 12 years and my farther was a hard working man. But he like to drink and when he got drunk it was like the fourth of July. But one thing I can say for him no matter how much he drank he always brought enough money home for my mother to buy us food and clothing. I mean for my sister and me.

"I can still remember where it all began. I was as old as the other boys but the only trouble was I was bigger than them. So when I came to school they all made fun of me and told me why don't you quit school. I looked old enough. But I was only 12-½ so I waited a year until I learned how to read and write and then I didn't come to school anymore. And when I did come to school I always had fights with the other boys. They told me I was big and clumsie and that they could beat me up, so I fight and I fight until they think different. And the teacher would say I am bullying them most of the time. He would tell me to go home so I would walk out of the school and hang around the candystore until 11:30 and then go home the teacher allways marked me present in school so I never came.

"I used to bum around the streets with older boys and girls. But

I always told them I was 16 so we use to go to some Dumpie Show that would open up at 10:00 and mush it up all morning long and in the afternoon we would do the same thing. The only trouble was we would be hungry because we spent our money on the girls to take to the movies so we would choose and the one that would go in a store and order a few sandwergeys to take out and when the man would put them in a bag the boy would grab it and run out. When I come home at 3:00 my mother would tell me her friend called her up and said she saw me around the streets and I would say awh your friend is seeing things and my mother would say be careful Bud one of these days you are going to get in trouble and I would say don't bother me and that night I would come home about 6:00 for supper and my farther would be sitting there stewed drunk and my mother wouldn't tell him what happened.

"The next day I get all dressed up and meet the boys. That afternoon it was a girls birthday so she had a little party and of course her parents were out. She was my age 13 but she told everybody she was 16. The fellows had told me to chip in some money so they could get a present for her. I didn't know it was 5 cases of beer. Well we went up her house it was a nice house and we walked in and saw her she was wearing a low cut evening gown it belonged to her mother because I seen her mother wear it when she went out at night. But I didn't say anything because I didn't want to hurt her feelings. Well I sat down with my girl and started talking and I lit a smoke up. I was smokeing since I was 7. But I wouldn't let my girl smoke. We drank soda and talked for about an hour when one of the boys brought out a few bottles of beer and said lets see who could drink the most. He was 17 years old and could take a little of it, but not a lot. So they started drinking, they drank for about a half an hour and when they were feeling high they all came over to me and offered me a bottle. I said no. But they said I couldn't take it so I drank a bottle. I didn't know there was whiskey in it mixed with beer. My head started to turn. I looked around and saw my girl lying on the floor next to the chair she fell out. I picked her up and said whats the matter she said she had a headache. But I could smell the beer on her breath so I put my arm around her and walked out of the house. I brought her to her girl friends house, she said she would take care of her.

"When I went back to the party I walked in and found most of the lights out. I found a needle on the floor. I didn't know what it was at first then one of the girls told me. They asked me if I wanted a shot. But I told them no so I sat down and started drinking soon it was 2:30 and the girl said we had to leave so we left. We walked through a quiet street and we saw a store the fellows told me to bust the window and they would watch for the dollysisters, I mean cops. Well I broke the window and took the money and threw it all over the streets. All of a sudden a man grabbed me and brought me to the police station and then about 6:30 my father came to get me.

"That monday we went to court and the judge let me go home and then I promised never to rob or drink again and my promise didn't last long. 2 Years later I was 15 and hanging out with boys 20 years old. I was in all Kinds of business fixing flat tires working in groceries and fixing bikes. I was making about 60 dollars a week and I liked to spend my money fast thats why I had so many friends. My mother told me to save some money but I told her I will start saving next week. But I never did. One night I came home from work all the boys were burning garbage it was a cold night. I went upstairs my father was drunk as usual and my mother was fighting with him. My older sister was still working. I went into the bedroom and put on my suit and topcoat and ran out without eating. I went to a resterant and had a bite to eat and then I went out and walked around the Block looking for the boys but nobody was around except the younger boys who were making fires or in the Hallway trying to win a few cents in a dice or card game so they could go to the show the next day.

"Then I met the guy I grew up with, he was a pool shotter and he was the champ around my way. He asked me where I was going and I said nowhere so he said Lets go to the poolroom. I told him I couldn't play the real reason was I wasn't old enough you had to be 16 but he insisted so I went. I walked 2 flights of stairs and opened a door and a cloud of smoke hit me in the face. There I

saw boys playing pool with fellows 20 and 21 they were getting
roped in for the nickels and dimes they got selling Newspapers. I
played one game with my friend and lost. It cost me sixty cents.
After that I went to the pool room every day and played by myself
until I Learned how to play a little.

"That friday I got paid 50 dollars went home and got dressed.
I told my mother I would get paid monday Because the Boss went
to the Bank. I walked out and went to the poolroom and started
to play By my self untill a fellow about 20 walked over to me and
asked me if I wanted to play just for fun. I beat him 4 games and
for a pack of cigaretts and a soda then we started to play for
money and my Luck changed and I started to lose my money.
Before I knew it I was broke so I went home and went to bed.

"It came Sunday and I had to get some money to give to my
mother. I couldn't tell her I lost it in a poolroom so I asked my
friend to lend me some money till next friday he told me he didn't
have it but he knew where I could get it. He took me to a man
and the man lent me the sixty dollars only I had to pay a hundred
back. It came monday and I got up to go to work when the phone
rang. The man said I have to lay you off because your school called
and said they were going to give me a fine. Friday came and I
didn't have the money to pay the man back so he told me he would
give me till next Friday to pay up or else. Now it was $140 dollars,
I had to pay interest every week. I tried to borrow the money but
I couldn't so I looked for a store to break into.

"That night me and my friend broke into a laundry and got
caught. They let us go home and then Monday they brought us to
court. My friend said I did all the planning and so they let him
go with probation and they put me in this State training school.

"I'm doing pretty good. I will be coming home in December. I
remember now what my mother usto say Bud be good or they will
put you away. I guess you never learn until its to late. I can't say I'm
all right because I'm not. All I have to say to other boys is to be
good, stay with boys your own age don't hang out in poolrooms go
to church stay away from boys who stay out late and get into
trouble its all right to have a girlfriend and take her out first make
sure your working. Don't borrow money from anybody and don't

drink Liquor when your at a party. Boys get into trouble when they stay around the streets or hang out in candy stores. Try to keep yourself busy.

"Boys that get into trouble usualay aren't there fault always. If the grownups would stop letting thear sons stay out 11 and 12 O'clock at night and if they wouldn't Let boys 14–15–16 in the poolroom they wouldn't lose the money their mother gives them to pay for their lunch in school. They should make the boys show their birth surtiffercate to prove they are 17 to go in a poolroom or hang out in candy stores or go to the movies during school hours. I understand they have a law out saying their not suppose to do this. They ought to be more strict on it also about boys having clubs in a store or cellar. I seen cops coming into the club I usto belong to and take graph so they wouldn't bother the boys when they had a party and got drunk.

"These store dealers should not sell the boys BB guns or pistels to boys without a Identerfercation showing that their 23 or over. I have seen them sell them to boys 16–17. Many of boys are put away because of this they buy a gun not because they need it because they want to show off in front off their freinds and then their big deals and when ther sent away they cry and say their sorry. But why are they put away? Because some Big dope sold them or taught them how to make one.

"I think all the people ought to wise up a little and get together and start writing letters to the state Department to build more boys clubs and PAL and recreations centers for boy to go so they can stay out of the streets. Don't forget the boys of today will be the Men of tomorrow so I hope that whoever may read this will try to do something for your son and you Neighbors sons. Just one more thing to you boys who may read this. I would probably say the same thing you are saying now if I were out there. But it so happens I'm not. But now I know different and I learned my lesson the hard way. Well I'll close now goodby and God Bless All of you your friend Bud."

By reading these seven stories, we come to the heart of the matter. A juvenile delinquent is not simply a thief, or a murderer, or a vandal, he is a troubled human being who steals or destroys as a result of pressures both within and without.

He doesn't just suddenly make the front page by committing a serious crime. The armed holdup, cases of assault, and so on, are usually the climaxes of a series of smaller rebellions against society. A child is a truant or runs away from home long before he "kills for thrills." Professor Sheldon Glueck and Dr. Eleanor T. Glueck, whose outstanding research on juvenile delinquency will be referred to throughout this book, made a study comparing five hundred delinquent boys with five hundred nondelinquent boys. (This material is contained in *Unraveling Juvenile Delinquency,* published for The Commonwealth Fund by Harvard University Press.) They found that 94 per cent of the delinquents had truanted while only 11 per cent of the nondelinquents had truanted. "Of the 474 delinquents who were truants, a third skipped school only very occasionally, while two thirds truanted persistently." In my own survey made in 1954 (see pages 355 ff.) of 208 girls at the New York State Training School for Girls at Hudson, 40 per cent said that they played truant often, and 39 per cent answered "sometimes." Of 208 delinquent boys in the New Jersey State Home for Boys in Jamesburg, 41 per cent played truant often and 46 per cent sometimes.

Many more girls are actually committed to institutions for such offenses as truancy and running away than boys are. It may be, because of our mores, that a girl will be committed for truancy or running away while a boy will be let off until he commits a more flagrant act. Often, too, a boy who runs away steals a car first and is therefore arrested for auto theft and not running away per se. Or if he truants, he spends his time with other restless boys breaking windows and stealing.

In *The Psycho-Analytical Approach to Juvenile Delinquency,* Dr. Kate Friedlander points out that the difference between delinquent and nondelinquent behavior is one of quantity, or degree, rather than quality, or kind. The superintendent of the New York State Training School for Girls, Mr. Abraham G. Novick, says that this is an important distinction. It means that the normal and the delinquent child possess the same basic drives and feelings, that the only difference between the two is that, while the normal individual has gained control over his impulses, the delinquent child expresses his aggression in overt acts.

So, regardless of whether a child is arrested for running away or for stealing a car to run away in, or for any other forms of lawbreaking that result from gang activity, the act itself contributes little to our understanding of delinquency. We must consider the causes in an individual's environment and personality that have made the act inevitable.

It is easy to say, "Lock them all up." It is easy to say, "We will have no part of them in our society." But it is not easy to forget them once you have spoken to them as individuals. I myself questioned fifteen hundred of them. It is not easy to get them out of your mind once you have eaten with them, once you have watched them on the playing field, once you have listened to them talk. They have an important message for society—a message that we can not ignore because whether we consciously recognize it or not, they are part of society and will contribute to it harmfully or constructively. And, in a way, this is *our* choice. As one of the boys in trouble expressed it in talking to me, "Help us—help us find ourself."

"What do you mean by that?" I asked.

"Oh," he answered, "I don't know who I belong to. I don't know what is good, I don't know what is right. I've never had a good home. I had my gang, that was all, but it wasn't good for me. I want, we all want help."

It is not delinquency that we want to examine, it is the delinquent, the individual human being.

3. The Home

*"I didn't have The Love that a
child should have . . ."*

It may be an old American saw that the "first hundred years are
the hardest," but the first *six* years are the most important for
determining our characters. During this early period, the most
essential person to the child is his mother. Nearly all of the child's
needs—physical, moral, social—are provided by the mother, the
most important over-all provision being that of giving the child
a sense of security. Psychologists' and physicians' reports demonstrate a baby's tremendous need for mother-love, while news reports and investigations show the dire effects the lack of it can
produce.

The great importance of the relationship of the child to his
mother is made clear in the observations of Dr. James C. Moloney,
navy psychiatrist on Okinawa in 1945. Dr. Moloney found that
an Okinawan baby is emotionally and physically very close to his
mother during the first two years of his life. When the mother
goes out into the fields, she rocks the child by carrying him
strapped to her back in a papooselike fashion. When the child is
hungry, the mother shifts him around and the infant suckles at her
breast until he is satisfied. He is not left to cry until an arti-
ficially scheduled time arrives. Nor is he given rigid toilet training. When he is ready for this training, it comes naturally.

Dr. Moloney observed, "Their life [under the long Japanese
occupation and later] has not encouraged emotional calmness, but
the Okinawans are calm in spite of it. By the time they are five they
seem to have such a sense of security that their minds survive even
catastrophe."

Then Dr. Moloney added, "I get similar accounts from our medical men all over the island. They rarely see asthma, allergies, hyperthyroidism, neurogenic dermatosis, varicose veins, or shock reactions to surgery. I've never seen an Okinawan faint. The pathologists made six hundred and fifty post-mortem examinations at one base. They confirmed these observations; they found few structural changes of the sort that result from mental tensions and pressures. When you compare it with our western world— where every two minutes a man, woman, or child enters a mental hospital for observation or care, where half of our hospital beds are occupied by the mentally diseased, where more than half the ills in the doctor's office are psychosomatic—Okinawa makes you wonder."

Not long ago, a doctor in charge of a South American orphanage to which many babies were brought reported that for no apparent physical reason, they gradually weakened and died before they were one or two years old. These children slowly lost their will to live, and little could be done about it. The nurses had a heavy load, each one having to care for about ten children. They had no time to give anything but physical attention. It was not enough. These babies died because of a lack of mother-love or from the lack of the attention of a mother-substitute.

During World War II, in Great Britain, when the children of London were in constant danger from the buzz bombs, the authorities quickly made plans for the mass evacuation of children. By the hundreds, by the thousands, from London as well as other danger zones, children were sent to comparatively safe homes in the country.

The farms to which the children were sent were as safe as any place could be in time of war, and they were able to provide fairly good food. The attention and sympathy which the children received surpassed what might have been expected in normal times. Yet, the authorities found that the children under five years of age who were taken from their mothers were extremely unhappy and apparently unable to stand this separation. While the children over five seemed able to adapt themselves to the change, the younger ones experienced a real emotional trauma.

The British evacuation proved that it is far easier for a child to adjust emotionally at home, regardless of the external difficulties, regardless of the problems, even regardless of the bombings, than to adjust away from home under pleasant surroundings and in safer circumstances.

The report "Maternal Care and Mental Health," issued by the World Health Organization, emphasizes that the effect on the physical health of infants deprived of maternal care can be serious.

"Direct studies," it says, "make it plain that, when deprived of maternal care, the child's development is almost always retarded —physically, intellectually, and socially—and that symptoms of physical and mental illness may appear."

We have seen that even when orphans or "temporary orphans" received the best of care, from the physical standpoint, if they did not receive the emotional satisfaction of belonging or knowing affection and love, they deteriorated rapidly.

The WHO report observes that there is a "specific connection between prolonged deprivation in the early years and the development of an affectionless psychopathic character given to persistent delinquent conduct and extremely difficult to treat."

Even though one may not agree entirely with Freud's statement, "The little human being is frequently a finished product in his fourth or fifth year, and only gradually reveals in later years what lies buried in him," enough data has been presented to prove how important it is for a child to feel wanted and loved by his mother from the very beginning, and to have someone upon whom he can depend for security. Rejection by the mother will almost always produce a traumatic effect on the infant's personality. Food, shelter, and love are the first needs of a baby. Love is the bedrock of his security; without it, he is alone in a world he does not understand. A child's desperate need for love is truly a universal phenomenon.

What happens when the mother love is absent, or hidden, or warped, or twisted into evil overt acts? What happens to the child of a mother whose natural instincts are perverted by ignorance, unhappy circumstances, external pressures, jealousies? Last spring the United Press reported this unhappy story: "Doctors fought today to restore the deformed body of Rose M., nine, who said she still loved her mother despite eighteen months of torture in which the mother:

"Twisted her arms until they broke 'with a crunching noise.'

"Struck her so hard in the face that she was blind in one eye.

"Beat her back into a mass of welts with a rubber hose.

"Knocked out six of the girl's upper teeth.

"Squeezed her hands until the bones broke.

"Smashed the girl's nose by breaking it several times with the hose and her fists."

Rose was found because a neighbor became aware of what was happening and reported it to the sheriff. The child was cowering behind a pile of dirty clothes when the police entered the flat; she broke into tears when she was told that she was being taken away from her mother. "I love my mother," she sobbed.

At first the mother calmly admitted the beatings and even told the deputies that Rose, her daughter by a former marriage, was "a good girl." Erratic and impulsive behavior on the part of a mother, aroused emotionally by various conditions and circumstances, must be analyzed before one can condemn her. This mother might be said to have been wrong on the surface, but underneath, she was right in her feelings. Later she sobbed hysterically, "Oh, my God, I love her. I'm sorry I ever hit her. I don't know why I did it. I'd felt bad. I wasn't mad at Rose. I was only mad at myself. So I took it out on her—I don't know why."

Extremely unnatural conduct on the mother's part results from her own experiences. It must be remembered that a parent may suffer as much from insecurity as the child of the same parent. Both suffer, but the child becomes the ward or charge of society as in the case of a New York woman who abandoned her two-year-old son to take a vacation trip to Florida. Some time earlier, she had signed over the custody of a six-year-old daughter on the back of a tavern menu.

These are extreme cases. It is more common to find a hostile, rejecting, or indifferent attitude on the part of one or both parents. Recently a nine-year-old boy ran away from the home where he lived with his grandparents. When the police asked him why, he told them that he had heard that his mother had asked the court to commit four of his nine brothers and sisters to an orphan asylum. The grandparents had not threatened him with a similar fate, but he "identified" himself with his brothers and sisters. A storm of anguished emotion was unleashed by what seemed to him another act of rejection by his mother. His release came in the form of muscular action. He ran and ran and ran. The fact that his mother placed him in the home of his grandparents and had asked relief from her duties in rearing some of her many other children *may* have been a matter of stern necessity rather than one of emotional rejection. But surely a loving and understanding mother could have explained to the child, with hugs and kisses and a few tears, that she was parting with her children because it was wise to do so and not because she did not love them. A sad and emotional parting would have been better than a cold one. The overt act of expressing love for the child could have prevented the trauma, the insecurity, and the fear that were, on the other hand, aroused in the child. His identification with his mother, through a benevolently emotional experience would have been far more preferable than his identification of himself with the seemingly unwanted brothers and sisters who had been "sent away."

Behind the rebellion of thirteen-year-old Maria, who was remanded for truancy to a detention home for girls, is a mother who rejected her.

"Nobody can change my mind, I still hate this place," Maria told me. "I've been here a month, and just don't like this place. I don't know why they sent me here." She stopped. "Oh, I guess maybe I do. I didn't want to go to school. They sent me here to this place for three weeks. I was in the seventh grade. I have nine sisters and two brothers. I'm next to the youngest. I didn't get along with my mother. My mother was mean to me, she always used to hit me. Why, I guess, she doesn't like me."

I looked at Maria, black-eyed, black-haired, a sweet-looking girl with a baby face. "Why? You're such a sweet girl."

"Tell that to her and she'd kill you," Maria said with fire. "If she thought I was a sweet girl, she'd help me, wouldn't she?" She hesitated, then continued. "She doesn't get along with my father. My father and I stick together like glue. That's why I hate this place. I want to go home, I want to be with my father. He's sick; he's got heart trouble. I want to be with my father. I want to help him.

"I got in bad with my mother when I was eight. She wouldn't buy me any new clothes. She wouldn't buy me anything. I liked school for a while, but I couldn't do my work. I had too many other things on my mind. I was thinking about my father all the time. I was thinking about why my mother doesn't like me. I asked her, 'Mother do you like me?' She said, 'No, I don't like you. I don't even think that you are my daughter. I wish that they would send you away from me.'

"The judge said to me, 'Maria, are you going to school?' I said, 'Yes, judge, I will.' Sure, how could a girl with so much on her mind? How can she go to school? I went two days, and then my mother started all over again. Said she wished the judge would send me away till I was sixteen, so I would learn my lesson. It was very miserable living at home.

"My mother ran around with another man. I saw my mother making love to this man in his car. I told my father. He told my mother she should be ashamed of herself; maybe that's why my mother is mad at me. Why should I like her if she doesn't like me? I don't bend down and kiss nobody's feet for nothing. If my mother would like me, I would like her."

Here is Maria's record as reported by her case worker:

"Maria feels in competition with other children in her attempts to gain adult love, and is inclined to try to eventually gain control of them so that she will have at least them for security. She acts childishly, exhibitionistically, to gain group attention. In relation to adults, Maria is guarded and unwilling to expose her own unhappiness. She is made unhappy and resentful by her mother's rejection. She'll need patient, long-term efforts to gain trust in women.

"At present Maria is isolated from others with her inner attitude being either I will try to ignore them, or have to fight with them. Despite this emotional isolation tendency, there is nothing in her test findings to indicate loss of reality contact or severe pathology.

"Maria is inclined to depression and to answers impulsively spanned to stress situations, but generally can act in a rather controlled manner. She senses her need for love but may be able to express it only in an orally demanding way. She is confused about where she belongs, or whom she belongs to. Maria needs help in working through her problem, and needs a chance to establish a warm relationship. When she gains the confidence to express her dependency need directly, she will probably lose some of her distress and defiance of authority, and be able to inwardly desire conformity to the pattern of society."

At the age of thirteen Maria is carrying far too heavy a burden for any child to carry. She is unable to understand why her mother rejects her, why she is friendless. Every child wants to be loved— and mother-love is basic to our very existence. Something dies within us if it is lacking—actual physical death in the case of a neglected infant; emotional death in the older boy or girl.

And that is why we have so many Marias in trouble.

If, during a child's early years, his relationship to his mother is of prime importance, as he grows older, the father's influence on the child grows too. The father represents authority and his method (or lack of it) in administering authority is of tremendous importance in developing in the child a respect for authority outside the home.

First of all, a child needs a "father figure." This means that he needs to identify himself with a person stronger and wiser than himself. Boys especially need to identify themselves with their fathers. Take the case of a boy who had been stealing, running away, playing truant. His father was unassertive, with a highly neurotic wife. When the parents came before the court, the father for the first time took hold in a masculine way. He began to assume the real responsibilities of a father. Since then, the boy has made an excellent record; he found his "father figure."

I interviewed a sixteen-year-old boy at a state training school. His name was Phil, and he had just arrived that morning. He was small of build, thin, looked about thirteen, although he was actually six-teen. He was fearful and furtive.

He was very unhappy at home, he told me, rejected by his father and stepmother. He had loved his mother who died when he was six. He wished she was still alive and could take care of him. He tried to become friendly with the brighter children in the neighbor-hood but was rejected by them. He was a quiet child to whom people did not pay much attention. He was not a troublesome child in school.

Later I observed that he stayed mostly by himself. He didn't come out of his shell. He needs to be brought out, I thought, in order to become a part of his own community.

And then I looked at the case record. He had an IQ of 106, slightly better than average. His drawings on the tests showed he was trying to maintain control of his feelings. Much anxiety was present in his relation to women.

The official report reads: "Philip was somewhat anxious in the interview situation. He responded in a manner which indicated that he was eager to please; spoke in a low tone of voice. He indi-cated very frankly that his trouble has been mainly in the home. He has been in conflict with his stepmother ever since he can remember. He describes her as an aggressive, loud, nagging type of person who is always criticizing him. She is also very strict; per-mits him to go out only two hours a day at the most. He has always resented her and doesn't believe that their relationship will ever be any better. He gave the impression that his father is sympathetic but rather passive. At least, he makes no effort to protect Phil from the stepmother. Later he brought out the fact that his father is inclined to believe the lies that the stepmother tells him about Phil and has punished him severely for things he didn't do."

Now, why did Phil come here? Stealing. He denies that he stole; he explains that a policeman happened to see him on the roof and got the impression he was intending to break into an apartment. Phil was on the roof because he had run away from home. He had done this a number of times before.

His father, on the surface, is for him. He wants him to go to college and study law. Phil had this ambition at one time, but now he is not sure what will happen to him in the future. He has some disturbing dreams; in one dream he is being pushed out of a window. In other dreams, he is being killed or is killing his step-mother. Yet, in talking to him, all you see is a well-behaved, quiet, mannerly boy.

What is the answer? Phil is not a serious delinquent but is an emotionally disturbed boy whose problems center about his relationship with his father and stepmother. He feels rejected by her and resents everything she does or says to him. His feelings about his father are mixed. He likes his father but there are indications of repressed resentment; his father doesn't protect him from his step-mother. Phil can not respect his father's weakness; he has no father figure to emulate.

On the other hand, many fathers are perfectionists. From her experience as a counselor in a well-to-do suburban county, a psychiatrist gave me this illustration of a father who asked too much of his child:

"I had a conference with a parent yesterday after seeing her child, seven years old. He was quite emotionally disturbed, and he is quite a behavior problem—very nervous, can't sit still, isn't willing to read. He fights constantly and children complain that he always gets them into trouble when he is around. The father, a service man, expects instant obedience from this child. The mother says that nothing the child ever does pleases the father. She is somewhat of a perfectionist herself, holding very high standards for table manners and behavior. Actually, both parents are trying to do a good job, showing in their high standards a way to help their child become a good citizen. Ironically enough, it is the pressure to meet these high standards that is causing the child's misbehavior."

More damaging to a child than the weakling or the perfectionist, is a father who is both demanding and inconsistent—a father who disciplines his children harshly according to the dictates of his own moods. The Gluecks found that 70 per cent of the fathers of five hundred delinquents were overstrict or erratic in disciplining their children. (Twenty-six per cent were lax or indifferent, and only 5 per cent were both firm and kindly.)

Betty's story, which follows, is a classic example.

"I am just fifteen years old. My name is Elizabeth or Betty as they call me. By "They" I mean the girls up here in the training school for girls. I wish I would have never come to this school. It is only making me worse instead of better. I was sent here for stealing and fighting. I first started fighting when I was six years old. My mother and father were very strict to us. My father didn't make much money. Our rooms were always dirty because we lived in the back of the building where all the garbage was emptied, and the dust used to fly in our windows, and my mother just couldn't keep the place clean.

"Every night my father would come home drunk on his pay that he spent on liquor. My mother used to yell at him for money but he wouldn't give her any, only when he was sober. I remember one night my mother told me she was pregnant again and I started crying. A few minutes later my father came in the door just as drunk as ever. My mother told him to get out because she couldn't put up with it any more. But my father didn't get out, he just swung his hand at my mother's face and then started beating her. Me and my sister and brother screamed so loud that my Aunt who lives under us came running up the stairs. By that time my mother was bleeding from her mouth. She was coughing up blood. My father left the house that night after beating me, my sister, my brothers and my mother.

"He hit us with a strap and it left welts on our backs and faces. The next day my father came home sober and told us he was sorry. We all told him we forgave him, but deep down in my heart I knew he didn't mean it because I knew it was going to happen again. And it did. That same day me and my sister ran away after school. We ran away because we were hungry and cold. We wanted food and warm coats, and most of all freedom. Because my mother never let us go out never—only to school. So we ran away. Not far, just a few blocks, but at least we did get some food. We didn't want to steal, but then I didn't know what stealing was. I was only six and my sister didn't know either.

"So we went into Super Markets and took cookies and bread and butter. We went into a building and buttered the bread with our fingers and ate it. After we finished our cookies we came out of the building, and it was dark out. I told my sister I was scared and wanted to go home because I had never been out at night before in my life. But we lost our way, so we just roamed around until one in the morning. We were walking down the street freezing and ready to drop when we heard this siren and it was the police after us. My sister got scared and ran into a building, but I just stood there because I would be so glad if a car did stop and pick us up. So my sister came out of hiding and got into the car that stopped in front of us. The police brought us to the police station where they asked our name and address and age. All we could tell them was my name was Betty. I didn't even know my last name. They saw we were freezing and hungry so they took us into a big room with benches. They sat us near the stove and gave us blankets and some rolls and milk. I don't know how long we were sleeping, but when we woke up, I found myself in my own bed.

"I got out of bed but couldn't go out of the room because there were wooden bars across the doorway.

"My father made them and put them up every night so me and my sister wouldn't sneak out into the kitchen and take food. I got out of bed and looked out the bars to see if my father was home or at work. When I looked out, I could not see his feet in the bed, only my mother's, so I took it for granted he wasn't home, so I woke up my sister and together we took down the bars so we could get out but when we got them down after an hour of noiseless work, we saw my father standing there in the kitchen with the 'belt.' We knew that there was nothing more to be said, but to get into bed and wait for the worst. My father followed us in and beat us until he made us say we were sorry and promise not to run away any more. Me and my sister just layed there and cried after he left for work.

"We were so sore that we couldn't go to school that day. That night me and my sister stayed awake all night planning on what we were going to do when we ran away the next day. The next morning we got up; it was Saturday so we stayed in the house all day; we didn't have a chance to run. We thought it was better to run away on Sunday anyway because my mother always sent us to mass with a dime a piece. So we waited.

"Next day my father was off from work, but we didn't care because we thought we would get so far away that he would never find us. But we didn't. We came out of our rooms, ate breakfast, and bundled up nice and warm, and went to church.

"But we never got there, instead we went down to the subway, God knows which one, but we took any one because we knew it would at least get us further away. So we snuck under the turnstile and got on the train.

"We sat on that train until we were the last two there. We got scared being alone, so we got off. We were in Brooklyn, but we didn't know it until later when we were home. We walked and walked until we were so tired and hungry that we fell asleep in a hallway. We woke up the next morning still in the same hallway with twenty cents to our name. With that twenty cents we bought candy, and we stole candy also. It was dark when we came back to Manhattan. We realized that we were gone almost two days. A few minutes later we heard a police siren; the car stopped, and we got in. Back at the police station, my mother came for us, but we refused to go; so they asked us why, and we told them about the beating we got the last time. So the policeman made my mother promise not to beat us. So she didn't. But, oh, I won't talk about how my father did. That same afternoon after school, I met my sister again, so we walked around for a half hour, but we got lost again, and then I was mad, and I knew that we would be in trouble.

"Then my mother put me in my room, put the bars up on my door so that when my father came home he would think I was asleep. But I couldn't lie and told my mother that I had played hookey, so that was when me and my sister were sent away for the first time. We went to a little home for girls and boys. We were there five months; then we came home. I'll never forget the day we came home.

"My mother came to get us. We both had on blue dresses that matched, and she brought us lollypops. When we saw my mother I was so surprised to see her not with a belly any more. I asked her why she didn't have a big stomach, and she laughed and said, wait till you get home.

"I opened the door and ran into my father's and brothers' arms which I hadn't been in the whole four months. They pointed to the bedroom, and I followed, and when I got there, I saw my baby brother. He was so cute, but mother never had time to look at us. She was so busy.

"One night I remember we were picked up at two o'clock in the morning and brought to the police station. Then we were taken home by my mother and got a bad beating with a strap from my father, and this time it was with the metal part. He beat us until my mother felt sorry and told him to stop. We were so sore we couldn't put on our ragged pajamas, so we had to sleep naked.

"A few weeks later it was Christmas. We didn't get nothing, we didn't expect nothing, because we never did get anything. On ———— was my birthday. I was eight years old. I didn't get anything then either, but I didn't care. A few days later, though, my mother took us all to the hospital and we got some toys that were left over from Christmas.

"Then I was sent to a foster home in Long Island. I was there for about two months, but then they sent me away because I stole $2.00 out of the lady's house. I went to another house on Staten Island. I was crying my eyes out when they sent me there. I thought that if I cried they wouldn't keep me there, but I got foxed because I was there for five and one-half years.

"My mother in this house wasn't different. I thought she would be, but after I was there a few months she made me work like a dog. I didn't mind it a bit, but then she made me clean the whole fourteen rooms in one day, every Saturday. She beat me with a stick. She was sixty-six years old and so was her husband. I hated her so much. He was quiet, and I thought he was nice, but I found out different when I went to him and told him that she beat me. He used to say good for you. I hated him after that.

"After I was there two years, I got bad. I started smoking cigarettes when the mother wasn't looking. Then I started stealing a dollar every day from her. Finally she found out about my stealing and smoking. She called up some one and told them to take me away. After that she started saying, after all these years I let you stay in my nice house, I clothed you and fed you and even had you make communion, and then you turn around and do this to me. I got tired of her preaching and asked when they were going to take me out of there. She said soon. I remember one day she told me she was going to adopt me, and I said "hell no." We got into an argument, and I was sent to another foster home. I was there a few months when they sent me home.

"I was twelve years old when I got home, but I didn't stay there long. My mother was starting to get strict. We never had fun at home together. We had to be in the house at ten, and we had to sweep all the floors and make the beds. We'd get up in the morning, and all we could have to eat was either a sandwich or a piece of cake. We ate in school.

"That's when I met Janet, my best girl friend. We used to steal together, and play hookey together and get in trouble together all the time.

"We started stealing. My mother caught us and punished us by making me stay inside after school for one month.

"The day that my mother started our punishment, my sister asked me to run away from home with her. We were coming home from school, and we went into the laundry until my mother got finished washing so she could take us home and start our punishment, by putting us in our room.

"We walked into the laundry, and my mother said: What are you two doing in here? Get away from me and wait outside because I don't want anyone to know you're my daughters. So I got mad. We walked outside carrying our zipper loose-leaf books when my sister said to me, "Betty I'm mad, let's run away from home." I said, "No, cause we'll only get caught and get another big beating." "We won't get caught," she said, "because I know where we can hide. And we're too old to get hit." So I said, "O.K."

"We hid for a while, and we saw a movie on 42nd Street, we saw a lady and we grabbed her pocketbook, and we saw fourteen ten dollar bills in it. One hundred and forty dollars.

"We didn't believe our eyes, but it was true. We didn't come home for a long time, I think almost a week. However, my father caught up with me one day when I was walking around alone and asked where I got the jacket and turtle-neck sweater and dungarees. I told him I robbed them, and he slapped me.

"I asked him where my sister Jane was, and he said she had been picked up too and was home. The next day my mother locked us into the house again. And that day she went to court, I think, and said that we better be sent away. Well, I've been sent to many homes, and finally got caught, ran away, got caught again. They sent me up to ———, that's where I am now. I've been here eight and one-half months. My mother has never come up to see us. Jane was here but I don't know where she is now. I think she has T.B."

I have given Betty's story at great length, exactly as she told it, because it is unfortunately typical—a domineering father, a neurotic mother, poor surroundings, lack of security, and complete absence of love. In her own simple, straightforward, almost literary form, she has spelled it out for us.

I spoke to a twelve-year-old boy in another training school. He had slashed the upholstery in a number of cars; he scratched the cars. He did this right after he was beaten severely by his father, he told me. He was so angry because his father had beaten him unjustly that he just went out and slashed up the first half-dozen cars he found. The judge gave the boy a choice of going home or to a training school. The boy said, "I don't want to go home, I'll go wherever you send me."

An investigator told this story: "Some time ago I had occasion to be in a school talking to the disciplinarian officer. He was telling me that they really didn't have any trouble in their school, everything was going along just great. And indeed it was, for at that very moment a boy was being knifed in the school yard. I went out to see what was going on, and a bit later I went over to the hospital where the boy had been taken. This was about a half-hour later, and the boy's father was present.

"The father was walking up and down the hall. His boy was in the emergency ward, quite seriously hurt. The father was walking

up and down, up and down, and was wringing his hands and saying to a friend of his who was walking with him, and then saying
to me when I came along, 'What can I do? I beat him every night.
I tell him not to go around with these kids. Just last night I beat
the daylights out of him.'"

These are the words of a misguided father. Too often the administration of authority becomes cruelty, though born many times of a
sincere desire to instill virtue. The results can be disastrous to the
child, the parents, and to society. Ben's case is a good example.
Ben's father boasted of the almost daily whippings he gave the boy
to keep him in line. Ben's mother boasted that she was firm with
her children, that they wouldn't go wrong. But what was the actual
effect of their rigid attitudes toward this sixteen-year-old? Ben gives
a frightening answer:

"When I started going to high school," he said, "I began to raise
holy hell. I have a mother and father, and every night they ask
me where I'm going, and they tell me to keep out of trouble. I'm
going to a playground, or I'm going to a club, I would say.

"'Please come home early,' they would say.

"I'd go to the corner, come home hours later. My father always
used to beat me, sometimes he beat me pretty hard with a strap.
I have three brothers and sisters and we live in a four-room house.
I slept with two of my brothers in the same bed.

"I guess I got in trouble three years ago. I sold firecrackers to
make money. Ten or fifteen of us went down to ——. We sold
these firecrackers and blew up the town. Charged forty cents a
pack. We paid ten cents for them. We got caught, but the cops
let us go. We went back to town and rounded up our gang and
said, 'Let's go in and fight them.' There were twenty of us.

"We found a nice place where we could have quite a battle. I
went over to these grounds and I grabbed a girl.

"I said, 'Come with me.' I made her walk away with me. They
wanted to jump me, but I had a knife in my belt.

"'Don't worry,' I said, 'I'll come back with my gang, and we'll
really go at it.'

"Well, we did. We won. But the cops got us again, and a couple of guys got their heads smashed open. We were put on probation, but still we had more gang fights. You know, we were called the Black Leaders, and we were fighting the Lucky Sports. There were so many of us guys on the corner that we had to break up into two gangs.

"I ran away from here six times. I was sent here by a girl. The cops tried to break up the gang fights. I got a job in a bowling alley, but my back began to hurt from bending down picking up pins, so I saw a couple of girls in a bowling alley. I went out with them. You know something, I had two girls. I was laying both of them. The boys in my gang wanted to come over one night to take a crack at the girl. I told that to the girl, but she refused. I beat her up bad. She ran home, and I ran after her. Her mother and father came, so I went away.

"They told about me, and I was locked up for a week. When I got out I beat her up again, almost killed her. I brought a lot of guys down to lay her, but after we got through laying her, I still beat the bejesus out of her. The court said we raped her. We all got sent up here.

"My parents come up visiting day. I write to them. I send them three letters a month. We live in a tenement house, a pretty bad neighborhood."

What is the story behind Ben? Pretty bad, the director at the public training school told me. Ben is pretty much of a show-off, a sex deviate, doesn't seem to have any moral or social scruples. He had found neither love nor understanding at home. He went to the corner drugstore and teamed up with older boys and girls in similar situations. He chose their standards of behavior.

"No one can call me chicken," said Ben. "By gosh, I'll show the best of them."

He told me wistfully, "When I get out, I think I'll make good. I don't think I'll get in any gang fights anymore."

Then he squinted cunningly. "You know something," he confided, "the first chance I get, I'm going to beat up my girl friend. She was the one who got me up here. The son-of-a-bitch. I'll show her. I asked the super for a weekend pass so I could go and beat her up, but he wouldn't give me no pass. I'm going to sneak out of here, and by God she's going to get it."

What can this case be called besides a series of failures? The father failed in spite of, and because of, his administration of authority. Institutionalizing Ben resulted in further resentment of authority. And Ben? How will he solve his conflict? Ben wants to "make good" and wants revenge simultaneously.

In attempting to understand why children choose certain behavior patterns, it is important to realize that children learn by imitation, and are more affected by what their parents *do* than what they *say*. Children are mimics, and the behavior patterns shown by their parents cannot fail to have a strong influence. Then, in rebelling against actions of their parents that they consider unjust, children will very often assume the very attitudes against which they rebel. It is not surprising, for instance, that Ben beat up his girl friend; he was familiar with this form of retaliation. It is through their early association with parents that children form their concepts of right and wrong.

Freud termed this sense of right and wrong the superego. It is equivalent to what is called conscience. According to Freud, "During the whole of man's later life it [the superego] represents the influence of his childhood, of the care and education given to him by his parents, of his dependence on them—of the childhood which is so greatly prolonged in human beings by a common family life."

The delinquent with defective superego has little guilt feeling or remorse. He does not represent the average citizen in conformity to conventional morality. This type of delinquent is usually the member of a gang and commits offenses with others rather than alone. He is more persistent in delinquent behavior than the others, less amenable to attempts to rehabilitate him. Again Ben is a good example.

A common effect that the example of a bad parent has is that of forcing the child to seek authority elsewhere. And because of the bad example of the parents, these children tend to seek an outside authority that is not much better!

Take the case of Ned.

Ned is a thirteen-year-old cited by Professor William W. Wattenberg of Wayne University in a study of juvenile delinquents now being conducted in Detroit. Ned's home situation is a bad one. His father is an alcoholic who has since received a prison sentence for assaulting his wife. Scenes of violence are frequent in the home. Ned boasted of having come to his mother's rescue on one occasion by knocking his father unconscious with a battery cable. Asked if his father punished him, the boy answered, "I dare him. He hasn't whipped me since I was eight years old."

Ned's contempt for his father extends to all five of his sisters. His attitude toward the neighborhood boys of his own age is, "They are all babies. They are chicken. Just touch them once and they cry." Accordingly, he goes around with older boys and works at odd jobs to get spending money. His detention resulted from this incident: Ned and a sixteen-year-old boy stayed at a girl's house until 1 A.M. Afraid to go home so late, he and his friend slept in a park and remained away from home for three days. Then, seeing a car with keys in it, they took it, intending to drive to Texas to see Ned's sister. At the time of his detention, Ned had already been arrested four times, twice for auto theft.

Even though Ned came from a fairly good neighborhood, he chose an older and experienced delinquent as a friend. Boys who live in slum areas have less opportunity to choose their companions. They are surrounded by bad influences, like this boy who wrote pathetically:

"Me and my mother were walking up from downtown and found out they had thrown out our stuff out of our house. We were thrown out. After that we moved to a different house on a side street. It was hard to make ends meet, but my mother did it. My father wasn't any good; he always got drunk and beat my mother up, and he never gave her any money. He always use to rob her purse and take her money. Later on I moved to a project and lived there for five years. During those five years, I got into a lot of trouble. Hanging around the wrong kids."

This boy was exposed first to the bad example of his father, then to that of "the wrong kids."

One father laid the foundation for his son's delinquency in a more positive way. His son made a practice of going to a local five-and-ten-cent store and bringing home kitchen gadgets. The father praised him for it. He would say that this was the smartest boy he had. Later, the boy told the police that he had stolen on thirty occasions and that no one outside his family knew about it.

A child learns a lesson in brutality when he is beaten or when he witnesses his father beating his mother. This not only breeds resentment in the child, but it undermines his feeling that his home is a warm and happy place. This is a feeling to which a child clings. Despite all that happens, the child tends to build up a rosy picture of his home. "My idea of paradise is my home," was the statement of one child whose parents sent her away. All the relationships within the family contribute to the child's picture of his home. And none of these relationships operate independently. The child's direct relationships with mother and with father are the most obvious determinants of personality, but these are interwoven with, and dependent upon, his parents' attitudes toward each other, and toward his brothers and sisters, too.

How compatible are the parents of delinquents? Though a child will usually deny that his parents do not get along, investigation of individual cases usually contradicts the child's statements. In many cases, these tensions result in desertion, separation, or divorce, and the child is deprived of a parent. A home where a child is thus deprived, by death as well as by divorce or separation, is called a broken home.

The correlation between the broken home and juvenile delinquency has been studied by many sociologists and case workers. The following chart is taken from my comparison of 208 boys at the New Jersey State Home in Jamesburg and the same number of girls at the New York State Training School in Hudson in 1954, and 500 boys at Jamesburg in 1937. Note the increase since 1937 of children from broken homes.

	From broken homes	*From normal homes*
Jamesburg Boys, 1937	28.0%	72.0%
Jamesburg Boys, 1954	60.6%	39.4%
Hudson Girls, 1954	77.9%	22.1%

The growing incidence of divorce and separation of parents is thus apparently causing increasing difficulties for children. The surveys summarized also show that broken homes come about not so much through the death of a parent as through divorce, or desertion, especially the latter.

At both Jamesburg and Hudson, for example, it was found that almost three fourths of the children were not living with both parents for reasons other than death, but because of separation, divorce, and for reasons like these:

"I do not know my parents."

"My father just took off."

"Father ran away."

"My parents were not married."

"I was sent away," was all one girl said!

A study made some time ago in Chicago of 362 delinquent girls showed that 67 per cent came from broken homes. In a control group of nondelinquent girls from a similar environment, only 45 per cent came from broken homes. It was also found that the chances for delinquency were fewer when one parent remains at home.

Dr. John E. Mohair, psychiatrist at the New Jersey training school, made this statement: "I've been here for two years. . . . I've analyzed 400 cases. . . . Present always is rejection of the boy in one way or another. . . . I'd say that between 60 per cent and 70 per cent of our cases come from broken homes."

These are approximately the same figures as those found in a recent survey of eighteen hundred juvenile delinquents at Bellevue Hospital in New York where 60 per cent of the children came from broken homes.

At the same time, however, many of these delinquents had brothers and sisters who were not in trouble. Problems of adjustments among teen-agers in broken homes and in homes in which both parents are present do not differ as much as might be expected, according to researchers at the State College of Washington. Statistically, broken homes appear to be the chief cause of delinquency. Yet, as the Gluecks and others have shown, you cannot rest there.

A report on a study conducted by Dr. Paul H. Landis, sociologist, showed that greater economic maturity was achieved at an earlier age among the boys and girls from broken homes. However, young people from homes broken by divorce or separation, particularly the girls, had tendencies toward extreme views. They are more likely to consider early marriage, or to be negative toward marriage, according to the report.

(The broken home is not in itself a *cause* of delinqency, but the emotional and physical deprivations implicit in it are. The broken home is only an outward sign that a child is not receiving the love he needs. When a father deserts the family, the child has been rejected by that father. But the child can have just as strong a sense of rejection when both parents are present. The break between the parents may actually *solve* a problem that is already having a bad effect upon the child. A complete home marked by dissension may be psychologically and socially more "broken" than a physically broken home in which the remaining members of the family carry on as a closely knit group.\

The Gluecks concluded that in the families of five hundred delinquents from both broken and normal homes the forces of disruption were greater than those making for unity. And this is the point. The real question is not whether a child's home is broken, it is whether whatever family he has acts as a unit—or is "cohesive," as the Gluecks define it. They found that only 16 per cent of the delinquents' families could be characterized as cohesive, whereas 61.8 per cent of the nondelinquents' families evinced strong emotional ties among the members, joint interests, pride in their home, and a "we" feeling in general. In about one fourth (24.1 per cent) of the families of the delinquents, as compared with only

0.8 per cent of the families of the nondelinquents, the self-interest of each member clearly exceeded the group interest; to the former group, home was "just a place to hang your hat."

Seven out of ten of the families that reared delinquent children failed to do things together that would lead to a sense of sharing. They held no family picnics, nor did they go to the movies together, or take walks, or ride busses or ferries. Eight out of ten of these parents were entirely indifferent or completely inhospitable to their children's friends. They just didn't want their children to bring their friends home with them.

In the Gluecks' study, eight out of ten of the delinquent boys reported that their mothers were not at all concerned about their welfare. Seven out of ten of the boys felt no attachment to their fathers; they didn't care for them at all. Eight out of ten of the same group of boys said their fathers were not concerned about them. They felt that their fathers had no interest in them, no interest in what they were doing, and didn't care about their future, or schooling, or any aspect of their lives.

Any element of cohesion in the family group is a step toward prevention of delinquency. The Gluecks found striking differences in the quality of family life in the two groups. In the families of the delinquents, there was less planning of household routine, a less cultural atmosphere, less family self-respect, less ambition on the part of the parents to improve their own status or that of their children. Standards of conduct were lower, and the supervision of the children lax. There was inferior provision for recreational outlets within the home as well as outside. They concluded, "Thus in the highly important quality that is both expressive of loyalty to the blood group and supportive of the individual in his sense of security—family cohesiveness—the delinquents were far more deprived than the nondelinquents."

This does not apply to families in low-income brackets only. Unfortunately, today we find a rising rate of delinquency among the children of families in the upper economic levels. We find that the son or daughter of a lawyer, a doctor, an architect, a professional worker, the sons and daughters of those who live on "the right side of the tracks" are more and more getting into trouble. They are getting into difficulties with the school authorities, the community, the police, and the courts.

I believe that this trend is based on the fact that these "privileged" children who become delinquent are deprived of the same sense of family cohesiveness that many poorer children are. Even when the physical well-being of the child is taken care of, the social-butterfly mother may be causing damage by denying the child his need for love and affection—even though her time is spent in service to what she considers to be worthy causes.

J. Edgar Hoover expressed this attitude in the spring, 1953, issue of *The Syracuse Law Review,* in an article on juvenile delinquency. He wrote, "The child who finds his parents too absorbed in vocational or social pursuits to provide him proper guidance and attentive care is one who turns from the home for understanding and recreation. In all too many instances his quest for understanding leads him to bad companions; his recreation consists largely of antisocial activities.

"During World War II a juvenile 'crime club' was broken up on the west coast when one of its members stole a bottle of gin, drank it, and revealed numerous crimes which he and his associates had committed. This youngster was a member of a gang of twelve boys whose ages ranged from nine to fifteen. Members of this gang admitted picking pockets, shoplifting, and burglarizing. So proficient had they become that a minor black market sprang up to handle rationed commodities and other merchandise which they stole.

"An examination of the backgrounds of these twelve boys showed that five of them came from homes in which both parents had been steadily employed. Two of the other boys, brothers, had been deserted by their mother. Their father left them in the care of a housekeeper while he worked. Another one of the boys came from a home broken by the desertion of his father. His mother worked to support her five children. Neglected at home, these boys fell into bad company and quickly adopted criminal behavior patterns which might have been avoided had their parents devoted sufficient time to their guidance."

Why blame these children for meeting in cellars, on the streets, in the poolrooms? Their families were not units; they were singularly lacking in cohesiveness.

The rejection of the child can take many forms. It is rarely a single act or a single experience, like a blow over the head. It can be manifested in various ways. Some of these forms are frequent beatings, face-slappings, turning away from the child's efforts to show his affection and to gain the affection of his parents.

The rejection by the parent may be something he says, like "Go away," or "Leave me alone," or "Don't bother me." Or the father or mother may threaten by saying, "If you ever do that again, I'll kill you, you little brat." Or it may be shown by a contrast between the attention given one child in the family and another. Many children have grown up in homes where favoritism was shown to a brother or sister and sternness to them. Not all such children become delinquent, of course, but in combination with other factors, this situation can be the determining one. To the child, it appears that if only his rival was not there, he would have the love he needs.

The case of ten-year-old George was reported by Charles E. Kennedy, chief of the Division of Child Welfare of the state Department of Public Assistance in West Virginia. George was thin and anxious-looking, just like his mother. She was worn out with her efforts to raise a new baby and act as a buffer between George and his stepfather, an aggressive young businessman wrapped up in two things—the little girl born to his present marriage and his business. George needed and wanted a father very badly, but the only man who could fill this role not only had no time for him, but gave all his attention to a baby sister. She, on her part, added insult to injury by taking from George the time and interest of his mother which at one time had been his alone.

So George stole candy from the store, money from a neighbor's house, small change from his stepfather's pockets, things that were lying around at school—in short, almost anything that was not locked up or nailed down. What did he do with the things he stole? He gave them to his schoolmates, to his teachers, even to his Sunday school teacher, saying, "This is for you because I love you." George has become one of our million delinquents.

Here is another case of a teen-age girl who felt bitterly the injustice of her treatment in comparison with the treatment received by her brothers and sister. In her words, she reacted against this by "being wild, going out and staying out until early in the morning. Giving my parents the 'don't care' attitude, bringing a regular disgrace upon my family."

She went on bitterly, "Far as I can remember my mother has always treated me as a stepchild. I was always the last to take part in anything. In other words, I played second fiddle. Yes, I looked nice in my clothes (when I got them). They were pretty and always clean. I especially want you to know that I was always beaten. If my mother was to argue with me, I would get beaten. I had better not say how if she argued with my brothers or sister they could walk all over the ceiling arguing back and saying and doing as they pleased. My brother walked out quite a few times and didn't come home until a couple of weeks later. Do you think my mother or father sent out an alarm? No. My sister walked out when she was sixteen. No alarm was sent out for her. My mother and father didn't touch them. But when I left home, and then I returned, I nearly got my neck broken. My sister, she was allowed to go with boys since she was fourteen. She's married now.

"Anyway the only time I got to see a boy I had to sneak. I had to sneak to really have fun. . . ."

Fourteen-year-old Honey told me a similar story when I visited a training school in the East.

"Guess my father died when I was about a year old," Honey said. "He drowned and several years later, my mother remarried. Everything went along nicely at first, but my father and mother quarrelled all the time. Then my mother had three other children, and I found that she didn't care as much for me. She was wrapped up in her own family. I was no longer part of the family. Real things in life didn't seem to mean anything. I wasn't wanted. I wasn't liked. I wasn't loved. I remember coming down on the stairs, I must have been five or six, my mother was giving a cocktail party, and I'd come down and make a fuss, and disrupt the party. No one wanted me around. Then later when I was eleven, I would be a tomboy and run around and try to attract attention.

"This went on until I was placed in a foster home," Honey added. "I liked being part of a family, the new father and mother were nice to me, but they didn't have the time to really talk to me. No one ever cuddled me. I ran away from there too. Then two years ago I was sent here. They said I was bad. I don't resent my own mother's attitude. Her life is wrapped up in the other three children. I get a letter from them maybe once every six months or so. When I graduated from junior high last year, they came to my graduation, but I don't know, I don't think that I enjoyed being home; I don't know now where I can go when I leave here. You know, I can't go home. Maybe I can get a job. You know, I want to be a nurse. I want to be nice to people and have a home of my own. I used to run away a lot when I was home. Guess nobody paid much attention to me."

Misbehavior like Honey's, used as an attention-getting device or a substitute for affection or in reprisal, may evoke expressions of parental dislike such as, "You are a wicked girl." Or, "You're no good." Or "You'll never amount to anything." And if the child felt wronged before, this is further proof of it to her.

Parental feeling produces like feeling in the child; parental lack of feeling produces an emotional disturbance tending to make the child neurotic or delinquent, or both, especially if there are accompanying circumstances or causes to support bad conduct. The child may withdraw into a fantasy world of his own; he may misbehave to gain attention; or the parent's hostility may arouse his destructive instincts.

Generally, children believe or say that they believe that their parents love them. Asked whether their parents loved them, 80 per cent of the boys at Jamesburg and 77.4 per cent of the girls at Hudson said yes. One out of five, then, felt unloved and was willing to admit it. But it is unusual for a child to admit he is unloved. In retrospect, the delinquent child's home life means affection and kindness to him although this is almost always a fantasy or a protective lie.

Nor will children as a rule blame their parents for their own delinquent acts. Asked whether their families had tried to keep them out of trouble, 99 per cent of the boys at Jamesburg said yes in 1937, and 94 per cent in 1954; 96 per cent of the girls at Hudson also answered yes. In 1937, 2 per cent of the youngsters questioned admitted their parents had helped them break the law; in 1954, 3 per cent of the girls and 3 per cent of the boys made the same admission.

"Whose fault is it that you are here?" we asked the girls at Hudson. Only 27 (of the 208) blamed their parents, 153 blamed themselves, 4 the police, 20 the court, and 13 the school. Since youngsters are reluctant to criticize their parents publicly, it is significant that over 10 per cent feel that their being institutionalized is their parents' fault, and next to blaming themselves, more gave this answer than any other.

In contradiction to what the children believe, the expert testimony at the Washington hearings of the Senate subcommittee investigating juvenile delinquency, practically without exception placed the onus for much delinquency on the shoulders of the family. Whether the family was broken, with one or both parents absent due to separation, divorce, desertion, or death, or the family was disorganized as a result of frustrations and instability, the end result was the same: maladjusted children who become involved in delinquency to obtain recognition and praise among their own peers. They wanted to express pent-up hostilities against those adults who neglected or abused them, or they wanted to obtain material goods the easy way—by stealing.

On the other hand, a child surrounded by a happy, healthy, wholesome home has a better chance of developing normally, even if his environment is poor.

And when a child says, as so many said to me in many different ways, "I didn't have the love that a child should have," there isn't much you can add. Unless we provide that love, unless we can help Betty while she is in the formative years of her life, we can do but little for her later.

This is one major problem in helping to reduce our delinquency rate. It is not going to be easy to supply love that is lacking. It is going to be even more difficult to provide a sense of belonging, of security, of happiness, to a child who has known no fulfillment of these basic needs.

But these needs must be provided for the more than 1,000,000 boys and girls in trouble.

"Thank God," a teen-aged boy told me recently, "my mother and father have brought me up to know what is right and what is wrong. I can go out on the weekend because I have to be in at a sensible hour. My friends have cleaned out a cellar, and together we have made a playroom. It keeps us out of trouble, and it is loads of fun."

"Do you know the boy up the street who got into trouble with the police for fighting last week?" I asked the boy.

"Yes, I know him," he replied. "He gets into fights with lots of kids, but I guess he is not to be blamed. His mother and father aren't living together. He doesn't really have a home."

Not really having a home can be defined in many ways. In terms of the reaction of the child himself, not having a real home means that he does not feel loved; it means that he feels rejected by one or both parents, that he feels his sisters or brothers have supplanted him, that he does not belong to a family circle. In this state of mind, a child is bound to look for compensations. When a child who has been rejected by her parents says, "Real things in life don't seem to mean anything," that child is open to the influences outside the home that lead so many to delinquency.

4. Slums and Gangs

"My main motive for stealing was the want of something to do."

Stressing the importance of the child's emotional environment does not, of course, preclude the importance of a good physical environment for the child. Obviously, if we are concerned with good homes for our boys and girls, we must also be concerned with helping to develop the opportunity for the parents to *make* a good home. If a mother has to rear her children in a slum, her task is made infinitely more difficult than it should be. She may often do her very best and still fight a losing battle.

Is there a direct relationship between juvenile delinquency and the prevalence of slums? We have enough evidence to convince us that the spread of "good" neighborhoods can help to reduce the delinquency rate. At the same time, it must be stressed that there is no concrete evidence that the slums by themselves create crime.

Various studies made of slum housing localities show that a family living in a blighted area and in overcrowded conditions suffers under handicaps unknown to a family living in more pleasant surroundings. Imagine the experiences of a child brought up in a slum environment such as those existing in one of our large Eastern cities. In one particular area surveyed, a woman with ten children lives in four rooms. Six of the children, and sometimes an even larger number, must sleep in one bedroom. The four rooms consist of a living room, kitchen, and two bedrooms. There is no bathroom; nor is there running water, or gas, or electricity. The family is required to use an outside privy or outhouse, which hasn't been cleaned for months. In the outhouse is a rusted pipe which carries the water supply for the entire building. The family must obtain water from this pipe and carry it inside to be used for washing dishes, cooking, and drinking.

Or take the case of the Willis family, who lived in a second-floor apartment of a tenement building. They shared a toilet on a rear landing with four other families. When they went to bed, they had to lock the bedroom door to keep out the rats that were too large to trap. They were in constant fear of drunks using the hallways of the building for sleeping quarters; they were constantly worried about the safety of their daughters in the street and in the halls of the tenement houses. There was open disregard for good moral conduct in that entire neighborhood. What chance would the four Willis children have, in spite of care exercised by the parents?

We must recognize that there can be no home life without an adequate home. When parents and children have to sleep together, sometimes five and six in a bed regardless of sex, in rooms used for all purposes, the impossibility of privacy, the tensions that arise from lack of sanitary facilities and from overcrowding, all combine to degrade the family where the very roots of its life should be growing strong and healthy—in the home.

Dr. Hans von Hentig, Yale University criminologist, says in his book *The Criminal and His Victim,* juvenile gangs "have two training grounds: slum life and prison life. . . . The slum boy inherits too much general hostility toward enforcers of the law. . . ."

Dr. von Hentig cites instances which indicate that the greatest incidence of juvenile delinquency is found in neighborhoods of bad housing and overcrowding. That does not mean, he points out, that either the students of the problem or those who are interested in good housing claim that bad housing by itself makes juvenile delinquents. No one who approaches civic problems objectively makes such a claim. But, he adds, what the students and the civic-minded people do say is that "bad housing is one in a complex of factors leading to high rates of juvenile delinquency, and that the elimination of the bad housing factor should help reduce juvenile delinquency."

The National Conference on Family Life has put it this way, "No program to strengthen the foundation of family life can overlook the influence of housing, the basic environment of domestic life."

While the slum clearance projects will not accomplish miracles, they have provided ample proof that juvenile (as well as adult) behavior does improve in a decent home environment. Careful studies made in many large cities show lower juvenile delinquency rates in public housing projects than in slums and in the city as a whole. According to the 1954 report of the New Jersey Bureau of Parole, in Essex County there are 257 juvenile parolees under the supervision of the bureau—186 boys and 71 girls. Of these 257 juvenile parolees, 151 came from the Third Ward in Newark, which is considered the worst slum area of the city. This means that one small blighted area of Newark has more than 50 per cent of all the delinquents in the entire county. Similarly, 55 warrants were issued for parolees of the Third Ward out of a total of 105 for juveniles in Essex County. Warrants are issued for recidivists— juveniles who commit further violations after their initial commitment.

Here is a typical case which illustrates the housing backgrounds of some of these young delinquents. Larry, aged fifteen, was paroled from a training school. Almost immediately afterward, he was charged with burglary. Larry's home was located in the worst slum area of a city, adjacent to the downtown commercial area. His family of five resided in two rooms consisting of a kitchen and a bedroom on the second floor of a frame dwelling. The furnishings of the two rooms were poor. The only facility was electricity; the toilet was in the back yard. The rent was sixteen dollars a month.

Larry was attentive and responsive during the time he was interviewed for admission to the state home, but his mentality seemed somewhat retarded. He appeared to be an unhappy slum-area child from a home of low physical and doubtful moral standards.

The evaluation: The boy's delinquency was apparently the result of his early exposure to a slum home, the report noted, in which the father—a reported drunkard—seems to have been one of the major disturbing elements. The mother's relationship with a lover for the previous four years was indicative of the low moral standards to which the boy had been exposed.

What happened when the boy was paroled again? Certainly if he was returned to a slum area, that did not help him in his adjustment. At the same time, we must also realize that, even if all the slums in the city were torn down, Larry would still be in a difficult spot because of his emotionally broken home.

Of course, extremes can be cited to suggest the viciousness of the unfortunate conditions in which some families live. For example, in one large city it was found that two adults were living with nine children in one room, sharing the same beds. They had resided under those conditions for two years. One of the children, a girl of sixteen, was suffering from cerebral palsy.

In another case, three adults and ten children lived in two rooms in a slum area. The children ranged from three to seventeen years of age, and the boys and girls occupied the same beds. There were two persons employed in the family, the father and one daughter. When they were urged to get better quarters, they pointed out that no landlord would accept such a large family.

In such atmospheres it is evident that moral influences may be weakened and that the temptation to delinquency strengthened. The miracle is that juvenile delinquency, adult crime, or even epidemics do not spread even further. It is a wonder that there is not an even greater breakdown of domestic relations than there is. Obviously the proper home background cannot exist when ten children and three adults live in two crowded rooms.

Pittsburgh made this startling comparison between conditions in the substandard Hill District and in the "good" residential districts. Where bad housing predominated, there were: 250 per cent more deaths from tuberculosis; 48 per cent more infant deaths; 127 per cent more fire calls; 87 per cent more policemen required; *267 per cent more juvenile delinquency cases*. Not all of these liabilities could be charged solely to bad housing conditions. The Pittsburgh report says, "But there was no doubt that unhealthy homes were the major factor."

Clifford R. Shaw and Henry D. McKay in *Juvenile Delinquency and Urban Areas* have shown that delinquency is associated with several other social problems common to the slums. Separate factors for which they obtained a high correlation to slum areas included poverty, tuberculosis, adult crime, and mental disorders. Their thesis is that delinquency, of the type serious enough to appear in court, is concentrated in slum areas of the American cities and then thins out until it almost vanishes in the better residential districts. They have found that over a period of some forty years so-called delinquency areas in Chicago have maintained their proportionately high rate of delinquency even though the predominant nationality of the areas has changed four times during the period. Children of all nationality groups have shown high rates of delinquency as long as they lived in these areas. When they moved to better neighborhoods, delinquency among these groups fell to the level of the new neighborhoods.

James A. McDonald, probation officer of Wichita Falls, Texas, points out that 60 per cent of the cases of juvenile delinquency in that city come from a district comprising one third of the city's area. In one area of bad housing in the district, juvenile delinquency is nine times as great as in a good housing area of similar size.

One delinquent teen-ager said to me, "The main thing that I didn't like was because in each one of our different houses, it was always a business section where boys and girls got in difficulty because of the environment. We didn't have the facilities for recreation, nor any of the things which interest teen-age children." As this child points out, it is not only poor living conditions which make a delinquent-breeding environment. What are the children to do with themselves in their leisure time? Another child says, "My main motive for stealing was the want of something to do." Is it surprising that bored children, especially if they are already insecure, choose adventure in the form of breaking society's laws?

In the exciting, stimulating, but little controlled and culturally inconsistent environment of the underprivileged area, the Gluecks say, boys readily give expression to their untamed impulses and their self-centered desires by means of various forms of delinquent behavior. Their tendencies toward uninhibited energy expression are deeply anchored in the malformations of character during the first few years of life.

Sixty per cent of the five hundred boys studied by the Gluecks said they rarely go to church. They did not believe in any kind of religious instruction or training. Ninety per cent of these children were chronic truants from school, as compared with ten per cent of the five hundred nondelinquents studied. Almost all of them hung around street corners, kept late hours. They made little use of playgrounds. They didn't like playgrounds. They started smoking early in life, at the age of five or six. They began dating early. And their parents didn't care.

One of the principal purposes of education is the worthy use of leisure time. The spread of delinquency shows partial failure by the educators to teach this, partial failure by youth to learn it, a widespread lack of physical requirements—such as buildings, equipment, leaders—and a partial inducement to criminality or vice on the part of vicious underworld influences.

How do young offenders spend their leisure time? And why do they choose certain activities?

The chart which follows is based on a comparison of a 1937 survey of 500 boys at the state training school in Jamesburg, New Jersey, and my own 1954 survey of 208 boys at Jamesburg and 208 girls at the state training school in Hudson, New York. (It should be noted that the percentages do not total one hundred in all cases because some children participated in either less or more than one of the specified activities.)

There is a marked difference in the way in which the delinquents spent their leisure time in 1954 as compared with 1937. The 1937 delinquents spent more of their time outside of school working or in sports and play. The 1954 delinquents—boys as well as girls—spent more time in loitering in the streets. This throws some light on the current number of gang wars that have made our streets into dangerous battlegrounds. The percentage of boys who loiter and run around the streets in 1954 is almost five times as great as it was in 1937.

How a boy or girl spends most of his or her time outside of school is indicative of the kind of life that youngster leads. Out of

CHART OF LEISURE-TIME ACTIVITIES

Activities	Jamesburg Boys, 1937	Jamesburg Boys, 1954	Hudson Girls, 1954
Sports and play	30%	25.0%	19.2%
Working	23%	14.9%	12.5%
Loitering and playing in the street	7%	33.2%	26.0%
Gambling	14%	15.9%	3.8%
Reading and other hobbies	4%	11.1%	6.3%
Paid entertainment	10%	11.5%	12.5%
Radio and TV	Not asked	22.1%	22.6%
Part work and part play	11%	37.5%	25.5%
"Hanging around boys"	Not asked	Not asked	33.2%
Had available playgrounds	82%	82.7%	85.1%
Made use of playgrounds	65%	37.0%	45.7%

208 girls at the Hudson training school, 69 of them wrote that they spent their leisure time "hanging around boys." This is a pastime which undoubtedly got these girls into trouble.

The part played by radio and television in the lives of these children is extremely important too. Today we find that more than one fifth of the boys and girls spend most of their time outside of school watching television or listening to the radio.

From time to time we hear that there is a correlation between the recreational facilities available to adolescents and the rate of delinquency. The figures presented by the various institutions under study do not substantiate that claim. It was found many boys and girls did have playgrounds near their homes, but for the most part they did not use them. Although proximity to playgrounds was about the same in 1954 as in 1937, far fewer boys and girls in 1954 than in 1937 reported that they used these facilities. Again, the rising incidence of street gangs is a reflection of the limited appeal that formalized playgrounds have for the adventure-seeking preadolescent and adolescent boys and girls. If this is so, then it is essential that the communities recognize the need to make the playground program more enticing. We can't force a child to use the supervised playgrounds if he prefers the unsupervised streets. But we can look into this problem to find out how our playgrounds can be improved so that they will not be neglected for street corners. Of course, providing playground areas *alone* is inadequate; they must be well equipped and must be staffed with experienced professional leadership. Just having so-called playgrounds, with little or no provision for equipment and leadership, is like having schools with no desks and no teachers—and still expecting boys and girls to be able to learn. Our best thinking must be concentrated on this question.

In this connection, it is significant to learn that today 35 per cent of the boys and 40 per cent of the girls questioned said that the reason they chose delinquent activities was because they "wanted excitement" and "to have fun." In 1937 only 9 per cent of the boys said that they got into trouble for these reasons. This disquieting rise in the number of boys and girls who become delinquents as a result of their hunt for thrills can be attributed partly to the increased restlessness and tension that characterize our way of life and partly to a desire to escape from family disturbances. So they seek their excitement and fun in antisocial activities.

The unfortunate thing is that there are so many older children ready to introduce the younger ones into the thrills of stealing and vandalism, gang wars and promiscuity. The contagiousness of the disease of delinquency is very apparent. If a child reaches adolescence and his important needs—protection and support, guidance, love, and security—are missing in his home, he turns elsewhere for the fulfillment of those needs. And an adolescent is more easily influenced by his contemporaries, especially those slightly older than himself.

In 1954, 41 per cent of the Hudson girls said that they had learned about things that led to their delinquency through older girls; 40 per cent of the Jamesburg boys said that older boys had taught them the ways and means of delinquency. In 1937, 44 per cent of the boys at Jamesburg placed responsibility for their learning how to be delinquent on older boys.

In 1954, 27 per cent of the Hudson girls said that they learned about delinquent activities through girls of their own age, and 37 per cent of the Jamesburg boys said that they learned of such activities through boys of their own age. Fifty-eight per cent of the boys at Jamesburg in 1937 made a similar claim.

If a child is influenced by the example of one or two children of his own age or slightly older—and we have seen that he is— he is even more susceptible to the influence of a group of his contemporaries. Adolescent boys and girls have always expressed their gregariousness by forming clubs or social groups. You can see gangs on almost any street corner, in small towns or in cities. Club members wear special sweaters or jackets, have pass words and initiations, and collect dues. There is often friendly rivalry between several groups. These things are considered part of the normal behavior pattern for young people. But because of the cloak of anonymity that shelters any member of a large group, the gang can and does foster antisocial behavior.

Unfortunately, we are hearing more and more about gangs that have gotten out of hand and become destructive. The pattern of the destructive gang is basically the same as the others—but carried to extremes. The uniform is apt to be more spectacular. For example, the recent (summer, 1954) police cleanup campaign in the Times Square section of New York City was made almost a simple task because the young hoodlums or gang members were identified by their dungarees, short jackets, brass nailhead decorations, and wide motorcycle belts.

Their mannerisms are also indicative of the gang influence. Their gait is chosen or developed. On entering a public place, the impression they make is of vast importance to them. What they call "the walk-in" is a studied attention-getting device.

Initiations may involve committing a daring crime rather than the conspicuous but harmless scrubbing of a railroad station with a toothbrush. And rivalries between gangs are not played out on a baseball diamond with bats and balls, but in the street with knives and zip guns. This is particularly true in large cities like New York, Chicago, Los Angeles, Cleveland, and Detroit. Juvenile gangs in these cities cultivate such intense hostile feelings toward each other that they frequently lead to bloodshed and actual killing. For children seeking excitement, the destructive gangs provide thrills with a vengeance.

We asked the boys and girls at Jamesburg and Hudson about their gang affiliations. In 1954, 56 per cent of the boys at Jamesburg said that they went with "mixed gangs"—"some of the members got into trouble, and some of them didn't." This compares with 57 per cent of the girls at Hudson. As for the "bad gangs that were mostly in trouble," 20 per cent of the girls at Hudson and 26 per cent of the boys at Jamesburg in 1954 said that they did go with such gangs.

The gang problem becomes more than statistics when we read what the children tell us—how hard it is to resist the gang's attractions or fight against its strong-arm methods.

The following is quoted from a report written by a boy who was institutionalized for truancy.

"I started playing hookie because there was a gang of girls and boys around my school. If you didn't do what they said they would all jump on you and beat you up and dare you to tell someone about it. I kept on going to school and getting beat up every day until I got tired of getting beat up so I stopped going and then the school called up to find out why I didn't come to school and my grandmother said she did not no so I stayed out about 2½ weeks and I came back to school and didn't have a note. I told them I'd bring it tomorrow but I didn't bring it. And I stayed in school for about 8 days straight and stopped coming again. Then I had to go to court."

The next case is that of a boy who came from a home where he was exposed to cruel and abusive treatment from a psychotic father who is presently confined in a state hospital. The mother found it difficult to care for her six children, of whom this boy is the oldest. The boy blames the father for his difficulties and seems attached to his mother. The family dwelling is described as substandard, and the family rely on public assistance for support. It is felt that this boy has been reacting to a very bad family situation, especially to his father's mental illness, and is constantly attempting to protect himself against hostility and rejection. With another boy, he entered a school lavatory unlawfully and at pistol point searched thirteen boys with the intent of stealing.

"My story begins back when I was a little boy shaking down the banana man. I was only nine years old at the time but do to the fact that I was living in a neighborhood ruled by the Sc gang I was forced to go along. So then I became a member of the Sc little fellows—thats when I really started getting into trouble but I didn't care. I was well protected. I started getting bolder trying to build a reputation for myself. I was now twelve years old and didn't care about any body so I stole my first Pistol and got three of the tots and went to the corner of ———. Nobody suspect four kids to do anything so we had the advantage. I told the other three to move away from me because I was going to light up then I lit guys ran everywhere and I ran two because I was empty. When I got back to the Turf I still wasn't reconized as a Sc. I didn't like that because I didn't like anybody telling me when to fight and not to fight I figure if I was going to be in the Sc little people I was going to be the big shot. I decided to become a bold guy. I didn't care if I went to Jail or not so I bought a nice pistol from one of the older guys and from then on I decided to keep me a joint [gun] for myself.

"I started to calm down and go to school because I had my rep and was going strong. I stayed in school for quite a while until I got restless again I never liked to stay in one place over a year so I started playing hookey until one day John law busted me down and ran up side my head from that day on I hated Cops and I still dont care for them but where I made my big mistake was doing the same thing twice in similar patterns thats what goofed me.

"Every time I did something alone I got away with it. All my fellows had been up but I never had, so they started calling me escape. Every time the cops busted down I was gone then I let it go to my head one morning I got up for school my mother told me to make sure I went. On the way to the subway I met one of the fellows he said there was a Boss flick and hoeurs and he would go pin [find money] if he could cop some bread, I told him to wait Id go get my piece because I wasnt down for going to school any way I went back home told moms I'd forgot something got my Joint and hoofed it back to my man. Together we went to this ───── high school and went in the bath room the period changed and 13 guys piled into the Bathroom. I took out my Piece and lined them up my boy pulled the frisk we got out and went to the show but the mistake I had made was wearing my special club jacket because nobody else had one like it they searched for me a month and a half than one day I got tired of coming in real late and leaving real early so I stayed in bed. Right there I goofed. the cops came that already had my boy so we went to court I refused to give up the gun so I was sent here my boy went home.

"P. S. They say this is supposed to be a training school I never had so much training on different ways of moving a hot car or larceny till I cam up here."

Listen to another sixteen-year-old boy, second oldest of nine siblings. His parents claim that his delinquent behavior stems from his undesirable group and gang associations. The father does not earn enough to support his family, and it is necessary for the Department of Public Welfare to supplement his income.

In the seventh grade the boy started to make a classroom nuisance of himself. Since 1952 he has been truanting and has behaved aggressively toward other children. At the detention home he expressed suicidal intent and was transferred to a hospital for observation.

His offenses: stealing from parking meters; fired three shots from a .32 caliber pistol in a movie theater. After being sent to a psychiatric ward for observation, he escaped, only to be caught after a month of freedom. But let's hear his story in his own words:

"This is how some of my trouble began," he wrote. "When I was smaller I started off by hitch-hiking trucks and buses. Then things started getting dead so I left my neighborhood and started to hang out in the projects. The projects was a big place to me when I first started hanging around there. I met a lot of girls and boys. So I began to really like the place the girls were different than around my way they liked excitement. And the boys were different. They dressed up real cool not like me with dungarees and sneakers. They wore flashy pants. I got introduced to them and thats when my trouble began. I started to robb stores in order to get the clothes like them. And be able to take the girls to the movies and have money during the weekend. Then I had to build up a reputation for myself, So I joined the gang. After about a month or so I got myself a girl, money and a reputation. Then a bigger gang started to hang around the neighborhood, but we didn't have a chance if we fought them so I joined them.

"I changed my high-school and went to a Vocational H.S. I went to class once a month sometimes didn't bother to go. I kept playing hookie and going to the show. So the school got after me. When I walked in to the class room the teacher use to say to stay out because I only fooled around in classes. Doing this things I worked my self a reputation in the gang.

"Then all of a sudden I stopped robbing. Because by robbing and fighting I got the reputation. So I had all I wanted. I got myself a job as a delivery boy. Made honest money, got myself a girl. That's when the trouble started.

"They thought I was getting soft so I had to prove I wasn't by quitting my job and having a fight with the boss. Everything was alright after that. A couple of weeks later I was caught robbing parking meters. I went to court and the judge put me in probation. A couple of weeks after that I went to some Elementary school and broke a boys head with a belt. We got caught so I went to court again. The judge put me in parole. About a month later I was caught on an assault and battery charge. This time I was put in the detention home. I spent Christmas and New Years there. Spending those holidays there was like going through hell.

"When I came out a couple of days later, I tried to go straight.

I got a job and everything was O.K. But one day my girls mother came down and told me that she didn't want me with her daughter. I kept going with her daughter, So her mother gave her a beating. I was mad as all hell, but I tried to keep cool. Then the next day I found out her mother punished her and wouldn't let her come down. It's things like this that make you hate everybody and rob or fight. I told her mother that I was going to school and worked after school and had quit the gang. But she wouldn't listen to me she told me that I was no good for her daughter. That made me real mad. I quit my job went home ate and ran away that night. Then I heard that my mother was sick because of my running away so I came back home.

"I still kept going out with the girl when I came back home so her mother threaten to put her away if I went out with her any more. I tried to tell her mother that I changed my ways, but she told me that was no good. This got me mad. So I told her if I'm no good I'm going back to the gang. . . .

"We had an argument with some other gang. That week-end I bought a .32 automatic. At first I bought it to sell for more money, then I decided to keep it. That Sunday when I went to the show I met the boys we had the argument with. Nothing happened at first we just sat down and cased the place. Try to find out how many boys they had and how many were packing [guns]. Everything was running o.k., Till one of them recognized one of our guys. They didn't know us at first but they knew my friend from their school. Thats when it started.

"There girls came over and took my girl to the bathroom to get my girl out while me and a few others went to the boys. I asked the gang where the boss was. At first they said none of my business. That's when I whiped out the automatic. They started singing a different tune. They told me he was downstairs. I waited and about ten minutes later my friend brought him up. I was going to blow his head off. He told me that what the girls were doing was there business. Thats when I shot at him. Everybody started running around the show so it was hard to hit him. He ran up against the Exit but before he could open the door I shot again.

This time he didn't move he just cried. I tried to hit him again but guess luck was with him. Then my friend yelled out that the cops were downstairs. So I shot again, and went out the exit. On my way out the manager of the movie asked me what was wrong upstairs. I told him someone was shooting fire-crackers. He ran up and I walked out.

"That night the gang was around looking for me for shooting at their leader. I went home and didn't come out. Till I could figure an angle. The next day I got picked up by the cops. The detectives asked the boy if I was the one that shot at him and he said no, he was scared. They asked me if I did it. I said no, so they worked me over. The boy kept saying it was dark in the show and he couldn't see who was shooting. So they beat me till I said I did it. Then they took me to the Assistant D.A. He checked up on me and asked me why I did it.

"The next day I was in court. They sent me to the detention home. Then back to court again. The Judge sent me up to the state school. But before we come up here they sent me to the detention home. Over there I started getting home-sick. I couldn't sleep at night thinking of all the trouble I gave my mother. So I got all confused and put my hand through a window. They sent me to ——— Hosp. The Mental Ward. I stoled the keys of the lady but I was caught trying to get out. I went to another Hosp. and from there I ran away. I was out for about a month, and was caught.

"And here I am in the state school. I've had time to think things over, and regret everything I've done. I found out that all I done was unnecessary. I just done it to get a reputation, and trying to get everything my way. But I find you have to take things as they come. You might be smart but theres always somebody smarter than you. I've been home on one visit and come back. I've been working hard to get home. So that my mother wont suffer no more. When I went down in my visit I quit the gang. Told them to get another patsy. I hope to go home and get a job as a painters assistant. All this I've done in the past was useless. I've learned a lot up here, more than I would've learned with the gang. And that is to have trust in myself. And to do what I think is right."

That was a boy who really wanted to "go straight," to break with his past. He couldn't throw aside his reputation, nor could he live it down. Can we blame the mother for refusing to let her daughter keep company with a "hoodlum"?

How typical of the hundreds of boys and girls in trouble with whom I spoke during this past year is the lad's reaction: "It's things like this [being kept away from his girl friend] that make you hate everybody." He showed this hatred by trying to blow off the head of a rival gang leader, by shooting, robbing, stealing, fighting . . . being a tough guy.

These boys have known failure. Success, a "reputation," has been gained only through overt acts, such as robbing and stealing and gambling and sometimes raping. They become successful in their own group. Yet they are unhappy in their success because they *do* recognize a difference between acceptance by their antisocial group and acceptance by a law-abiding one.

Not all delinquents are gang members, nor do all the boys who live in slum areas belong to gangs. But gang membership is frequent among city boys who become habitual delinquents, as Helen L. Witmer reported in a study prepared for the federal Children's Bureau.

The Gluecks found in a recent study that more than half the training school boys were gang members as contrasted with less than one per cent of the boys from similar neighborhoods who formed the control group. This would indicate that work in the gangs is an important avenue by which delinquency may be reduced.

The gang appeal—its excitement, its adventure, its deep loyalty, and its group award of approval—is difficult to overestimate. And boys and girls who are emotionally disturbed will band together not merely for excitement but also for protection. Being fearful, suspicious or hateful of adults, they turn to their own peers, for better or, often, for worse. That being so, it is essential that the constructive aspects of this kind of grouping be so strengthened and the destructive aspects so eliminated, that gangs become focal points for improved citizenship.

Slums and gangs go together. But the solution is not that easy. By eliminating slums we do not necessarily eliminate gangs. The growth of unwholesome gangs has been an unfortunate phenomenon in present-day American life. We find these gangs in economically well-to-do suburban communities as well as in the slum areas. We must look beyond physical poverty. Emotional undernourishment is not only a characteristic in the lives and homes of the lower economic brackets. Children left alone, deprived of parental love, affection and supervision, will form their own peer groups, regardless of slums or of palaces. A fifty-thousand-dollar ranch house, without love, is far worse than a twenty-two-dollar-a-month, rat-infested cold-water flat, with emotional security, kindness, family cohesion, and parental love and understanding. On the other hand, the temptations found in substandard housing areas are often too great for the average boy to overcome.

In spite of the complexities, it is clear that the slums must go, that gangs must be deflected from their devastating activities.

5. Physical and Moral Roots

"Nobody wants me."

One of the basic elements of a favorable environment for a growing child is stability. In addition to the unfortunate effects that emotional instability of the home can have on a child, preparing him for delinquency, a correlation has also been found between delinquency and the physical instability of the home.

A recent study, *Towards an Understanding of Juvenile Delinquency* by Bernard Lander, suggests that the point that is crucial in explaining delinquency rates is social disorganization. What Lander says in effect is that it is not so much a deteriorated slum area that causes delinquency as it is an unstable area. If a slum area that has not changed in over fifty years is compared with one with a population that changes every five or ten years, the statistics show that the stable slum area has reduced its delinquency rate, while the area that is in a constant state of flux continues to develop delinquency at a higher rate.

In other words, according to Lander's findings, one of the causes of delinquency (in addition to conditions in the home and in the community) is mobility of population in a specific community.

This is brought out in the present study. I found that time and again the children in trouble had no real community roots. They had moved from home to home, from town to town. Sometimes the youngsters had lived in a dozen different places within a two-year period. They were upset at this lack of stability, although they didn't express it that way. Perhaps the words of a thirteen-year-old boy who had not known a permanent home in his lifetime best express the cry of these troubled children: "We've moved so much in the last few years that I don't know where I belong. I have no friends. They've made their own lives before I get there."

More than half of the girls at Hudson, and 45 per cent of the boys at Jamesburg in 1954, lived in their last place of residence for two years or less before they were institutionalized. A substantial number had lived there for one year or less; while a sizable proportion had lived there for less than six months before they were sent to training schools. In 1954, 134 of the 208 Hudson girls and 59 per cent of the Jamesburg boys said that they had moved from one to five times, or even more, during the past five years. In comparing the home backgrounds of five hundred delinquent and five hundred nondelinquent boys, the Gluecks found that more than half of the delinquents had been uprooted eight or more times during their lives.

When a child thinks of himself as a transient, he is much less inclined to be governed by what society thinks of his behavior, and he has a harder time finding constructive outlets for his energy. As one boy said, "The reason I think I don't like school is because I traveled so much and didn't stay in one place to learn."

Even more disturbing to learn about than the transient children are the virtually homeless children—the children who have gone from one foster home to another. As an illustration, here is the story of fifteen-year-old Larry, born out of wedlock, who has spent his life in a variety of foster homes and institutions. His mother openly rejected him and did not want the child home. He did not see her for the first thirteen years of his life. The father never took any responsibility for the boy. The mother's family includes members with serious criminal records, with mental deficiencies and serious emotional disturbances. As a child the mother had been adjudged a juvenile delinquent; she has a court record, a history of venereal disease, and has had at least four out-of-wedlock children.

In his various placements, this unwanted boy of hers has had difficulty in adjusting and has manifested various symptoms of emotional stress and tension. He has never had an opportunity to put roots down in any one place. He was picked up wandering around the streets. When brought to his mother, she refused to take any responsibility for him.

And this is what Larry wrote down about his life:

"My story begins [fourteen years ago]. At this time I was in a home
in ———. I was there because my mother and father separated
and my mother could not take care of me. So the welfare department thought I should be sent to a school until I was old enough
to know what happened to my parents. I stayed there until I
finished the fifth grade. While I was there I got into a lot of trouble.
But after a while the brothers straightened me out. Each summer
I would get a job at the beach. I would save up all my money
and buy myself some clothes. In the winter I would work in a
parking lot or I would shine shoes after school. On Holidays I
would go to a movie, or I would go visit one of my friends.

"From there I went to [a private training school]. I liked it very
much. I got into a lot of trouble in [the training school]. I ran
away a couple of times, I stole a few things, and I had a lot of
fights with staff members. I stayed there a year and a half. While
I was there my social worker told me about my family. When I
heard about my family I ran away from the children's home. After
a few days I came back. I was back a couple of months when one
day my social worker called me in to see him. When I went in
to see him, he told me that my dean the superintendent and the
assistant superintendent had a conference and they decided to send
me to live with my grandmother. I stayed with her for only a
month because she did not have any room for me. So one night I
told her that If there was no room for me there I was going to go
back to [the training school]. So that night I went back.

"I stayed there for a couple of days. Then I asked my social
worker if I could go see my mother because I hadn't seen her since
I was a year old. When I saw my mother she said she had no room
at this time. So I could not stay with her. So I started to roam the
streets. About two o'clock that morning a cop picked me up for
vagrancy. A couple of days later I went to court. I told the judge
what happened. So he told me that I would have to go to a school
until they could find foster parents for me. I got mad so they sent
me to ——— Hospital for observation. I stayed there for a

month. Then I went back to court, and the judge said that he was going to send me to the [detention home] for a few days; then I was to go to [a state school]. So one Friday afternoon some other boys and myself came to the school. I stayed in there about four and a half months."

All children need a sense of permanence and security—and privacy too. "All I want in my entire life is to have a key of my own," Ralph, a tousle-headed lad of fourteen told me. He had always lived in foster homes; he had never had a room of his own where he could go in and close the door. Many times in the places he had lived, the door was closed and locked after him. All this boy wanted was a room that he could enter and turn his own key—a key which symbolized a home of his own where his individuality would be respected.

When a child has lost both parents, he may very well become delinquent because of the community's failure to provide for his welfare. A shocking example of this failure was presented to members of the Advisory Council of Judges of the National Probation and Parole Association by the director of the California Youth Authority, Herman Stark. He told of "a ragtag army of homeless children, some as young as seven years old, being shunted from state to state by officials anxious to be rid of them." He said that California received an average of two thousand waifs a month. He added that other states, including Florida, also get such children.

Mr. Stark reported that in some cases the hopeless youngsters, usually working westward, receive as little as fifty cents to "get out of the state." He did not identify the police departments that sometimes "chased along" the children. He asserted that the children were "just loose kids" who had no parents.

He went on to say that in some cases official agencies finance the children's crossing of state lines. After one state pays them to move to the next, the second state gives them a small sum to move on again. When the waif gets to California, the youngsters are rounded up and shipped eastward in four trains a year, along with older boys involved in criminal cases. The latter are accompanied by policemen. At each key city en route a passenger car is detached from the train, and the children are scattered back to their home communities. Those wanted for criminal offenses are turned over to the local police.

Can anyone doubt that a large percentage of this "ragtag army of homeless children" will inevitably become juvenile delinquents?

The New York Citizen's Committee on Children reported this grim case of one child of the nearly twenty thousand children who look to the committee's Foster Care Program for help. Billy, a thirteen-year-old Negro boy, was separated from his parents by the children's court because of their neglect. In July, 1945, when Billy was six, he was placed in a temporary shelter. At that time he was "co-operative, willing, friendly."

Here is a brief summary of Billy's case history:

January 1947. Billy has been living in a *temporary* shelter for two years. Ten institutions were approached, but all failed to accept him. Billy has become withdrawn, showing a constant distrust of adults.

August 1948. A psychiatrist reports: "Billy is shy and unresponsive. He does not feel free to express himself. He is insecure, dull and unhappy. He has had little chance to develop at a normal rate."

January 1949. He is quarrelsome, aggressive, without friends, disrupts the routine of the dormitory, has temper tantrums. He feels threatened.

February 1950. Five years have passed since he entered the temporary shelter. He says he gets "sick" when he sees other children leave. It makes him "mad" to see them go. He now presents a real problem in social relationships.

September 1950. Billy is finally placed in a foster home. His progress is good until his foster mother suddenly becomes too ill to care for him and he is returned to the shelter.

February 1951. Billy is sent to Bellevue Hospital for a psychiatric examination. Here it is found that "in a more stable environment he would develop well, emotionally and intellectually. His disturbance is ascribed to lack of stability in his back-

ground. He presents good potentials if handled with understanding in the next few years. He will become increasingly disturbed if he does not experience some security."

July 1952. Renewed efforts are made to place him. Every possible child care agency is approached in vain. Finally, as a last
resort, Billy is committed to a state school for delinquent boys.

If Billy "goes wrong," the finger of blame can be pointed in just
one direction: at society—at you and me—for having given him no
chance to "go right."

A child needs to have roots in order to attain successful social
and emotional growth. With constant shifting from one neighborhood to another and from one city to another, he does not have
the chance to feel that he *belongs* to any community, to become
identified with it and attached to it, and to share his love of it and
loyalty to it with others.

What about Donald?

He is eleven, of average intelligence, IQ about 106.

He didn't deny—in fact, he almost boasted about it—setting fire
to a garage. He couldn't explain why. He said he couldn't remember all the fathers and mothers that he lived with, foster parents,
that is. Almost without reason, he began to cry and smile at the
same time.

"I'm not crying," he said, as he wiped away the tears.

He refused to permit his emotions to come into the open. He
desperately tried to be happy or at least to give the impression that
he didn't feel any emotions.

I looked at the recommendation of the psychiatrist: "It is felt
that there is a good possibility of reversing the course of this boy's
personality distortion. . . . This has been fairly well demonstrated
by his extreme compliance and former record while in the institution. Attempts should be made to secure a very selective foster
home, preferably one where other children are not present. And the
foster parents should be able to provide cultural and intellectual
stimulation commensurate with this boy's functional potential. It is
of course necessary that there be a very sincere feeling of affection
which can accept him despite minor transgressions."

Donald was saying, "My father was a mechanic. He never worked much. I don't know where he is now. My mother—oh, she got married again. I have five brothers. I don't know where she is. She left us two or three times."

And I turned again to the psychiatric report: "The mother deserted the family twice, the second time was given six months in a county jail. The mother was an inadequate homemaker. She kept a dirty house, neglected her children by not feeding them properly, nor mending their clothing. She has shown no interest in the children since they were committed to the foster home. Her present whereabouts are unknown. The children's paternal grandmother paid an occasional visit to the foster home. Her present address is unknown."

And then followed a list of Donald's placements:

1945—(Aged 2) Emergency foster home placement
1946—Foster home placement
1947—Foster home placement changed to another part of state
1951—Placement with relatives in another state (Virginia)
1951—Placement in another state (Pennsylvania)
1951—House of Detention (Philadelphia)
1952—Camden County Children's Home (private agency)
1952—Camden County Detention Home (county agency)
1952—Camden County Children's Home (2nd time)
1952—Camden County Detention Home (2nd time)
1952—House of Detention (Philadelphia; 2nd time)
1952—Camden County Detention Home (3rd time)
1953—New Jersey State Diagnostic Center
1953—Foster home placement (rural)
1953—New Jersey State Home for Boys

I looked back at Donald. Fifteen times since the lad was two years old. Fifteen homes, and the boy is now only eleven. Imagine, if you can, how you might feel if you had lived in fifteen different places, in ten counties, in four states in just nine years of your life—and you were now just eleven years old!

He was about to leave. "Cottage father said if I was good I could go home," Donald told me.

Home? Where is Donald's home? What kind of roots can society provide for children like these? This is a question that demands an immediate answer from society in terms of better foster homes and institutions.

A broader question, and more complex, is: How does society itself influence delinquency? Just as all the relationships within a family react on each other in a dynamic way, so society and the home and the institutions of society form a dynamic chain. Parents are the products of their homes and of society, and society is a community made up of many parents. These relationships are a kind of infinity of interdependence. Therefore we cannot truly separate the home from the influences of society and of our particular times (or vice versa) any more than we could separate the home from its physical characteristics. It is possible, even necessary, to look at juvenile delinquency as a symptom of a more general sickness of society.

The United Nations Department of Social Affairs report, "Children Deprived of a Normal Home Life," observes that the development of our industrial society has changed both the structure of the family and increased the tension in it. It has changed it from a unit economically and socially more or less self-contained to a group compelled to rely for its support on goods and services secured from the outside. The change brought about by industrialization may provide the opportunity of reaching a higher standard of living for a greater number of citizens. However, the great strain laid upon the individual due to insecurity of employment and also to an ever-increasing specialization, monotony in many kinds of work and the absence of satisfying compensation in the way of rest, relaxation and the variety of occupation, affect the family's material circumstances as well as its internal relationships.

The UN report observes that anxiety in the home, caused by these conditions, may affect the parent-child relationship seriously. Children whose mothers are working full time, and whose physical and psychological needs are not fully met, may often be emotionally and even physically deprived.

The report stresses that such a child may be affected not only in regard to his physical health, but also mentally and emotionally, to the detriment of his adjustment to his family, school, and community. During World War II and during the Korean conflict, schoolteachers encountered the phenomenon of the "latch-key child," both of whose parents were working, many of them long overtime hours. The child saw his parents much less frequently than during peacetime years. The volume of delinquency was very high during both periods. Although there are clearly various other contributing factors for this increase, many of the teen-age offenders of today are the latch-key children of yesterday.

The rise in vandalism and delinquency is linked to world social tensions by Mrs. Lillian L. Rashkis, specialist in the field of emotionally disturbed children in New York City for more than twenty-five years. As supervisor of the Board of Education's schools for problem children, she has charge of eighteen hundred or more disturbed youngsters each year.

Although twenty-five years ago many of the chronic truant types lost interest in school because of restlessness, or because they could not absorb elementary subjects, today's crop of rebels, Mrs. Rashkis said, have somewhat different symptoms. Today many of the youngsters seem to have turned against society, probably because of the tensions that stem from the modern world's attempt to recover from two wars. A parallel tension, she noted, exists in the home.

No one need press the point that wars, natural disasters, and similar dislocations bring about family breakups and other types of disorganization or rootlessness which affect the behavior of children. Examples of disorganizing factors that have affected the home since the onset of the Industrial Revolution are many. They have been multiplied and accentuated by the advances—or regressions—of science during the past fifty years. We have increased numbers of mothers going to work, entry of fathers into military service, widespread acceptance of violence as a way of national and international life, and the confusion among unstable and immature personalities as to how far violence, rather than reason, may be applied to achieve selfish ends without social censure or punishment.

That we are living in times of great tension and rapid change goes without saying. What effect the threat of atomic war may have upon the increasing incidence of delinquency, we do not know. We do not know either whether the fact that this is the first American generation that has had to do peacetime military service is a factor. We do have evidence that some teen-agers adopt an irresponsible attitude of "What's the use—we'll be called into the army anyway," but their feeling does not seem to be typical.

Speaking before the Senate subcommittee investigating juvenile delinquency, Morris R. Taylor, executive director of the Robert Gould Shaw House, at Roxbury, Massachusetts, said that today's youth, those under twenty, have seen nothing but abnormal times, depression at birth, and war later. Many boys and girls, he said, feel that they have nothing to look forward to.

The boys know they must go into the army, and with most of the young men gone, the girls cannot look forward to proper courtship and early marriage.

Along a similar vein, Dwight S. Strong, executive director of the Citizens' Crime Commission of Massachusetts, observed that there is much adult moral laxity both in personal living and toward corruption in public life. "We think it's smart when someone gets away with it," he said. "We have been taught 'not to be caught.'

"Let me be specific," said Mr. Strong. "A group of teen-age boys recently discussed their problems very frankly and openly. They knew that the corner bookie operated without interference from the police. And they proceeded to name places like poolrooms and bowling alleys where gambling and betting on the numbers took place all the time.

"In fact, the boys themselves admitted that they placed bets with the bookies. Yet if they played on the street, the police would be called and they would be promptly dealt with.

"They sort of respected the bookie, too. He was well dressed, drove a late-model, expensive car, had an easy life, and lots of money.

"On the other hand," Mr. Strong continued, "their schoolteacher presented just the opposite picture. The teacher was struggling to make ends meet, was not well dressed, and his car was nothing to rave about. He was lucky if he had one, even."

In her testimony before the Senate subcommittee, Dr. Martha M. Eliot, chief of the Children's Bureau, pointed out that people all over the country are asking whether or not we as a nation are experiencing a breakdown in the exercise of responsibility by parents. "Breakdown," she stated, "I believe is too strong a word for what is happening in most families. In many cases I think it is indifference, lack of understanding, perhaps ignorance, confusion. In a good many situations, parents are at a loss to know (1) what is the reason for their children's behavior, or (2) what to do. Many parents do not seem to realize that what they themselves do is taken as a model by their youngsters. Minor delinquencies, minor infringements of the law on their part, may be accepted by their children as all right. And then, when the children go and do likewise, the parents and others wonder why.

"It is hard even for the most thoughtful families to find the answers to some of the problems precipitated by the pace and the tensions of our everyday city life. Many, many parents are struggling with these questions. Most of them, I believe, are coming out on top. Some, no doubt, are not. But together we have to find ways to help them realize that the old standards of family living still have much merit and attraction for youngsters even in our modern life.

"But we have to go beyond that and see what the community must provide to help families meet these problems."

Certainly one factor contributing to juvenile delinquency today is the breakdown of respect for authority. We find in our gang group that the authority of the police, of the courts, of the parents, of the teachers, is sometimes completely unrecognized. Defiantly, with scorn and impudence, many young boys and girls ride roughshod over any authority that attempts to restrain them. Two thousand young high-school boys and girls have wreaked havoc in a New York subway train and terrified passengers, guards, and police; youngsters of twelve or fourteen have terrorized, not only their classmates, but also their teachers; hoodlums of fifteen or sixteen have attacked armed patrolmen—these facts grimly indicate the dangers that lie ahead.

A report made by one of the community committees set up in Chicago reinforces Dr. Eliot's statement by suggesting that a lack of respect for authority is an adult failing which is communicated to the child. The report reads, "A pattern of delinquent conduct first gets established in a community because its adults have compromised their own moral standards. This is usually brought about by forces beyond their own control.

"Where the struggle for material advance is most intense . . . even adults will frequently stifle their scruples. Accumulative effect of such acts breeds an attitude of indifference with respect to the opinion of conventional society. Concomitant with this attitude is a falling away of interest in the character and reputation of the community. There develops a kind of personal isolationism in which people enter into an unspoken agreement not to meddle in the affairs of their neighbors in return for a free hand in carrying out their own affairs.

"In such a situation it is easy for the greatest variety of moral views to spring up and exist up side by side in the same neighborhood. Honesty and frugality live side by side with cheating and waste. Respect for law and adherence to the commandments are jostled on the crowded street by cynicism and greed.

"What we see in children as delinquent conduct is often no more than the inevitable effect of such a community atmosphere. When children are confronted with conflicting systems of moral value, they themselves fall into conflicts and confusion. In such a community the time-honored controls of parents over their children are broken, and without these controls, waywardness achieves full play. Under these conditions children inevitably develop a habit of delinquent behavior which, as they are passed along to younger children, become neighborhood traditions.

"When these habits and traditions are coupled with a persistence of the conditions which originally gave rise to them, delinquency becomes a fixed characteristic of the community."

When Fairleigh Dickinson College in Rutherford, New Jersey,

conducted a survey of twenty-five hundred students at twenty-seven New Jersey high schools, as well as a thousand college students, the results were in some respects astounding. Three fourths of these young people said that they did not consider lying and cheating as being acts of delinquency. Twelve per cent of the youngsters did not consider stealing particularly wrong, and 9 per cent would not agree that it is delinquent to rob. Fifteen per cent of the students could see no delinquency traits in destroying property, and 17 per cent did not feel that sexual offenses should come under the heading of delinquency.

Some of the students observed that stealing is all right if no serious damage is done or if you can get away with it. One youth's justification for juvenile thievery was this: "When children see and hear of police taking graft, parents fixing traffic tickets, friends smuggling perfume across the border . . . they feel that they, too, can do something and get away with it."

Where does the responsibility for the development of this moral code rest? Nearly half of the high-school students fixed it on themselves. Almost as many blamed their parents. Among the college students, 75 per cent of those polled fixed chief responsibility on the parents. Among the high-school students, the local community, the church, and the government were also listed in that order.

The majority of the young people questioned in the Fairleigh Dickinson survey listed as a prime cause for delinquency the desire of a youngster to be a "big shot" on the campus, at the prom, or on the street corner. Thrill-seeking placed a close second, and too much idle time, and parental delinquency followed, ranked in that order.

One of the students with keen insight observed, "Juvenile delinquency is a result of lack of parental love, lack of religious training, and a lack of faith."

The children and young people who took part in this survey are more fortunate than the delinquent; they are going to high school, are completing college, and come from the so-called best elements of the community. Yet, even among this group, we find a wide difference of opinion as to what delinquency is. In general, we find a lax moral attitude concerning honesty.

Commenting on the study, ex-Senator Robert C. Hendrickson observed, "America's children are no better morally than the adults who have callously laid the framework for wholesale delinquency." The moral values of society are thus transmitted from one generation to another.

In addition, the vulgar realism and adult sophistication of much of our literature and entertainment, the sensational parade of scandals and half-truths in some lurid and irresponsible newspapers and magazines, complement the examples of adult dishonesty which a child does not fail to discern. Some have been inclined to emphasize the influence of such forms of entertainment as a major causative factor. The answers of the boys and girls questioned at Jamesburg and Hudson would not seem to support this theory. Only 10 per cent of both boys and girls blamed newspapers, magazines and comics for their troubles. Four per cent of the Hudson girls and 7 per cent of the Jamesburg boys named television and radio as the source of their ideas. Neither does the influence of movies seem to be very great in 1954; 3 per cent of the Hudson girls and 7 per cent of the Jamesburg boys said that they got their trouble-making ideas from the movies. In 1937, 38 per cent of the boys at Jamesburg blamed the movies. It is doubtful that the movies alone could have caused trouble for more than one out of three of the boys at Jamesburg in 1937, but it is significant that they themselves thought so. Today we hear a great deal about comics, radio, and television as causes for delinquency, just as movies were under fire in the thirties. When a child says, "I got my ideas from television, movies, radio, crime comics, newspapers, and so on," we must not accept such a statement on its face value alone. Certainly from reading and looking at pictures, a child learns *how* to be bad, but it is false to call this a *cause*. The desire to be bad, the need to be bad is already formed.

Bertram M. Beck, director of a special juvenile delinquency project of the Children's Bureau, stated at a convention of the National Congress of Parents and Teachers, "The spread of delinquency through economic levels of our communities is a danger signal that must not be ignored. It is a sign of social decay and a signal that our social institutions are losing their capacity to perform a primary function—namely, the inculcation of a sense of social and moral values from one generation to the next. . . . There is a pronounced relationship between a world in strife, a world seeped in aggression, and acts of aggression on the part of today's youth.

"As we meet here today," Mr. Beck continued, "we as a nation are threatened by the aggression of Russia and her satellites. We live in the knowledge that out of this threat may come global warfare and the use of means of warfare that can spell annihilation of the world as we have known it. It is our great tragedy that, rather than face up to this awful reality as a united people, full of purpose and dedication and firm in our belief of the ultimate triumph of our democratic ideas, we are squabbling amongst ourselves, turning upon one another. . . . It is this lack of unity, of faith, of sense of dedication and purpose, it is this lack of a feeling of 'we-ness' which lies at the base of our problem of delinquency today. Unless we can pull ourselves together and subscribe to and live by the fundamental social and moral values that have made us a great people, we obviously cannot transmit those values to young people."

Mr. Beck's argument may be essentially sound. It may be overstated in its omission of qualifications. Certainly it raises certain questions about the family as the focus of delinquency. When there is a state of national tension due to war, or the threat of war, delinquency rises (conversely, the incidence of adult crime drops). On the other hand, during depression years delinquency falls although there is also a feeling of national tension. During periods of prosperity, delinquency rises.

Whatever the causal relevance of these great national changes, there is not much that we can do about them immediately. Moreover, the people and organizations interested in decreasing juvenile delinquency are not likely to be in a position to do anything to affect these external conditions. Again we must remember that there is a double problem in juvenile delinquency: how to reduce its rate of increase and how to reduce its "normal" volume. If the external causal factors behind the increase in rate are beyond our control—except in the sense of constantly warning people not to let their sense of social and moral values become dulled—then we must act to improve conditions on more immediate social levels such as the community, the school, the home.

If, by effort at this level, we can reduce over-all delinquency by 75 per cent, we will have accomplished much, even though the cyclical patterns correlated with war, peace, prosperity, and depression still occur. This is not an impossible nor Utopian objective. Mr. Beck recognizes this point when he says, "Recent studies have demonstrated that the essential difference between the delinquent and his nondelinquent peer is that the latter has benefited by good parent-child relations, particularly during the first six years of life. There are parents who are so fortunate in their own personality that, despite the storms of neighborhood, community, and world, they can give to their children an essential sense of belonging that inoculates them against the economic and social forces that promote delinquency and other types of character malformation. There are parents who are so firm in their own convictions about right and wrong, who offer to their children such admirable sources of emulation, who guide their children so skillfully, that no matter what these children experience in school life, they will be exemplary members of our community."

From his many months of study and research on the delinquency question, Senator Hendrickson concluded that delinquency arises out of society's failure to provide for children's normal emotional and physical needs on the one hand, and, on the other, failure to protect them from baneful community influence.

"We would all agree," he said, "that our knowledge is not sufficient nor our tools so well developed as to enable us to protect all children from damage. But both our knowledge and tools are well enough advanced for us to know that neither mere repression nor one new playground is ever the answer to a community's problem."

All who have looked into this basic problem agree, too, that there is no one answer. As we have seen, there are a great many factors that enter into the picture. But the issue cannot thereby be cast aside as being too difficult. Too many future young Americans are involved for us to be either complacent on the one hand, or harsh and uncompromising on the other.

Just as we are pressing ahead to find the causes and cures for polio, cancer, and multiple sclerosis, so we must press forward to eliminate the causes of juvenile delinquency. Then must come the preventive as well as curative remedies.

6. Who Are the Delinquents?

"My attitude is pretty bad, but I hope with God's help I can straighten out."

I asked delinquent boys and girls to write down their stories. I asked them to tell me why they thought they had gotten into trouble. Here are their answers, which illustrate how each child reacted to a unique combination of the factors that have been discussed in the preceding chapters. These are the boys and girls talking. The spelling is their own. The ideas are theirs. And so is the unhappiness.

The boys wrote:

"Well, I didn't get along too good with my mother & father and I was not interested in what whent on at home and just didn't care. I had some good friends that I really enjoy to be with and I think if more people would try and talk to us insted of trying to use the rubber hose on us and beating our brains in That less Boy's and girl's would be comeing hear. Maby if thire wear more club's and less of pool rooms we would proubly not be hear right now. In school if they would let me have something to say about what I would like to do insted of them telling me."

"I started to get in trouble a year ago. I feel that I am not liked as much as my step brothers. I got along good until my mother & father seperated. I go to church every Sunday. I hope that when I get out I won't come back again. In school on the outside I didn't like English because I couln't get along with my English teacher. Some reasons I got up here was, I used to steal things, small things. Then when money had been stolen I'd been the first one accused.

I came up here for stealing five dollars, no one in my family believed I was innocent, but in my heart I know I didn't steal it."

"I have been a problem child ever since my mother and father seperated in 1941. My mother got along fine with my stepfather until he was killed in 1945 after coming home from war. I have 1 brother & sister, half brother & sister that is, I usually got along with them, except that I always had things my way & when I didn't I was mad.

"I have been moving from place to place ever since I was 2 years old. I never had any jobs except cutting grass & delivered papers.

"Movies has always excited me & I think I used to do my wrong things from them.

"I really & truly can say that I never was in serious trouble. There is only one thing I have to learn how to do & that is get along with people, my attitude is pretty bad, but I hope with God's help I can straighten out."

"I got along in school okey but I always used to fool around and I'd get left back and I'd be about thirteen years old in the second grade and I'd feel like a dum bell and thats why I disliked school.

"I had a step father and he was always strict with me and disliked me a whole lot. and I'd start running away and started stealing for food and money. and thats how I started getting in trouble.

"I got ideas from television, movies, radio, crime, comics, newspapers, and so on."

"I moved around alout. I don't like home. I whould like to be put in a forster home. My farther is to lazy to go to work. My life is half good and half bad mostey bad. Will you try and help me out. I really can't blam my mouther and father I am in here for sex now. But will you please get together and help me out. try and get me in a forster home."

"My mother had gotten devorsed from my father, because he was an alkaholic.

"She then married again, and her my sister and our new father

could be used as example

moved to a rooming house in —— about a month later we moved to a new 1 family house I was then 7 my mother and farther were getting along fine, but then I keep getting sick and they had small arguments that didn't amount to anything. My new father hardly ever drank. Only on holidays, I have never seen him intoxacated ever. When I was nine my little sister came into the world and then everything was fine no more arguments, and as my sister got older they started to argue and in my heart and mind my father was to blame but I believe that my mother had her part, I never had any argument with my sisters that amounted to anything and they weren't often at all.

"I was about 12 when I first started to get into trouble, small thing like braking windows but later I start to break into houses, naturally I got caught and was sent to [a clinic]. I stayed there for 3 months. I was released on probation. I stayed out of trouble for 4 or 5 months, then again I broke into houses and did a few things that I didn't get caught doing, but I got caught at last. I was then sent to ——. I ran away a few times but got caught.

"I went home [19 months later], when I got home I stayed out of trouble for about 3 months. I got Polo I was cured and out of bed about a week when I stole a car and went across the state line and gave myself up, when I left I had 5 cents and when I gave my self up I had 5 cents. I went to court and was released. About 4 months later some boys and I stole some liquor and got drunk and I got caught, the mayor of the town got me out of it. About 2 months later I set a fire cracker off in school and was sent to ——.

"P.S. If you can think of something that will help me, or you can figure out my future please tell mister —— and let him read this over and he'll know who I am. Thank you. I am Glad to help."

"I got along with my mother and father and brothers and sisters, I have lived in my own town all my life and only lived in 2 different houses. And I hated to go and sit in school all day and waste my time when I could be out making money. I didn't have many jobs I only had 2 once I sold papers but for the last 5 years I worked with my father. I made all the money I wanted but I liked to steal just to see if I could get away with it."

"Most of my life I have lived in ——, all but the year after I was born. I have lived in a flat in an average neiborhood until 6 or 7 years ago, then my parents bought a house in one of the better neighborhoods.

"I have led a good life, with the exception of the past 7 years when I started hanging out with older guys around the ages of 18 to 20. I started getting in trouble. We never did anything real wrong except staying out late & drinking in fact within six or seven months of the time I started going around with them after I started staying out late they kept me out of worse trouble such as robbery. I didn't steal until I stopped hanging out with them. My main motive for stealing was the want of something to do."

"My main problem was I lived in [a small town] for 8 years, & then moved to N.Y.C. on —— St. and the west side & was doing good for a couple of years & met up with a certain Boy by the name of Billy, & he taught me how to steal & smoke & get into sex with girls & all this was in the big city & then my parents moved back to the country & I tryed to get away with a few things & then everything exploded & I got caught and sent away . . . and [later] was sent to this place for fourteen months & got into trouble up here & now I am working my way toward a furlough and parole. I hope you understand my problem."

"I did not get along good in school. I was born in —— I have wonderful parents, they were always trying to set me strait. If only I hadn't went with the wrong crowd."

"My parents fought a lot and my father married again. Get along good now. Moved about 20 times in my life. Ran away a lot. Came here for running away with my girl, stealing cars, breaking entering, etc. Was alright in school until High School. Got in with a gang and got caught with homosexualist. Reasons I stole was for money, excitement. Ran with older kids. Some are in Derdentown & Annandale [institutions]. I drank a lot. sometimes stay away from home for two or three days. Once rolled a queer and took his car and went to N.C., stayed away from home for 3 months. Lived by stealing down there. Came back and didn't steal for 4 or five months but stole a car with my girl and got caught. We were going down south.

"What happened is not my families fault. I had a good home life. My family tried to stop me from doing all these things."

Nor were the girls reluctant to tell their stories:

"My father died four years ago. I got along very well with my sisters and my brothers. Having sisters older than me made it more or less quite difficult for me at times. To explain myself more freely, I'll say that my sisters having all grown up and gone thru their various experiences only tried to prevent the same things from happening to me. Like any other teen-age girl, I was stubborn and bull-headed and wanted to be independent and do exactly as I wished, not caring about how it reflected on my parents.

"My parents didn't live in very many houses. Up to now, I can only remember three houses that we have lived in. The main thing that I didn't like was because in each one of our different houses, it was always a business section where boys and girls my age got in difficulty because of the environment. We didn't have the facilities, for recreation, nor any of the things which interest teen-age children.

"My school experiences weren't any different than any other boy or girl. I liked school up until my freshmen year of high school. Then I started skipping school and not doing my home work or even paying attention in class. That is where I made my mistake because if I had attended school and had done my work I would most likely be very much interested in my education right today. Don't misunderstand me, because I am interested in it, but not so much as I should be. Education means quite a lot now-a-days in applying for a job and for your own personal use.

"I haven't had one steady job, I have never applied for one. When I did work it was only little odd jobs like helping out in a restaurant, working in a toy shop or helping out in Beauty Parlor. I didn't receive a salary, it was just in a sense of being helpful and being friendly.

"My childhood was not a very happy one and I wouldn't want my children to ever have to go through it. My father drank too much and when he came home he use to take his mean-ness out on his children.

"I grew up to be more and more independent as each year passed by. Up until I was 14, I didn't have any particular problems. Then I met a girl who was three years older than me and who was much more mature in her thinking than I was. She seemed to attract me and I foolishly decided to follow her and imitate her. I started drinking and smoking and all the other little minor things that arise from mainly that. To me at the time, I was a pretty important person and I wasn't doing anything out of the way. If only I had stopped right then and there.

"Now as I think over everything that has happened to me, I come to realize that there's only one reason why I found myself and started thinking about love, affection, kindness, friendship and understanding. That reason I am so very proud to let everyone know. I have found God to be always by my side only before I never bothered to turn to him. I'm so happy I've found him and that I use him in my every day living."

"I was born in a large residential section in ———. Since my parents were divorced since I was 18 months old I lived with one for awhile and then with the other for awhile. I have two sisters. I've went to a number of different schools one of which was a private school. My parents and their friends have always wondered why I turned out to be the black sheep because I was considered to be a girl with a high I.Q. and a good sense of responsibility. I don't know just what got me started off on the wrong track but I started hanging out with a bad crowd on the other side of town & we stole & played hookey and got into gang fights & other types of trouble. The school brought me to court about my hookey playing. I was sent away.

"My parents were considered well to do and had highly respectable reputation in the communities. I got anything I wanted & still do, maybe that was the trouble I was spoiled.

"When I get paroled I'd like to finish school & go to a tailoring school & then open up my own little shop.

"Up here I've learnt quite a bit about the business from our tailor teacher & he thinks I'm a very good pupil. I also have the knowledge of a few different languages, French, Spanish, Portuguese & Latin & would like to learn a few more."

"I was born in ———, my mother is very nice, but my father drank a lot and my sisters & brother and I got along nicely. My mother and father were separated. My mother always was moving to another house. I didn't like to go to school because I didn't have nice clothes, and I was very bashful. The only time I got in trouble was when I didn't have anything else to do."

"I don't remember anything that hapend until I was five years old. When I was five I was sent to [an institution], because my father & mother were seperated & my mother was sick. After I was in [the institution] for two years I moved to ———. My mother & father went back together again. My mother died when I was nine.

"Sometimes I use to think I hated my father because he use to beat my mother. Very often my father would drink. When I was almost ten my father raped me & then I ran away from home. I never told anyone what happened until I came here. After I had ran away from home so many times I was sent away again. I have been in about nine Institutions. I have been here at the Training School for almost a year and six months. Since I have been here I think I have grown up more. I use to run [away] just for the excitement but now I am not interested in running any more.

"Since I have been here I think there has been a great improvement in this place. The girls have more privileges & they don't run as much as they use to. I have two sisters and four brothers we are all seperated now.

"When I leave here I will be going to a foster home. I want to go back to school . . . after I finish high school I think I will go to college & study to be a psychologist."

"I came to New York when I was about eight years old. About a month after I went to school close to where I lived at. I liked it very much. I got along with the boys and girls. And it made me happy to be there. Then I graduated and went to Jr. High School. I did very well until I got to the ninth grade. I got pregnant. I still went to school until I became 3½ month. And I left, then the school and court check on me, and made a big issue out of this whole thing. I went to court and then I went to ———. And then I came home, and had my baby. Then I started staying out late at night. And sometime I didn't come home for a week or the next day.

"My mother and father they use to sit down and talk to me for my own good, but I use to laugh inside. I didn't pay any attention, I went on doing the same thing. I went to court again in August, then I went to [a shelter]. I use to go to court every Wenesday. Everytime I go, they tell my mother that I'm comeing home next Wenesday, it never came so I never went home. Well, the last time I ever seen a court was the day the judge sent me to ———. I got along "fine" until almost time for my name to come up for "Parole." Then I came to cottage ———, it is very sweet and I am doing "very nice." They have very nice House Mothers.

"I think this school is very good for girls to 'forget the past and plan for the future.' I can write this because I have learned that and a lot of other things and am very thankful to this whole place. Well I have a wonderful mother and father, also a smaller brother and it is one happy family. I have never heard my mother and father fuss or use bad language around me and my brother, also I can say is I hope that I can go home soon so I can make up to them. I know as long as I have 'Faith in God' everything will turn out 'okey.' "

"Well to start I don't know my real parents. I stayed in a home till I was nine years. I was to large for my age so I didn't have

The Love that a child should have & The Things Like clothes & nice Little Things So I Stold them from my Gardion. She got prety mad and kicked me out. Then I lived with a Miss ——— who ran a very Bad house So she used to Beat & Kick me around like a dog. I got tired of it & ran away. I was sent to [a school] one year & 3 months Then to ——— Hospatil. I have no Sister or Brother. I have never Been stradle [settled] down I have all ways Been on The go. From Place to Place I have had many Bad Experiment all throug Life I have Been in many Little difficut I have Been in 21 Shelters 3 Hospital I have been in 18 School I didn't get along very well cause I didn't look nice in grown up clothes and the kids pick on me & Beat me up & took my Lunch & 10¢ wich was carfare & chase me all over. I couldn't take it cause I was afaird of Life I still am afaird to faice facts. I had 3 jobs in Baby sitting & earns for diffrint people. I was mis Lead by the wrong People & got in a lot of difficult & kick around some more. I have 3 wishes all my Life to have nice & kine people have a nice home & nice clothes."

"The way that this all started was when I was about 5 years old my mother and father separated and my father took custody of us children which are my sister & Brother and myself. While my father worked he boarded us three kids out by the week and came to see us week ends. Then my mother happen to find out where we were and came to see us. My father found out that she was coming to see us so he didn't like it. Then he said he was going on a two weeks vacation and he took us kids with him but when we were on our way he told us where we were going which was ——— and that we weren't coming back.

"Then my sister wrote to my mother and told her where we were. So my mother came and got us. Then we started going out and we got mixed up with the wrong gang and started staying out late at night against my mothers will so I was then placed on probation and was told to be in at a certain time but I still went up on my own when my mother threw me out of the house and I got out and under age my probation officer had the cops out after me so I kept hiding out so they couldn't catch me. But when I went out to this womans house I use to board with was when I got picked up.

"I was placed in a Detention home in my town until my court trial came up. Then I was sent here to ——— which I didn't like but I realize now that it wasn't only my fault but that it is going to do me a lot of good.

"The reason I did this was because my mother use to always argue with me and I couldn't stand it anymore. So my father came to my school to see me on the sly and wanted me to go back to Arizona with him. So I went with him. Now I hate my father for what he did that was he had sex relations with me so I put him in jail from five to six years. And I have had that on my mind as it is not easy to forget.

"I went to school regular when I was home as I liked school very much. As if I didn't go to school that would only make me in more trouble with my probation officer."

"In the year ——— the month of ——— I was born. Shortly after my birth I lost both of my parents. Taken into a forster home I began what one might call the childhood of an orphan. Though this mishap took place a few years before, willing was my new family. My sisters and I never had the opportunity of living together, scattered; we (actually) weren't because all of us lived in the same neighborhood but did not realize the nearness.

"As time passes I fall into the dark haze of what is called 'Juvenile Delinquency.' The reason is simple. At the time of my thirteenth year, I decided to be a wild chick as I had seen my friends doing. To start the fling of bad behavior, keeping late hours semed to be a great hobby of mine, the environment (meaning my friends) indulaged in late car riding, parties and other social gatherings; wanting to be a part of the crowd, despite my parents warning; the late night owl hours was a joyous continuence for me. Mother, thinking on my behalf, placed my case before the court. I brought all this upon myself.

"I was the type that wanted to follow the crowd, I did but got stuck."

Who are the delinquents? They are children with problems too big for them to handle. And they are all individuals. By recognizing the existence of a complex combination of traits and characteristics that make each child unique, we understand one of the reasons for the fact that one child may become a brutal killer and his brothers and sisters become useful citizens.

For in spite of emotionally disturbed homes, in spite of unfavorable surroundings, not all children fall prey to the disease of delinquency. The point should be made that some children are more susceptible to the disease than others. Just as many people have a predisposition for tuberculosis and will, under certain circumstances, suffer from this disease, there are children who have an emotional predisposition for delinquency. This means that under certain conditions—especially conditions in the home environment—they will almost certainly become delinquent children, or, if their environment is favorable to them, their energies may be channeled constructively.

The children who wrote these stories all tell of their individual rebellion against the conditions and attitudes that surrounded them. Poverty and slums, for instance, may have combined to produce a delinquent boy. Yet, as has been pointed out, two boys reared in poor, underprivileged homes in the slums of New York will develop into two different persons. One may become a distinguished governor, a man greatly admired and loved; the other ends up in Sing Sing prison. Similarly, poor schools may cause different reactions in different children, and bad companions likewise may turn one boy into a juvenile delinquent and leave another relatively unscathed.

In a family ruled by an overstrict father or an unaffectionate mother, four of the children may compensate for their resulting emotional problems in a socially accepted way. The fifth may be unable to cope with the situation and compensate by committing antisocial acts. In the case of a young arsonist and potential murderer, we find that as the last of eight children in a home ruled by a fanatically authoritarian father and an ineffectual mother, he was probably the most neglected of all the children, and, at the same time, that the most was expected of him. In any case, his reaction to his home surroundings was not the same as that of his siblings. His personality was such that he reacted in a more forceful and more overtly antisocial manner to an impossible situation.

Potential juvenile delinquents have emotional manifestations that can be recognized at an early age. They tend to be hostile, defiant, suspicious, resentful. They have a deep feeling that they are not wanted or appreciated. They often tend to be parasitic, wanting to be looked after and being unable to take care of themselves. They also frequently have a strong desire for power and position.

The Gluecks have found that, on the whole, the delinquents are unco-operative, unconventional, nonsubmissive to authority, independent, and uninhibited. They generally are lacking in self-criticism and are stubborn and eccentric. "They are less fearful of failure or defeat than the nondelinquent. They are less concerned about meeting conventional expectations and are more ambivalent toward, or far less submissive to, authority. They are, as a group, more socially assertive. To a greater extent than nondelinquents, they express feelings of not being recognized or appreciated." In almost every respect the delinquent is an unhappy and dissatisfied person; he is emotionally disturbed.

A child who is hostile, defiant, resentful, suspicious, and stubborn is unlikely to cope with the problems of life with which he will be confronted as he grows older. Perhaps, being unable to cope adequately with his problems, he just cracks under the strain of temptation or the strain of bad companions.

Summing up, the Gluecks suggest that delinquents as a group are distinguishable from nondelinquents in these respects:

   Physically, in being essentially solid, closely knit, or muscular.

   Temperamentally, in being restlessly energetic, impulsive, extroverted, aggressive, destructive—traits which may be related more or less to the erratic growth pattern and its physiological or emotional consequences.

   In attitude, by being hostile, defiant, resentful, suspicious, stubborn, socially assertive, adventurous, unconventional, nonsubmissive to authority.

Psychologically, tending to direct and concrete, rather than symbolic, intellectual expression, and in being less methodical in their approach to problems.

Socio-culturally, in having been ruled to a far greater extent than the control group [the nondelinquents] in homes of little understanding, affection, stability, or moral fiber by parents usually unfit to be effective guides and protectors.

While in individual cases the stress may be contributed by any one of the above pressure areas, in general the high probability of delinquency is dependent upon the interplay of the condition and forces from all these areas, the Gluecks report.

To learn more about the causes of juvenile delinquency, particularly why in the same family one child might be a serious delinquent and another a well-adjusted individual, Drs. William Healy and Augusta Bronner conducted a specific study for the Institute of Human Relations of Yale University. One hundred and five boys who had been repeatedly delinquent and 105 nondelinquent siblings of these boys were the subject of study. These children and their families and surroundings were studied in great detail. For the delinquents and their parents, treatment services were provided.

The psychological aspects of delinquency causes were later expressed in this manner by the psychologists: "It finally appears that no less than *91 per cent of the delinquents* gave clear evidence of being or having been very unhappy and discontented in their life circumstances, or extremely disturbed because of emotion-provoking situations or experiences." In contrast, these researchers found similar evidences of inner stresses in only 13 per cent of the control group. They added: "And here it should be said that in our concern not to overstate the contrasts we have ruled out cases in which emotional discomforts seemed comparatively mild and have included controls about whom there was some doubt concerning whether or not to any considerable degree they had suffered emotional distress."

Attempts were made to involve the delinquents and their parents in treatment so that the possibilities of this form of child guidance work for delinquency reduction might be adequately explored. Half the boys were found to have abstained from delinquent conduct during the two years between the end of treatment and the follow-up study.

The delinquent boy becomes delinquent, then, not because of a desire to be "bad," but because of a driving force within him that demands expression. The normal child suffers less from such emotional attitudes as excessive anxiety, feelings of insecurity, helplessness, and defeat. We are convinced, however, that the delinquent is not a schizophrenic or a person who has a deep-rooted psychosis. The Gluecks found that the psychopathic personality is rare in delinquents. They did find that many of the youngsters were in need of psychoanalytical help, but that is a far cry from their being psychopaths. It is encouraging to remember that a predisposition for delinquency can be combated by a favorable environment, that criminals are not born that way nor are they incurable.

They *can* be helped. There is no sense in the remark of the law officer in Washington who said that these things have been going on for a long time, and "there is very little we can do about it." There is a great deal we can do about it. However, the "we" must include all the adult members of every community, so that there will no longer be: rebellion against unfair punishment, a lack of a chance to act in concert with parents, constant mobility with its accompanying lack of belonging and security, repeated failure in school, alcoholism of parents, lack of parental love, defiance of authority to show the child's individuality, seeking senseless thrills, bad companions because of a lack of supervised play, lack of religious training, violent scenes between parents, and the resentment of all unfair shows of authority.

These factors in the cause of delinquency must be understood by all adults as clearly as by the pitiful youngsters who have experienced and expressed them. I've spoken to them. I discussed their problems with them. They are not defeated, they are looking ahead. But unless they get immediate, sound help from society, they will not have much of a chance.

7. Two Views

"If more people would try and talk to us insted of beating our brains in . . ."

An angry, indignant community now seeks to end juvenile delinquency by the woodshed method. The cry has arisen in ever-increasing volume, "Let's get rough with these little hoodlums and punks."

"If I get a bad kid here, I smack him," an attendant at one of the training schools told me. "I take the kid's pants down and whale some sense into him."

Proponents of the good old-fashioned woodshed method of enforcing discipline earnestly believe in "whaling some sense" into our delinquent and predelinquent children. The tone of their arguments varies from hysteria to sarcasm. Unfortunately there are some judges who assume the latter attitude. According to a story appearing in a newspaper early in the year of 1955, an eighteen-year-old man, who pleaded guilty to a charge of stealing, was sentenced by a certain judge "to a spanking with a ping-pong paddle until his seat is a pink-red." His father told the judge that it had been five years since the boy had gotten a spanking. Said the judge, "You can't cultivate a farm if you don't take the weeds out, and you can't cultivate a child without inculcating respect." I seriously question the value of a ping-pong paddle as a means of inculcating respect—especially in an eighteen-year-old.

Even for young children I would question such measures. On January 9, 1955, a thirteen-year-old boy shot his stepmother because, as he told police, "she was too strict and picked on me. She said I closed the door too hard. She said I wore my shoes out too fast. She said I scuffed up her rugs when I walked." The policy of over-

131

strictness does not work in the home; nor will it work when applied by society.

As we become more and more baffled at the increasing incidence of delinquency, we become more and more on edge and disturbed. Indeed, an air of near hysteria has developed in this country today. A newspaper editorial in one of the large metropolitan newspapers said not long ago that use of the woodshed method is called for and called for at once. The newspaper said, in part, "A stout strap, vigorously used at home, can often do more good than repeated summonses to adolescent courts. It can and should also be used on parents themselves when obviously needed to drive home plain parental duty."

A formidable example of this new trend lies in the comments, recommendations, and suggestions made recently in New York State by the Kings County Grand Jurors' Association. These are contained in a statement made by that association on March 16, 1954, a statement which consists primarily of a report submitted to the Executive Committee of the Kings County Grand Jurors' Association by its Committee on Juvenile Delinquency, Crime Prevention and Prisons, with the concurrence of the Committee on Law and Legislation.

The report starts on a note of panic. "Owing to the shocking disclosures as printed in all the New York newspapers, the general public has been made aware of the deplorable conditions now existing in our public school system. The handwriting has been on the wall for a long time, as evidenced by the many reports our committee has submitted on this subject during the past ten years. . . .

"The time has now come for more stringent measures. The co-operation of all is essential, parents, children, corrective agencies and administrative powers. Measures must be taken to eliminate shootings, muggings, stabbings and vandalism in our schools. Above all, respect must be inculcated for older people, teachers and established authority. Protection must be granted to teachers in the classroom, both from students and from parents. The City administration and the Courts must support the teachers and police officers in their efforts to maintain proper discipline. Without adequate discipline, students are at loose ends, not being able to control themselves. They end up by becoming antisocial and finally become a menace to themselves and to society."

The report goes on to criticize comic books and television crime broadcasts. It asserts that progressive education and so-called self-expression in schools should be changed. "Self-expression among the youth should be kept within proper limits." It recommends the addition of several thousand patrolmen to the police force, that policemen be required to carry their sticks when on patrol duty, that all children be fingerprinted. It asserts that current laws providing special treatment for youthful offenders do not act as a deterrent to crime, concluding: "We believe that it actually makes it easier for juvenile delinquents to get away with practically anything, with a mere tap on the wrist as punishment. A far worse result, we fear, is that many of these problem children end up with the idea firmly implanted that they are heroes, or at least misunderstood martyrs, because of the coddling they receive, instead of the correction they should get."

The cry for action, for punishment, for a positive stand on the question of delinquent children, is not one that can be overlooked. It might be well, however, for those who advocate the woodshed method to examine carefully their philosophy. Where will it lead them?

One specific answer is given by Leonard W. Mayo, chairman of the national Midcentury Committee. Dr. Mayo said that from time immemorial measures such as flogging have been advocated by the ignorant, the desperate, and the fearful. According to Dr. Mayo, it takes more than just a strapping to cure delinquency. As a matter of fact corporal punishment may merely harden the delinquent in his belief that he is alone in the world and that he has been deserted. The child does not need a flogging as much as he needs understanding.

There is no such thing as a "born" bad boy. Every boy is born with the equipment to be good. There is, however, the unhappy boy. And if you scratch the surface of the bad boy, you will find an unhappy child. The president of the Citizen's Committee on Children of New York City, Mrs. David M. Levy, writes, "Behind today's headlines of crime and juvenile delinquency stands a small, sorrowful figure—yesterday's unhappy child who somehow failed to take root in a secure home."

Writing for the same committee, Mrs. Helen W. Puner asks, "What are the hot angry facts? Children brought to court are troubled children crying for help. It's misery that's being expressed in their destructive behavior. They are children who have been deprived of things all children need to grow constructively—of emotional stability and discipline, of love and protection, of social acceptance and opportunity, sometimes even of physical nourishment and care. The world they know is at best indifferent; at worst, hostile. By their behavior they are repaying hostility with hostility, destruction with destruction, indifference to their needs with indifference to society's needs. Rejected by their parents—and, by extension, the world—they are in turn rejecting the world around them."

Still another committee, the Citizens' Emergency Committee on Youth Problems of School Districts 12, 13, and 14, reacted to the lurid newspaper articles on conditions in New York schools and to the critical claims that modern education methods are to be blamed for juvenile delinquency and acts of vandalism. This group believes that our education programs benefit the majority of the children. And it points out to the critics that if juvenile delinquency is to be attacked effectively, the sources of evil must be properly identified, and that the blame must be placed not only on administrative and disciplinary failures in the schools, but also on "the real causes of teen-age delinquency—on the doorstep of families broken by violence and illness, on crowded slums, inadequate law enforcement, inadequacies in some of the children's courts, and many other conditions which are breeding neighborhood crime."

These statements, of course, do not delineate the full profile of juvenile delinquency, nor define it. They do not indicate explicitly what we should do. However, they show the important difference of attitude which various groups of people are taking toward the problem of our troubled children. Above all, they point to the need of our solving the problem of juvenile delinquency. As expressions of opinion they are a part of the activity—the co-ordinated social activity—that will save us from becoming an increasingly criminal society.

The special appeal of the argument made by these citizens' committees is its rationality, its thoughtful concern, its quiet willingness to examine the entire situation before taking abrupt action. It has the persuasive tone of prudence and responsibility. The focus of its attention is the human being, the child—whom we must love, cherish and provide for—and not the mischievous or appalling act he may have committed.

The attitude of the opposed group, at its worst and most dangerous, is emotion (in the objectionable sense), reactive rather than thoughtful. It represents the type of identity thinking that we share with the lower animals. Teen-age purse-snatcher with slip-knife = evil = crime = danger = FEAR = HATE! Hit him over the head! Lock him up! Punish him! Don't care if we kill him!

More formal statements of the reactive attitude may take this form: Let us stop listening to the soft-hearted, muddle-headed do-gooders and uplifters. Let the patrolmen carry their clubs at all times. We must stop this coddling of juvenile delinquents.

The neurologist and semanticist tell us that, when a person indulges in reactive thinking, his cerebral cortex, which is regarded as the seat of consciousness, is like a machine that is idling. The problems of a modern, complex, technological culture cannot be solved by other parts of the brain. In fact, that culture cannot survive. It will destroy itself.

The delinquent child, like other children, is trying to solve personal problems. Consciously or unconsciously he is trying to get something he wants. What he wants can, perhaps, be best expressed in terms of feeling. He certainly wants pleasurable sensations, the taste of candy, for example. He also wants to be loved and accepted. He wants a sense of accomplishment and fulfillment, of equality among those with whom he comes in contact. Moreover, he wants to satisfy the expectations of others. On an unconscious level, he wishes to satisfy a wide variety of impulses of whose nature he is only dimly aware. Negatively he is striving to escape from unpleasant sensations, from hate and rejection, from the disagreeable, the unpleasant, from disappointments, abuses, cruelties and dangers.

In other words, he participates in the human condition. What distinguishes him from the nondelinquent child is that his methods, his solution to his problems, are both self-defeating and socially unacceptable to a degree that marks him for special attention. In this way, he is comparable to, but not to be confused with, the psychotic and the neurotic personality since his general method of solving problems is notably different from the average and more or less successful patterns of human behavior.

As part of the woodshed technique there has been considerable agitation for the punishment of the parents of delinquent children. The suggestion has been made on frequent occasions that the parents of the child who, for example, commits vandalism in a park should be forced to pay the damages incurred.

Robert Moses, New York City Commissioner of Parks, is one of those who have called for the fining of parents whose children commit park vandalism. He suggested that if the parents were responsible for the activities of their children, there would be less damage to our parks. The damage done by child vandals, he noted, already runs into hundreds of thousands, and will soon run into millions, of dollars. He warned that conditions were getting worse. And then Mr. Moses voiced a rather widely held attitude when he suggested that we should let the "uplifters take this thing and let them administer the system. If we wait for the great and glorious time when persuasion can be used to prevent vandalism, we will have terrific bills to pay."

On January 7, 1955, the *Chicago Tribune* reported the story of a grandmother who received a ten-day suspended jail sentence because her grandson was found twice in the streets in violation of the Chicago curfew ordinance.

The ordinance requires children under sixteen to be off the streets at night, but they may stay out until 11:30 P.M. on Fridays and Saturdays. The parent or guardian may be convicted if a violation is repeated.

The fifty-nine-year old woman was warned by the judge that she would have to go to jail if her fifteen-year-old grandson was found on the streets again in the late evening. The grandmother was also warned in October when her grandson was found with other boys in an automobile in possession of brass knuckles and a knife. The boy was again picked up in December in an areaway of his home as he was returning from a movie. The grandmother was then charged with contributing to the delinquency of a minor and was arrested.

Who is this woman? She was described as a tiny, gray-haired, kindly looking woman. When questioned she explained that the boy's family "broke up" four years ago. She doesn't know where the boy's father is. The mother contributes to the boy's support.

The youngster's record in school was described as "pretty bad."

"I'm going to be lenient in view of the fact that you are not his mother," the judge said. "I want the boy to understand that it will be his fault if you have to go to jail."

Will it be, really?

Can we expect a frail fifty-nine-year-old woman to control an obviously emotionally disturbed boy whose parents have left him? Here we find the kind of situation that seems to add up inevitably to a delinquent child. We have the broken home. The poor school record is another warning sign. So are the bad companions—brass knuckles and a knife suggest more serious rebellion than merely violation of a curfew.

The basic question: What good will it do to send an elderly woman to jail—whether for ten days or ten years?

Jailing or fining parents or guardians of children who commit delinquent acts can not be truly effective. We would still not know *why* the child acted as he did; he would still go untreated. Fining parents, in my opinion, is on the same level as the old-fashioned hookey cop who grabbed the truant by the scruff of the neck and tossed him back into the classroom. When recess came the child left again, and the truant officer, often on his bicycle, would make a mad race to drag him back to school again. The fact that the boy was reacting to unbearable home conditions was of little concern to the attendance officer. He was paid to see that the boy went to school, and that was that.

Similarly, jailing or fining a parent for a child's misdeeds is the most superficial manner imaginable of handling the problem. This belief, indeed, was the one that prevailed at the recent conference called by the federal Children's Bureau. The conference report, "Parents and Delinquency," presented the views of psychiatrists, psychologists, sociologists, and social workers who deal with delinquents and their parents, and said, in effect, that putting an absolute liability on parents for the delinquency of their children would be unfair and ineffectual and might even make matters worse.

"As parents we must be clear and consistent in our discipline and hold children accountable until they have demonstrated their right to increasing freedom.

"We cannot, however, in good conscience, hold parents wholly responsible for delinquency as long as there are wars, or fathers are in the armed services or on night shifts and therefore are token fathers, or when divorce is so frequent."

A child who knows that he is loved can accept discipline, even the woodshed type. A girl who had run away from one of the training schools said to me: "Oh, my housemother, when I returned, hugged me and kissed me and spanked me. It was wonderful."

We wouldn't have many delinquents if their mothers hugged them and kissed them, and when necessary spanked them. Unfortunately, however, the stern disciplinarian is too often a mother or father or other adult who cannot offer love along with discipline.

If the child is beaten and disowned emotionally and physically in his home and then is again beaten and told that he is a failure by the courts or the training schools, he will perforce accept that verdict. He will not understand why he is "bad," he will only know that the adult world has already labeled him a pariah.

The woodshed technique may be valuable or even necessary in some few instances. But to advocate it, as some do, as a general philosophy, will do considerably more harm than good. There is little if any evidence that corporal punishment serves as a deterrent to delinquency in children. Nor is it possible to find evidence that punishing parents will effect a desirable change in the young delinquent. The day of retaliatory punishment is over. The day of the various cruel and unusual disciplinary measures used in courts, in training schools, and in police stations, is, or at any rate, should be, behind us.

On the other hand, constructive discipline is essential to the preservation of the interests of the community. When a boy of sixteen has reached the stage where he holds society in contempt and is ready to become a killer, then he must obviously be taken in hand and made to see that he cannot single-handedly challenge the laws governing society. Even so, this boy may be desperately in need of help at the very time of his greatest antisocial act. The time that society must show its greatest mercy is the time when the boy shows himself to be most disagreeable.

An editorial in the New York *Herald Tribune* commented, "A little more toughness by police and courts might work wonders in raising the standards of juvenile behavior by applying pressure at the family hearth." A little more pressure would be advisable, perhaps, if that pressure were followed with help in securing guidance, counseling, and aid for the parents as well as the child. The parents are the ones who have nurtured their children and, consciously or unwittingly, set them on the road to becoming good citizens or potential criminals. And too often it is the parents who need help as much as the children.

Most of the proponents of the woodshed school of discipline are very sincere in their belief that it is necessary to punish the child or his parent if we are to cure the evil of delinquency. An outgrowth of this "let's-punish-the-punks" school has been the so-called Chicago Plan. Under this plan young offenders who are brought before the boys' court in Chicago have their cases continued. They are then placed behind bars in the newly established juvenile cell blocks in the Cook County jail. They are given what the state attorney called a taste of jail, or a taste of punishment, first, and then they are put on probation.

The warden of the jail prides himself on being a man who will put up with no nonsense. "These kids come in here and they're smart-alecky," he observed. "What they need is a hairbrush. Well, we can't do that, but the jail will take the smart-aleck out of them."

This is a too easy answer to a most difficult problem. It follows along the line that society has rules, and whether you like them or not, you must obey them. You would obey rules if you played on a baseball or football team; therefore, you must obey the rules when you play on the team that an adult society has set up. What's wrong with this philosophy? The answer is fairly obvious. Not every lad can make the baseball or basketball team. And not every lad is competent to understand, let alone obey, the rules of society.

What about the neurotic delinquent? His act frequently grows out of internal conflicts. Will being put behind bars help him?

And what about the social delinquent? He may live in a blighted, underprivileged community in which he is pushed into antisocial acts almost against his will. If his home situation is also unhealthy, he will have been punished, neglected, and rejected all of his life. Punishment is something that he has come to expect. If the Chicago Plan, or any similar plan, punishes him further, he isn't exactly surprised. But at the same time he isn't helped to understand why he must obey the rules of the community.

And what about the accidental delinquent? He may have committed a crime almost innocently, or at any rate not because of a confirmed pattern of delinquency. Is he then to be severely punished also? And if he is, will that punishment create a feeling of bitter resentment in him?

There are other than tough ways of dealing with delinquent children. These are the scientific ways, the psychiatric ways, the ways of those of us who believe that each child is an individual, and that any individual is worth helping.

Bertram M. Beck suggests that there are far more effective methods than the old-fashioned type of punishment.

"New ways of dealing with delinquents," Mr. Beck observes, "do not advocate a mushy sentimentality or a coddling of these youths. They do advocate both an art and a science of both firmness and kindness, meeting the needs of the youth as they can be perceived through the application of what we know of human development. To carry out these new ways there is demanded, for example, that our juvenile courts have a staff of trained probation officers.

"Only 11 per cent of all the juvenile officers doing probation work in the United States have the necessary professional training. In half of the juvenile courts in the United States, there are no probation services. To remedy conditions like this," Mr. Beck states, "to give new ways a chance, their first chance, is the hard answer to the problem and the answer that most people do not want to hear."

Harsh punishment of young offenders has been tried in this country and in many other countries, now and in the past, and it just has not worked. Back in the early days of this country we found that children were treated as adult criminals. We have a record of a child of eight who was hanged for maliciously burning down a barn. A child of ten was hanged for killing his companion. A girl of thirteen was burned to death because she had killed her mistress. In 1828 in the state of New Jersey a boy of thirteen was hanged for an offense he committed when he was twelve.

This tough attitude did not deter criminals in the past. We cannot expect that it will today. Is it fair to call a child of eight, or even thirteen, a "criminal"? Does he know or understand society's rules?

As a matter of fact the back-to-the-woodshed cry is not a new one. About a century ago the great educator, Horace Mann, commented on the same trend in these words: "Governments do not see the future criminal or pauper in the neglected child, and therefore they sit calmly by, until roused from their stupor by the cry of hunger or the spectacle of crime. They erect the almshouses, the prison and the gibbet, to arrest or mitigate the evils which timely caution might have prevented. The Courts and the ministers of justice sit by until the petty delinquencies of youth glare out in the enormities of adult crimes; and then they doom to the prison or the gallows those enemies to society who, under wise and well-applied influences, might have been supports and ornaments of the social fabric."

Today we frequently hear the suggestion that the police should use night sticks on juvenile delinquents. Parents are advised to use the slipper and the cat-o'-nine-tails. Indeed one judge boasted in court, in threatening a seventeen-year-old with physical punishment, that he had a cat-o'-nine-tails hanging in his home and that his children certainly knew that he would use it and behaved themselves accordingly.

These methods—night sticks against children, jails for children, and prison for parents—may be recommended by some, but we cannot condone it. Although the juvenile crime rate increased by about 45 per cent between 1948 and 1953, the lasting answer is more psychiatric help and less switch and slipper.

Speaking from two decades of experience as a judge Justine Wise Polier, in *Child Study* magazine in the summer of 1954 (published by the Child Study Association of America), points to the failure of this technique. Justice Polier observed that many of the children who appear before her or before the juvenile courts, come from homes not only poor but torn with dissension and unrest. She observed drily that in England when the penalty of pickpocketing was public hanging, which was intended to punish the culprit, avenge society, and deter others, the ceremonies were found to be field days for other pickpockets, including small children, who were also hanged if caught. Here is the woodshed technique at its worst —yet it did not act as a deterrent. Fear never breeds true respect for authority.

There is no evidence that severe punishment of itself given to children or their parents has any effect whatsoever in curbing juvenile delinquency. Conversely it is difficult to measure its ill effects. But it is essential that we recognize the need to bring about better understanding of the entire issue.

WOULD HORSEWHIP PAIR IN TOT'S DEATH. This news story reported that an angry magistrate had said he'd like to horsewhip an unwed mother and her shiftless lover, accused together of beating the woman's little boy to death.

The magistrate said to the couple, "I don't know whether they'll return an indictment against you. But I know what I'd do. I wouldn't indict you. I'd horsewhip you."

It was later found that the mother was a deformed, semi-hunchbacked woman who was 4 feet 8 inches tall. Since she had had a miserable life as a child herself and was deformed, it is not difficult to visualize the emotional punishment which she had received at the hands of society and which she in turn took out on her own child. Instead of wanting to horsewhip this neurotic mother, the magistrate might well have assigned her to a two-year program of intensive psychiatric treatment. At the end of that time, or if necessary twice that time, the woman might have returned to society as an adjusted individual. Too late, of course, to save the life of her young boy. But not too late to salvage and rehabilitate a living person who might become a valuable member of society.

Judge Samuel Leibowitz of Kings County, New York, said in sentencing a sixteen-year-old boy with a long record of delinquency, "These kids are desperate, vicious and depraved, and the approach of the courts toward dealing with these vicious young thugs must be reappraised and altered."

Yes, our attitude must be reappraised and altered. Because they *are* so desperate and depraved, it is essential that society do more than merely punish its "vicious young thugs." It is necessary that we do whatever is at all possible to rehabilitate them. No matter how long a sentence is given to a child arrested as a juvenile delinquent, the punishment alone will not prevent him from developing into an adult criminal and may in fact add to that possibility.

It is difficult to "get tough" when you remember the backgrounds of so many of the children who are in trouble.

In visiting Children's Village, a private treatment school in Dobbs Ferry, N.Y., I found that to use the paddle or the switch would be compounding an injustice to which many of the boys have been subjected since they were youngsters in diapers. They always expected and received beatings at the hands of their fathers or uncles or mothers, or the neighbors or the police. They never knew what it meant to be a normal, loved child in the household or the community. They were always "bad," bad because they were not given a chance to be good; unhappy because they were never given a chance to be happy.

Harvey is one of these children:

"I was Borne in New York and never got to know My Parent only My sister and I din't get to see much of My sister I grew up in brooklyn at a Mrs. —— house I lived there I stole and took money then when I was 11 years old she had to go to the hospital and I was taken to Mrs. —— to live I lived the a year and the I sent to Mrs. —— I lived until I started to steal I went to school and done my work I only had one habit and that was stealing and now Im up here."

How would you get tough with eleven-year-old Harvey, who was "Borne in New York" and never got to know his parents? He was moved from one foster house to another, and before he was eleven he began to steal. It doesn't call for a professional staff of psychiatrists, sociologists, and clinicians to explain why Harvey expressed his resentment against insecurity and indifference in the only way he knew, by stealing, but they are needed to change him into a happy, adjusted child. What type of punishment do young boys and girls like Harvey deserve?

One indignant mother expressed the view about delinquents held by a large majority of the community when she wrote in a letter to a newspaper: "Let's move out of the area of 'why did they do it' to the area of 'they can't do it any more.' That means," she said, "more policemen, many more. It means more cops for the protection of the people and the capturing and destroying of killers— no matter how or why they got that way."

That mother has every right to be indignant. We must agree with her that something must be done. More police is a partial answer, as the Harlem experiment in the fall of 1954 showed. When the New York City Police Commissioner added 250 patrolmen to a small Harlem area, the crime rate decreased dramatically. There were fewer arrests, less robbery, fewer holdups, and much less crime generally in this area. The residents expressed relief at this improvement in their neighborhood. Police can help keep crime down. But the night stick alone is not enough. We cannot hope to keep our youth, or our adults, from prison by police measures alone. Unless we find out how and why a thrill-killer got that way, and how and why a boy of fourteen became a destroyer of property and a thief, we will never learn how to prevent other children from following in their tragic footsteps. Certainly it is the better part of wisdom, to say nothing of humanity, to adopt the line, for example, of the Berkshire Industrial Farm school at Canaan, N.Y. There, in healthy surroundings, boys who have gotten into trouble work with each other, and the authorities in charge seek to discover why they got that way. Understanding this, it is possible to take steps so that "that way" may disappear and a delinquent be rehabilitated. At the same time we learn more about how to prevent other children from becoming delinquents.

Let's look at one of the boys at the Berkshire training school. When Eddie was six, he witnessed the killing of his mother by his stepfather. At the age of eight he was misbehaving seriously in school. He fought with other children, took their money and belongings and disrupted the entire class. His aunt, who cared for him after his mother died, told the teacher, "Hit him whenever he acts up. That's what I always do."

We need not belabor the point that when Eddie witnessed the killing of his mother at the age of six, he witnessed something that he would not easily forget. No amount of punishment will erase the memory of what he saw, or his traumatic reactions to the experience. He had seen more violence in his six years than any child should see. If he continues to be exposed to violence, through his experience with his aunt, in school, and elsewhere, Eddie will merely be convinced that the adult world in which he is living is one that only respects, understands, and practices the blow over the head or the smash in the face.

Even from the practical standpoint, punishment simply does not help the child become a better citizen, whether he has had Eddie's experience or the brutal experiences of hundreds of thousands of other children. Fortunately, the Berkshire school does not condone hitting him over the head. Through a policy of patient, sympathetic, humane reorientation, Eddie has developed into a stable, happy member of his own community. Love was substituted for hate, the book for the birch rod; understanding replaced indifference. Eddie is accepted as a human being, as one who has feelings, emotions, likes, and dislikes. And soon we find that the many Eddies who come to this and other good training schools respond as happier, less hostile boys to a kind of society they never before knew existed.

Recent studies show that prisons often do not correct a criminal's tendencies. Many come back. In one Massachusetts state prison, 70 per cent of the inmates had previously been in prison. In the Eastern Penitentiary of Pennsylvania, 67 per cent of the prisoners had served time in the past. In New York, as much as 80 per cent of the men sentenced to prison had previous criminal records. In one analysis, twenty-seven hundred of them had been arrested a total of ten thousand times. In Michigan, jail inmates consisted of 63 per cent who were repeaters. In Washington, D.C., 70 per cent were repeaters, while in Louisiana the figure was 80 per cent. If punishment per se prevented repetition of the crime pattern, for adults as well as for children, something might be said for the use of the woodshed technique. It just doesn't work out that way.

The late Judge Joseph N. Ulman of the supreme court of Baltimore, in talking before the Conference of the International Association of Chiefs of Police, expressed a pessimistic view of punishment by itself, through incarceration, as any kind of remedy for delinquency. The young, he thought, deserved more. And he said, "The young offender, the offender still in the formative period of his life, the offender who might be rehabilitated and set upon the right path, we deliberately force into a lifetime of crime. And then we arrest him again, and try him and send him up again—and again—and again—all for no good to him, no good to the family, and no good to society."

Punishment has always been the way of dealing with lawbreakers, and punishment has always failed as a deterrent to crime. We can go all the way back to Old Testament days, where it is written in the Book of Deuteronomy, that a stubborn and rebellious son, a glutton and a drunkard, should be taken before the elders of the city, and stoned to death.

We have outgrown that point of view, I hope. Far better is it to try to help, to try to rehabilitate the son instead of stoning him to death. Yet if we are not careful we will find ourselves retrogressing in the handling of our delinquents because we shall succumb to the pressures accusing us of pampering or coddling "bad" children. Children should be coddled, particularly if they have been as unfortunate as that lad who witnessed the killing of his mother. In many instances the provision of long-overdue affection, warmth, interest—coddling, in fact—is the first and most important answer to the child's needs.

Not long ago the newspapers carried the story of a judge in Germany who hated to send young persons to jail. He earned himself the title of the "Chocolate Judge" after he sentenced a little girl, convicted of stealing chocolates, to donate a candy bar each week to an orphanage. In another case a seventeen-year-old boy was convicted of stealing a motorcycle. The youth stood trembling before the judge.

"You will never know the beauties of nature if all you do is to drive like a madman," the judge observed. He sentenced the youth to serve a year-long membership in a walking club.

"Except for obvious criminals, most young people have simply gone astray and must have another chance," this judge said. "In fact, society owes them another chance. They must perform some good deed related to the bad."

The jurist has seen juvenile delinquency drop 40 per cent in the area he served during his term on the bench.

This is not, of course, a scientific study. It may be that a 40 per cent drop in delinquency is far too much to credit only to the approach this judge is using. But there is more than a little science implicit in his approach. There is a recognition that treatment of the young offender, other than a routine administration of punishment, other than the use of woodshed techniques, should certainly be considered. It is not enough to become angry at an already angry boy. It is just at the time that that boy is in his greatest difficulty, in his greatest disgrace, that we must show him the greatest affection and understanding. Surely it is impossible to accept the argument that most of these young boys and girls are not worth saving but only merit punishment. Because these youngsters have shown signs of mental or moral or emotional deterioration is precisely the reason why the woodshed technique is the one that should *not* be used.

The modern approach utilizing all available facilities, and creating new ones as they become necessary, is the approach that eventually will succeed in reducing our delinquency rate as nothing before has ever done.

This is not wishful thinking. We have enough evidence today to prove that the preventive and curative measures employed in treating potential or actual delinquents are far more effective than punitive measures. Throughout recorded history, punishment has been used . . . and it has failed. Why not try another, more scientific, more realistic approach?

It is not an either/or proposal that confronts us. Surely there are times when the woodshed is necessary. No one would want a dangerous hoodlum, whether he be twelve or sixteen or twenty, let loose upon society. He must be put behind bars or in a psychiatric ward until he has been educated to behave. No one advocates letting lions or tigers loose on the streets.

At the same time, coddling or taming is essential if we are to prevent many of the future tigers from threatening the safety of towns and cities. Sometimes the little bit of affection, of understanding, of security that a troubled child may get at the crucial moment of his life may turn him from a potential criminal career to responsible citizenship in his community.

That is our goal. And it is worth making every effort, no matter how difficult, to reach it.

8. The First Line of Defense

*"I cannot conceive of a case of
spontaneous delinquency . . ."*

"The solution to the problem of juvenile delinquency," said J. Edgar Hoover, head of the Federal Bureau of Investigation, "lies in an intelligent co-ordinated adult action—action which demands full co-operation of adult society, social agencies, and law enforcement."

Applying that formula implies three specific steps: (1) early detection of children who are going to become delinquent, (2) a program to help these children adjust adequately, and (3) a program to rehabilitate those children who may already be delinquents.

The four thrill-killers of Brooklyn who went about beating vagrants in parks and horsewhipping girls, who beat one man to death and tossed another one half-unconscious into the East River, allegedly came from "happy" homes. People who knew them found it hard to believe that they were capable of doing what they did.

I am unable to accept the thesis that basically these youngsters had "happy" home lives. From the parole officers' and social workers' reports, from reports of the psychiatrists who interviewed the families, we know that there was some emotional disturbance that was not discernible on the surface. We know, for instance, that chronic truancy is one indication of a seriously maladjusted child —a potential delinquent. We know that one of the four Brooklyn youths who wantonly killed and tortured victims in the park played truant on twenty-two days of the previous school year. Prior to that time he had been absent from school only two days during the year. The abrupt rise in his truancy rate could well have been an indication that something was going wrong.

In a century of service, the Community Service Society of New

York City has worked with large numbers of delinquent boys and families in emotional trouble. The society has found that juvenile delinquency is not a sudden, isolated incident. A child doesn't just "go bad" suddenly and without cause. It is a long-term process starting from early childhood. The frustrations, hatreds, despairs, and bewilderments of the child are nourished until the breaking point is reached. The nature of the particular trigger that sets it off is relatively unimportant. But Bernard Fisher, research associate, observes, it is rarely spontaneous: "It is true that in some cases the juvenile misdeed appears to be without explanation. I am quite sure, however, that appearances in these instances are deceiving and a closer study would unearth the causes—causes that might have been detected long before. I cannot conceive of a case of spontaneous delinquency and I certainly never encountered one."

The majority of the delinquents we studied at two training schools, were between thirteen and sixteen years of age. About 70 per cent of these young people had been to court on two or more occasions before going to a training school. Indeed it is known that the largest number first appeared in court between the ages of eleven and thirteen. Almost half of those studied in another group of five hundred older delinquents showed signs of aberration at the age of eight, or even younger.

In my own study I found that both the boys and girls started to break the law at a rather early age. Among the boys committed to Jamesburg in 1954, 35 of the 208 boys said that they had started to break the law before they were nine years old; 19 of them were nine years old; 16 were ten years old; 12 were eleven years of age; and 32 were twelve years of age. Thus we find that more than half of the boys had started getting into trouble by breaking the law when they were twelve years old or younger. This percentage is probably larger; 31 boys said that they didn't remember when they started to break the law.

Among the girls at Hudson in 1954, a similar proportion—just about half—had already broken the law by the time they were twelve years old. If 50 per cent of the boys and girls who end up in institutions get into trouble before they are twelve years old, obviously we must look beyond the child himself for the cause of his wrongdoing. And we must help these children faster. Most of the children in these training schools were fifteen or more (72 per cent of the boys and 65 per cent of the girls). Something could have been done between the time when these children first got into trouble and the time when they were committed to institutions three or more years later. Beyond that, something could have been done even *before* their rebellion resulted in overt, antisocial acts.

Dr. Fritz Redl, chief of Child Research for the National Institute of Mental Health, told the members attending a recent conference that no one can tell whether or not a child will turn out to be delinquent five years later. "Some children," he commented, "prepare for the delinquency pleasantly and quietly."

This statement would seem to be somewhat exaggerated inasmuch as the Gluecks have found a formula that can, to some extent, predict the onslaught of delinquency. Certain forms of behavior, both in and out of school, indicate the potential delinquent. The fact that almost 90 per cent of the occurrence of traits characterizing a delinquent appear in children before they are eleven years old is an indication that the behavior pattern that characterizes delinquency is formed at an extremely early age. This pattern, formed so early in a child's life, would seem to contradict Dr. Redl's statement that no one can tell whether or not a child will turn out to be delinquent five years later.

The Gluecks set up five factors that could be included in a prediction table for future delinquents: (1) discipline of boy by father, (2) supervision of boy by mother, (3) affection of father for boy, (4) affection of mother for boy, (5) and cohesiveness of the boy's family. Whether we agree or not, we must recognize that these five factors are basic in the consideration of our present delinquency problem. But the question of semantics beclouds the picture. Not many parents would agree on the definition of the terms "discipline," "supervision," "affection," or "cohesiveness."

What is discipline? To one father it may be a strict forcing of the child to "toe the mark." It may take the form of harsh punishment. To another it may be a lenient let's-work-it-out-together attitude.

"I've always been strict with Jim," a worried mother told me recently. "I thought that was the way to make a man of him. He never dared talk back to me. If he did, I'd smack his face so hard he'd know it for a week. His father was weak . . . he'd never say no to the boy.

"But," she continued, "he's twenty now and I know he never laughs. He never talks to me. He goes into his room in the evening and stays there by himself, listening to the radio. I told him he's like a boarder in the house. He seems to be afraid of me. I can't get through to him."

What is affection? It can be interpreted differently by every parent. To some it is a complete domination of the child, to others a smothering protectiveness or an uncritical acceptance. Whatever it is, a child knows when it exists and misses it strongly when it is lacking. He knows too when an outward show of affection disguises rejection.

Or supervision? What are its limits? Do we supervise a six- and a sixteen-year-old in the same manner? And to the same degree? "My father never lets me go out on dates," a sixteen-year-old delinquent girl said. "I was supervised, all right—I couldn't even go to the movies or school dances. Had to be home by nine o'clock. My father didn't trust me. So I ran away. I couldn't take it any more."

Family cohesiveness? We know that the pressures and distractions of modern life in many cases have destroyed the unity of the family. Each member has different interests. They meet at meal-times only. The family picnics, square dances, and automobile outings are disappearing.

Without quibbling over terms, we can recognize that an over-strict father or mother, an unsupervised home, a child who does not have affection, or who does not have strong family ties, has less of an opportunity to develop into a wholesome individual than the one who does get adequate affection and supervision. The Gluecks' factors can be useful in developing a preventive program.

The New York City Youth Board is conducting an experiment in two schools. Of 223 first-grade children, 75 boys have been selected on the basis of the five factors as being potential delinquents. Half of this number, those in one of the two schools, will receive concentrated treatment wherever possible. The other half, about 35 boys in the second school, will receive only the limited treatment offered to any child in the New York City school system.

The experiment may prove, according to those sponsoring it, that potential delinquents can be accurately predicted and, once discovered, they can be effectively treated. If at the end of four or five years we find that the boys who received special help were deflected from the course of delinquency, while those who received no special help developed patterns of delinquency, we shall have proof that remedial treatment can begin in the first grade in our public schools.

This will undoubtedly be one of the most important educational discoveries of our day. It will be as valuable as the pioneer work being done by Dr. Jonas Salk in the attack on polio. If the schools can serve as the focal point in the preventive program, we will have made tremendous strides toward eliminating delinquency. And the cost will be far less than it is at present. It is easier to help a child of six than to help one of sixteen.

Those operating the experiment in the New York schools find that the problem of treating the delinquent is not easy. A six-year-old child is not always ready to discuss his problems, if indeed he is aware that he has any. It takes a great deal of tact, effort, energy, and wisdom on the part of a trained social worker or psychiatrist to get to the fundamental issues involved. But there are ways of doing it. Frequently the play technique is utilized to reach the mind of the child. Playrooms are equipped with such objects as modeling clay, paints, blocks, games, toy furniture, and little dolls. The emotionally disturbed child may sometimes utilize these toys in ways that reveal his inner feelings to the trained observer.

One social worker told the story of a boy and the grandmother who often cared for him. From all outward appearances the grandmother appeared to be gentle, kind and devoted to the child. "But one day," the social worker said, "for no apparent reason the kid took a female doll, shoved it into a bathtub and turned to me and said, 'That's grandma, and I'm drowning her.'"

The social worker later found that the grandmother was at the root of much of the boy's trouble. The social worker continued, "I invited the grandmother to come and talk to me, and we talked about the boy's problems. She was genuinely interested and then suddenly she suggested, 'Why don't you cut out part of his brain?' and then she told me all about a member of the family who had undergone successful brain surgery. She thought brain surgery would cure just about anything, and often brought it up to the child."

It is not difficult to imagine the effect of a suggestion like that upon a boy if it is repeated time and again, as it was in that household. And it would have been difficult, if not impossible, for his classroom teacher ever to have been able to detect the problem involved without the help of the clinic.

It is very possible that the 223 first-graders who entered school in September, 1954, and who will be watched by trained Youth Board workers, will hold the clue for a great many answers to the riddle of what can be done to check the growth of juvenile delinquency in this country.

In a symposium on the education of emotionally disturbed children, Dr. Louis Hay, New York City school psychologist, commented on the fact that the school is the child's first and most sustained contact with a social institution other than the family. If the school can provide early detection and treatment of emotional disturbances, the number of permanently or seriously troubled children will be reduced substantially. Dr. Hay pointed out that, despite the multiplicity of the symptoms of maladjustment, troubled children might be nurtured to more adequate functioning in guidance classes designed to meet their needs.

Ward T. Miller, superintendent of schools in Wilmington, Delaware, said, "I believe it is possible for trained, observant teachers and psychologists to detect serious emotional disturbance, in the childhood years, in potential juvenile delinquents. Such trained teachers and psychologists need to be able, after detection, to refer such children for expert psychiatric diagnosis and therapy or suitable follow-up."

Other educators and authorities in the field are of the same opinion.

L. Kenneth England, supervisor of attendance for the Birmingham, Alabama, Board of Education is convinced that early detection by teachers and school guidance clinics is possible: "With remedial treatment applied, with parental co-operation, many children can be saved."

School superintendent J. W. Edwards, of Portland, Oregon, made this revealing observation, "In practically every case of murder, or major crime, for that matter, Portland schools had a record on the youth that would predict the act. We have a number running loose now about whom we shall probably—and unfortunately—be able to say, 'I told you so.' We may miss a few, but not the majority. Most of them can be identified in junior high school, from Grades Seven to Nine."

The burden of early detection of disturbed children must fall on the teacher. Despite the importance of specialized personnel, classroom teachers must be the first line of defense against the spread of delinquency. This does not imply that they should become psychiatrists or even amateur clinical psychologists. It is not delinquency itself that a teacher should detect, if she is adequately trained, but those emotional disturbances within the child that may prevent him from developing into a normal, law-abiding person. It does suggest, however, that if the teachers have smaller classes, if they secure better working conditions, if the salaries are made attractive enough to recruit the most sensitive and the most qualified persons as teachers, then teachers can be of enormous value in detecting potential delinquents—and helping them to secure guidance and treatment—long before these children come before the courts or become involved with the police.

What qualities should a teacher have to do this important job? The Bank Street College of Education of New York City listed the following abilities and skills that characterize a good teacher:

She utilizes a nonpunitive way of dealing with out-of-bounds behavior, and she exerts authority without requiring submission.

She gives support to the child in the face of conflicts, failures, and obstacles.

She creates a classroom atmosphere in which children can grow according to their own needs and capacities for each stage of growth.

She sees each child as an individual.

She helps the child get satisfaction through achievement and competence of his work rather than through competitive activity.

She has a stable personality, combining warmth, spontaneity, and sensitivity to others.

She has beliefs, ideals, and a quality of devotion to a way of life that is transmitted to children in the atmosphere she creates.

She knows the world in which she lives and likes it.

These traits are not found in every teacher. But they are very important. It is essential that our teachers strive to attain them, that we work diligently to bring such teachers into our schools—teachers who love children and who recognize their needs. And the teachers themselves, as the Bank Street College points out, must be stable and emotionally mature. Unless we have happy teachers, we will not have happy children. Neurotic teachers will of necessity contribute to the unhappiness and emotional disturbance of their pupils.

The great influence a teacher can have for good or bad is shown in these excerpts from the story written by a thirteen-year-old boy now detained at Warwick:

"Well my story begins when I was at school when I was living in Manhattan. It was the first day I went to school. I liked it. I liked it only because I was in kindergarten. It was fun. I was the teachers pet. . . .

"Then I went to school for my 3rd grade I had a young teacher she treated me good and I went to school all the year with out any trouble from any one. . . .

"The next school year I had a Teacher who was the kind of teacher who is scared of her own shadow. The first thing you would do she sent a card home and tell your parents you are not doing to good in school. I soon got tired of all of that and decided to do something about it. So at the end of that school year I broke out all of the window in that school, and on top of that I threw ink all over the classrooms. . . .

"Then I went to the eighth grade the teacher told me I wasn't worth a dam and that was in October so I didn't go to school no more since then.

"Then the truant officer took me to court. The judge sent me to the youth House. It was like trying to put the fire out of hell! . . ."

⊛ . . . night have been put out of this child's private hell if his
        . . . had affected him like the young one he had in the

PP . . . wnell, United States Commissioner of Edu-
        . . . ree obstacles that prevent the teacher from
        . . . children: "(1) Some teachers are not properly
        . . . the needs of pupils who should have special
        . . . these needs; (2) many teachers are not given
        . . . ow pupils as individuals; (3) many teachers are
        . . . onal assistance to deal with problems which they
        . . . not know how to treat."

        . . . these obstacles, Dr. Brownell proposed these meas-
        . . . each teacher a group small enough so that she can
        . . . ch them as individuals. (2) Provide adequately pre-
        . . . rs who understand how to work with children and
        . . . are interested in working with and helping them, and
        . . . demonstrated their ability to work constructively with
        . . . 3) Provide some specialized staff to help teachers with
        . . . problems involved in learning, recording, and interpret-
        . . . haracteristics of each pupil and his home and neighbor-
        . . . sychological, medical, and social services to deal clini-
cally . . . otherwise with youngsters needing care beyond that which the teacher and principal can provide are also needed. (4) Unite parents and school leaders in support of school programs and procedures which seek to solve the problem of delinquency at its roots.

The teacher's duty to impart formal knowledge or various skills may be the least important one in dealing with the young, especially in cases where there are recognizable symptoms of potential delinquency. The emotional needs of the child, especially in the lower grades of elementary school, are of tremendous importance. There is need for understanding and sympathy and for a willingness to work with the child.

The teacher who possesses a majority of the eight traits listed by the Bank Street College of Education will be quick to recognize the beginnings of frustrations which lead to delinquent behavior.

It may seem that there is a wide gap between a classroom situation and delinquency, but there is not. The child who cannot recite the answer to a question and is passed over by the teacher may never acquire the information (or skill) needed for the next step in the learning process. He is unable to do his homework or the next assignment. He lags behind the class with a feeling of neglect and frustration. From being unprepared with his homework is but a step from staying away from school. While out of school with nothing to do, he will find opportunities to do the wrong things and companions with whom to do them, and end as a delinquent or be apprehended as a truant.

We know that delinquents are often retarded in school. For instance, in testing 345 delinquent boys, at the National Training School for Boys in Washington, D.C., it was found that 33 made normal progress in school, 12 were accelerated, and 300 were retarded from one to five grades when they were compared with normal boys of their ages. The Gluecks also found that 41 per cent of their delinquent cases were two or more years behind the grades proper for their ages.

Dr. Louis E. Raths, professor at the New York University School of Education, analyzed three doctoral studies completed recently under his supervision which were concerned with ways in which the emotional needs of children affect their learning processes. Research and field studies included development of a teacher-education program to sensitize trainees to psychosomatic difficulties, the relation of emotional needs to critical thinking, and the facilitation of learning through meeting basic emotional needs.

Dr. Raths said that his work "pinpointed eight basic emotional needs of children which are perhaps more important than their academic needs." These needs are (1) the need for belonging, (2) the need for achievement, (3) the need for economic security, (4) the need to be free from fear, (5) the need for love and affection, (6) the need to be free from intense guilt feelings, (7) the need for personal integrity, and (8) the need for understanding and knowledge.

The doctoral studies show that psychosomatic illness affects learning. If teachers could actually know the innermost thoughts of many of their students, they would likely discover that often some of the children are crying from within. The concerns of some children are so great that they are likely to sit in school classrooms brooding, thinking, analyzing, and worrying about the problems, anxieties, fears, tensions, and frustrations which are so real to them. As teachers engage in their courses of study and in the activities they plan for the subject or grade, many children are victims of emotional problems. As these frustrations in the children continue, and as the teacher tries to fulfill her objectives for the subject or for the grade, more obvious and observable evidences of tension often arise in the form of physical illness.

These conclusions are reached by Dr. Raths: "Given a child with a health problem affecting his school progress, the chances are great that emotional factors play a large part in the condition. As teachers get to know this individual, as they study his home, his problems, his anxieties, his frustrations, his fears, his ambitions, his progress, and the conditions which aggravate his health problem, they have some basis for arriving at hunches as to probable unfulfilled needs. If an attempt to fulfill these needs employs a consistent, continuous course of action designed constantly at fulfilling a particular need, improvement begins to occur. Improvement may be observed in school attendance, in a reduction of intensity and in frequency of the psychosomatic condition, and in academic work. Improvement may be a slow process and may not follow a common pattern.

"Yet, given continuous and consistent therapy in fulfilling emotional needs, progress occurs. As the process goes on, a plan of continuous appraisal is necessary as a means of identifying appropriate changes in procedures. If parents likewise attempt to work with the child in a manner consistent with the plan described above, greater progress occurs."

Another research study, completed by Emmy Drake Jenkins of Adelphi College's School of Social Work (New York), also shows that a child who is failing frequently cannot do better even if he tries. The study shows that children who are poor pupils generally come from unhappy homes; the emotional disturbances of the children prevent their doing satisfactory work in school.

This study of the influencing emotional factors involved in the cases of twenty-five children referred to a child guidance center for learning difficulties showed an overwhelming proportion of unhappy, confused youngsters, the offspring of similarly unhappy parents. The children were of normal intelligence; for the most part, their parents were well educated and, in a material sense, they were reasonably successful. However, reports of the parents' emotional lives presented a dark picture. Of twenty-one sets of natural parents, only four reported that they were compatible. Ten sets were separated or divorced. However, the effects of these physically broken homes on the children appeared to be not very different from the effects on the children of seven sets of parents who remained together "for the sake of the children," under conditions of extreme friction. The theory of mental health specialists who believe that unhappy children often grow up to be the unhappy parents of more unhappy children is supported by this study.

Added to the pressures already existing in most of the homes were the emotional difficulties that revolved around the children's school troubles, the Jenkins study suggested. The tendency of parents to measure good school achievement as evidence of a child's development aggravates the difficulties when the child begins to fail in school. Miss Jenkins observed that all sorts of unfortunate attitudes on the part of parents grow up around the child's failure, further complicating an already difficult situation. This study adds proof to the theory that, if we want our schools to do an adequate job, we must work closely with the homes and parents, as well as with the pupils.

It is essential that we recognize the individual difference among children. It is also important that we offer those who are gifted an opportunity to develop within their potentialities. But if we place too great a burden upon a child, if we set standards so high that he cannot meet them, he may withdraw into a world of his own fantasy. It may be a totally unreal world into which he withdraws to escape the difficulties of life in general and of his home environment in particular; he is in danger of becoming a dreamer—and even a schizophrenic.

On the other hand, he may rebel.

We are constantly asking our children to be, not the way they would like to be, but like their classmates, like their brother or sister, or like some other child. We want our children to conform to please us; their own desires and abilities are often overlooked. We want to wear our children like medals, to show them off to our friends and neighbors. We want to use our children to fulfill our frustrated needs and wishes and dreams. But in so doing, we often warp the very lives we would encourage. In trying to make the child conform to our own views, proper as they may be, distorted as they often are, we are harming him beyond measure.

Our schools stress mass education. All of our classrooms, with commendable exceptions, are too large. On a nationwide basis we have an average of thirty children for each teacher. In order that each child may receive the attention he requires, we know that a class should have no more than fifteen or twenty pupils, at the most. How can we expect a teacher to develop the potentialities of all her pupils if she has at most five or ten minutes to give to each child during the course of the day?

In some school systems we have developed what is known as continuous promotion for the average child. Yet in most instances we fail a child for not being able to keep up with his normal class. If that child is working already to the height of his capabilities, we are indeed doing him a tremendous injustice. What is even more important, we are frustrating him. At the same time, it is not wise to promote a child into a regular grade if he cannot do the work. We must not give him a false sense of security. We cannot fool the youngster; he knows that he is not measuring up to the capabilities or the standards of his classmates.

How is such a dilemma to be resolved? I believe that we must develop a program in our schools in which our children can move ahead at the pace that is best suited for them. That does not mean that we should coddle them. Rather, it means that we should develop a code that will permit children to secure the best schooling they can get to meet their own levels of response. It means that the community must spend more time and money in making schools more inviting to those young boys and girls who now dislike school to the extent that they simply stay away, and end up by becoming confirmed truants. They get their first contact with the police and then later with the courts as truants.

In order to do this, we must assume that the teacher is an emotionally mature person who is not easily thrown off balance by a nonconforming student. The teacher who is unbending herself, who is autocratic in her approach, will receive more antagonism than support from her pupils. There is a sound middle course for the teacher to follow between the extremes of rigid control and no control at all. If we substitute the word "guidance" for "control," we have the key to this middle road.

The emotional atmosphere of the school itself gives us the key to this problem. If a teacher or a school is cold and forbidding and rigid, then the maladjusted child, generally coming from a cold and forbidding and rigid home, will fall into a pattern of behavior at school identical to his pattern at home. However, if the teacher and the school radiate friendliness and a genuine respect for each child as an individual, the youngster will begin to adjust and grow in an atmosphere of understanding and attention and warmth.

At the same time the teacher needs the encouragement of knowing that the community recognizes the deep-seated, deep-rooted problems involved. The teacher and the school can achieve the maximum results only if they receive the maximum support from the community in general, and from the parents in particular.

9. Guidance for Delinquents

"Maybe if my mother had had a chance to talk with somebody when she was young, she wouldn't be having a nervous breakdown now."

It has been suggested as a solution for delinquency that children be allowed to leave school earlier, at fourteen or fifteen. Is this even a partial solution? I doubt it.

A great many delinquents do leave school at an earlier age than nondelinquents do. In 1952, 61 per cent of delinquents who were from eight to seventeen years old were not enrolled in school, as compared to 39 per cent who were. Two things are clear: (1) delinquent children, who are frequent truants, do not want to continue in school and drop out at the first opportunity, and (2) the children who drop out are deprived of the guidance and stability that schools should provide.

Indeed, there have been suggestions that the length of compulsory school attendance be increased rather than decreased. The recommendations made to the Senate subcommittee by a series of witnesses from Denver, for instance, included suggestions that the compulsory age for school attendance should be raised from the present requirement of eight years of formal education or up to the age of seventeen to twelve years of formal education or up to the age of eighteen. The Denver group also proposed that school curricula should be modified to meet the needs of nonacademically oriented students.

The most telling argument in favor of school for delinquents is that the schools can do so much to help these children. Not only that, the schools can do more to help them, perhaps, than any other social organization. What can the schools do? What are they doing? Let us be specific.

163

Probably as good a program as can be found anywhere is the one that has been established in Philadelphia where a Case Review Committee has been set up. The committee, working as a group within the school system, considers cases of acute behavior problems, of emotional disturbances, and suggests treatment that is appropriate for the individual child involved.

Six years ago, when a twelve-year-old public school pupil was murdered by a sixteen-year-old boy attending a private school, a wave of hysteria swept through Philadelphia. Panic-stricken parents demanded that the public officials take proper action to prevent such vicious crimes. At that time the Case Review Committee was set up to see what could be done. The committee, which meets weekly, is made up of the superintendent of schools as chairman and the directors of the Medical Services, Pupil Personnel and Counseling, and Special Education divisions of the Board of Education.

During a period of five years the committee has considered 480 cases. The case log has been stepped up in recent years. Most cases of maladjustment are handled by teachers, attendance workers, counselors, psychologists, and nurses in the particular school in which a case arises. The committee handles directly only such acts by potentially delinquent children as sexual aggression, rape, arson, sexual perversion, attempted suicide, and assault and battery.

Through the efforts of this committee, children who are actually dangerous to others as well as to themselves and who might require residential care are sent to the juvenile court. As a matter of fact, more than two hundred children whose cases have been considered by this committee are now making good adjustments in school, and their progress is being followed closely by the committee. What is most important is that, because of this teamwork approach, the committee has been able to secure for these children the kind of help they need in order to solve their problems.

To show what the schools can do in this field, I want to cite some of the actual case histories taken from the records of the Philadelphia schools, where the Case Review Committee is in operation.

Here is the case of a lad we will call Arthur Jones. He was ten years old when he first attracted the attention of the Philadelphia school authorities. The teacher referred him to the committee. He was ranking lower and lower each year in his standard tests. His IQ dropped from 120 to 91. The teacher thinks he is bright. He has a charming personality. There is a new baby in the home and the teacher thought that perhaps Arthur was jealous, but she found that she was still unable to get at the roots of the boy's problem. She therefore placed the case before the committee.

It was found that Arthur had repeated colds, sore throats, constipation, and poor appetite. It was obvious that something was bothering the child and that he could become a serious problem.

Here are the counselor's rough notes of a series of interviews with Arthur, which took place over a period of two months:

"Interview with Arthur: Quite concerned over failures. Blamed much of this on the baby. Nobody has time to hear his spelling, etc. Hopes baby isn't walking by July 18. That's his birthday and he doesn't want her messing around during his party. He has nosebleeds and headaches now, too. Father is going to take him to hospital to see about them.

"When he grows up he's going to be a detective. His uncle got killed that way. He guesses he'll be in a box himself.

"Arthur is pretty desperate to get attention for himself."

"Interview with Arthur: Began on spelling. Jumped to arithmetic. Needed help with trial divisor. Back to spelling again. But at time to go lingered to tell me how baby sister wakes him up in morning and how his cousin is an artist and he hopes to make his mother as proud of him, too, someday, as his aunt is proud of his cousin. Remembered how his little girl cousin could tie her own shoelaces at three years of age and he couldn't tie his at five years. Even a baby on their street—only three years old—could tie her shoelaces and his, too.

"He can't draw—he doesn't like it. In spelling list his most difficult word was 'husband.'"

"Interview with Arthur: Brought out spelling list. Had difficulty learning it because mother had to go to her sister's and didn't help him. Discarded that, saying he knew it—did long divisions.

Can do them. Makes careless mistakes. Agrees his mind is on other things like 'Will I get promoted?' and 'Why can't I learn like other children?' etc. Asked if I thought he'd be promoted and I asked what he thought. He knows he's better than some children. 'I'm sure I'm not as slow as those children, but——.' I said he wasn't satisfying himself. 'That's it. I want to be as good as anybody.' Went right into his sister's Easter oufit. She has a pink dress he likes and a pink coat he doesn't like. He got new suit, etc., but not a new coat. I asked if he'd like me to talk with his mother about his work. He would but he didn't think she could come on account of the baby, but he'd ask her. Went on to tell of sleep-walking and nightmares. Then to his mother's talkativeness. 'Don't get her talking,' he said like a man. 'She'll go on forever.' Then he added, 'And here I am going on just like her. Goodbye.' "

"Interview with Arthur: Did a lot of arithmetic. Chided himself on careless mistakes. I said he was confused. 'I'm worried about a lot of things,' he said. I agreed that both at school and home there were things to worry about. 'Yes, at school I worry about not getting along. I'd hate to be left down and not be as good as the others. At home—there's nothing there to worry me. Now this arithmetic, etc., etc.'

"I asked if he had asked his mother about coming in. He had but she said she couldn't make it. I asked if I might send for her. 'You'd better let me ask her,' he replied. I said he already had. 'But I'll ask her again.' More concern about this today.

"At time to go sat down wearily in chair, 'I have a lot of worries,' he repeated and went into all his school problems again."

"Interview with Arthur: Talked a little about baby sister and his efforts to help her to walk. Then went right into arithmetic. After a while I asked if he thought all this work was helping him. He thought so until he finally decided it was his worries which kept him back in his work and it was them he had to bring out down here.

"Says he can read teachers' minds, but he doesn't know why his teacher looks at them so funny and he demonstrated (exactly as his teacher does look when she goes off into a daydream as she has a habit of doing). Says his mother is coming in to see me. I sent her an invitation by mail."

"Interview with Arthur: Talked most of time about his problems —trying to live up to ideal set by parents. He must not fail in work. He'd disappoint them. Confusion about why he isn't doing so well. Some talk about baby sister and how she takes up parents' time. A little comparison of how it used to be when she hadn't arrived and he was center of attention.

"Said his daddy was passing the school with him one day and he showed him my room, but daddy said he'd leave school business to mother. Mother may come in next week, he said.

"Arthur has to be all his parents want him to be to successfully rival baby."

"Interview with Arthur: Same pattern. Showing increased dislike for teacher and her attentiveness to him. Is able to express this verbally.

"Mrs. Jones in after I wrote a rather urgent note. Very quiet, shy young woman. Did not realize how much Arthur has changed. Realizes he is jealous of baby but doesn't know what to do about it. Tried to get her to see she must give him equal attention as baby gets if possible. Make a fuss over him. Let him help with baby, etc. Get husband to do same. She will take him for psychological examination."

"Interview with Arthur: Teacher had reprimanded him for untidiness. (Arthur is usually spick-and-span.) Today his shirt had buttons off. 'I just picked up my play shirt and put it on. I was so sleepy this morning.' Mother does not always get up with him. He feels very bad about his appearance and the teacher made him feel worse. 'She says I never comb my hair, and I do every morning.' There was much talk on this and finally he blurted out, 'This afternoon I'll wear my Easter pants and a white shirt and a tie. Maybe that'll satisfy her. What's she want anyway? Maybe she wants me to be a girl and wear skirts. Anything I hate it's skirts! I don't ever

want to wear them, but I guess that's what she wants.' I asked if he'd want to do that much for his teacher. He mumbled something about satisfying her for once. I said maybe he'd like to be a girl, that girls do get a lot of attention. 'They sure do, but I don't want to be a girl. I wish I knew what she wants.' Arthur's antagonism to his teacher has grown in the last month. I wonder if he's project- ing onto her his feeling about his mother. His teacher happens to be pregnant and it's rather evident so that the older children may be talking about it. Arthur may have heard about it. Since this antagonism has come out his teacher has decided he is lazy and not really trying.

"Today Arthur said he knows his work but when he goes to do it, 'it's like a wall is between me and the work.' He demonstrated a barrier with his hands. I said his worries came between him and his work. He passed his hand over his face like an old man. 'I got a lot of worries. Now I have to go back to that room and as soon as I go in the door she'll start on me.' I said he might like to be ignored. 'No, not ignored, but—isn't there a medium way to treat people?' "

It does not take much insight to see that Arthur was headed for a serious emotional disturbance unless something could be done and done soon. Well, in this case, something has been done.

The committee talked to the mother, talked to the boy, talked to the teacher, and Arthur is now doing good work. He is back to his 120 IQ standard and the child seems to be happy. Of course, it will require more than a promise on the part of the parents to participate in the program. It will need a deeper understanding into why the young lad slowly began to deteriorate. It is extremely helpful, though, to find the causes of the disturbance at an early date.

Here is the case of Alfred, who was eight years old and in the third grade. His case typifies what can be done with the co-opera- tion of a school teacher, a school counselor, and the parents.

Eight-year-old Alfred found his problems almost unbearable. Here is the report of his school counselor:

"1/8/51. Referred by teacher because of continuing aggressive behavior and inability to get along with other children. Constantly reported by safety and service guards for infringement of school regulations in yard and hallways, and by classmates for hitting, punching, annoying them in dressing room, in line, etc. Teacher indicates he is sly; she seldom is able to 'catch him,' but the repeated and varied complaints from the other children are, to her, convincing evidence of his troublesome behavior. Concerning his attitude toward school work, she notes an extreme lack of perseverance. When anything becomes difficult, he quits, then looks around for someone to annoy. His school record indicates unsatisfactory ratings in behavior throughout (except 1B). Subject ratings reasonably satisfactory."

"1/15/51. Teacher had requested interview of mother to discuss the problem, and, after finishing her interview, brought her to my office asking if I would care to talk with her at that time. Although I had not yet seen Alfred, and would have preferred at least one interview with the child before seeing the mother, nevertheless, I took advantage of this opportunity.

"She was obviously a greatly disturbed person, spoke freely and in a friendly way immediately. Throughout the interview there was repeated expression of self-blame; a great deal of guilt was expressed. She is aware of all the trouble Alfred causes, of the fact that he is wild, often unmanageable. She wonders how the teacher stands him. She can't trust him out of her sight five minutes. He is impudent, defiant, completely ruined, and it's all her fault. He wouldn't be that way if she hadn't spoiled him, and now it's too late. She can't do anything about it because she's let him go like that too long. I knew how disturbed she must feel to realize that her little boy is having so much difficulty, both in school and at home, and to feel that she herself is responsible for it all.

" 'Yes, I knew all the time that I shouldn't do these things,' she told me, 'but I'm soft and I always give in to him, buy him everything he wants. First I say no, then when he's at school I go out and buy it to surprise him when he gets home, and then he doesn't even play with it—a few minutes maybe, then he throws it aside.'

"I knew how confused and disturbed she must feel, not knowing just what to do next—loving him so very much and being hurt so very much by things he does. I wondered if it seems perhaps as if he just does these things sometimes for that very purpose—to hurt her. She is sure he knows how much he can hurt her and it does seem as if he sets out deliberately to do just that. We agreed that it gives him perhaps a feeling of a great deal of power to know that he can have control of a situation, that he can hurt her deeply whenever he wants to. She indicated that it must be just that way because the relationship with his father is so completely different. There is no trouble at all when father is at home—everything serene. Father says no and means it. And that's all there is to it. There's no begging or pleading or crying.

" 'His father never buys or gives him a thing! Yet he's more fond of his father than he is of me,' she said. I knew how much that, too, must hurt, when the boy means so much to her. I wondered if sometimes things like that make her terribly angry with him. She agreed vehemently—there are times when she wonders how she can go on.

" 'I'm very nervous anyway, and lose my patience easily. I can stand him so long, then I really give it to him. I hit him and hit him, sometimes without even knowing why. Then he cries; then I cry and tell him I didn't mean it, and it's a mess. He knows what he can do to me.'

"I know how discouraged, even helpless at times, she must feel. I wondered if things have always been like this. They have, ever since he was a little baby. She used to carry him around every minute—scarcely ever laid him down. He cried a lot and she didn't want him to disturb others in the apartment. I wondered, too, if his crying gave her another opportunity to hold him and to love him. She agreed. She'd wanted a baby for so long. Since he's grown up she can't take her eyes off him or he gets into trouble. He is always fighting with children in the neighborhood. Mothers are constantly ringing her bell to tell her Alfred has hit other children. There have also been constant complaints since he started school from teachers about his poor behavior.

"She can't send him to movies on Saturdays until exact time for show to begin. If she lets him go earlier he gets into a fight and gets thrown out. I thought it seems terribly necessary to him to prove his importance as a person in his relationship at home, in school, in the neighborhood. I didn't suppose there are ever times when she finds it possible to commend him for something he has done well.

" 'No! Never! I'm afraid he'll turn around and do the opposite next time. My husband praises him sometimes, but not me.'

"I knew it would be awfully hard for her to let go her hold even a little bit, to place any responsibility on him for growing up, because it would be almost like giving up her baby. She agreed that she hates to see him grow up. He is the only baby she'll ever have. It must often be almost more than she can bear. She seemed somewhat relieved as she left and asked if I thought I might be able to help him. I explained that I'd be seeing him soon and that if he felt he wanted to work with me on his problem we would arrange to continue and that we all might then work together toward helping him. She felt sure that he would."

"1/19/51. Alfred is an extremely disturbed boy. Quiet, unresponsive, resentful at first of what probably seemed to him facing one more person against whom he must defend himself. When I recognized this fact with him and we clarified the counselor's function he began gradually and then completely to open up with a great deal of negative feeling. There's nothing but trouble at home. Mother always hollers at him, constantly finding fault.

" 'No matter what I do, she hollers,' he said. 'Even when I try to be good and do what I think she wants me to do, it ain't right. She hollers.' I thought that must be very discouraging. He agreed and went on. 'Then when father comes home mother tells him the bad things I did and then he beats me. She hits me during the day, then he comes home at night and hits me again.' I wondered if perhaps he resents what seems like paying twice for the same offense.

" 'Yeh, but I keep on doing it. Might as well. I get hollered at anyway. Mother won't ever let me have kids in to play in the house or in the yard, and I'm ashamed to play all the time in their yard and never have them in mine. Lots of times she makes me stay on the step. Then when kids see me they call me chicken and I don't like it.'

"I wondered if he gets so mad at mother sometimes that he sets about deliberately to do things he knows she doesn't like. 'Yes, I do. I do things I know she doesn't like because she does plenty I don't like!' And somehow you feel better satisfied even if punishment follows. He agreed.

"I wondered if he felt this difficulty at home had anything to do with the trouble he has had in school about which his teacher had spoken to me. Yes, he guesses so. Plenty of trouble in school too. I thought perhaps he doesn't like school too much. No, he doesn't—never did. So every morning when mother calls him to get up, he stays in bed and she gets madder and madder. Then when he gets to school he gets blamed for pushing in line, tripping kids in the room, when it's always another guy that does it.

" 'Safeties pick on me, other kids pick on me.' I knew he must be a pretty unhappy little boy to have just no place where he can go and feel completely comfortable. He agreed and began to cry.

"He told me then that his mother says he's to leave home when he's eighteen— 'So I guess I will.' I wondered if that was a rather frightening thought—to be grown up and have to leave home. 'Yes, but I guess I'll know what to do. I'll have a job.' Then he told immediately of not having been able to go see the New Year's parade (more than a month ago) because he couldn't go without his shoes. He clarified by saying he could put his shoes on, but he can't tie them himself, and his mother had refused to let him go if he didn't tie his shoes. We discussed feeling of wanting sometimes to be a baby again, to have mother do things for him, have none of the responsibilities that go with growing up.

"Yes, sometimes that is the way he feels. Seemed anxious to continue counseling help, and we arranged for conferences twice a week."

"1/22/51. Alfred arrived promptly. Looked much less tense, more at ease. Told me he'd been out sick this morning—feels better now though obviously still has a cold.

" 'My mother said to tell you I was fairly good lately.' I wondered how he felt about the situation. 'I feel better, things weren't near so bad at home. My mother didn't holler at me so much. She hollered, but not so much.' We agreed it was a good feeling that things between him and his mother seemed even a little better, that he feels even a little better.

"We talked of liking to be bad sometimes, of doing things we know other people don't like. Yes, he likes to do that sometimes. Remembers last summer he liked to do as many things, break as many rules as he could, to see how long it would be before he got thrown out of the playground. I thought perhaps he uses that technique on mother sometimes too—a sort of game to see how long he can remain in control. He chuckled as he agreed. (More smiles, fewer frowns in this interview.)

"Talked of going to the movies. He likes to go with his boy friends. Only has three—wishes he had more, but he doesn't think the other kids like him. Mother makes him go to the movies alone because when he's with boy friends he always gets into trouble. I knew how much he'd rather go with his friends, especially since there are just three of them who must surely be very important to him. How much fun it is to share the experience of a movie with someone you like and who likes you.

"Told enthusiastically of one of his friends' lighting a rag on a stick and waving it around. This seemed to be his favorite friend and he told of several deeds of daring which this boy has to his credit. I knew how very much he himself would like to do daring things, hard things that would make other boys, other people, feel that he is grown up and important. He agreed completely but doesn't know how to go about it.

"I wondered if it is some of this same feeling of wanting to be grown up, wanting the kids to think so, that gets him into trouble in school too. Yes, he thinks maybe it is. Often things are going along O.K. in the yard or in the line, then all of a sudden a kid punches him or bumps him.

" 'I can't let him get away with it, so I slug him, then the kid tells the safety or the teacher. I hit him and I get the blame.' I thought it must be pretty confusing and disturbing. If he doesn't hit back he must feel that the boy and his other classmates will not respect him, will think he's afraid. If he does, there are consequences in the form of punishment. I didn't wonder he found it hard.

"He mentioned twice during this interview that he likes to come and talk. Thinks it helps because things don't seem bad like they were. He feels better. I thought it must feel good to be a little less worried, a little more comfortable, and perhaps as we continue working together we will be able to help him straighten out further these things which are of such concern to him. His relations with his mother and father at home, and with classmates in school. We agreed that there will be times when things seem to get bad again —mother will become difficult, trouble in school, he himself will get that gone, hopeless feeling of 'what's the use?' We agreed to work on facing these possibilities too."

"1/25/51. Alfred: This time smiling and assured. Began even before he got seated to tell me things are better than they ever were. 'I never felt so good! Mother doesn't holler at me hardly at all. She lets kids come in my yard and even in my house to play.' He had a friend in all Sunday afternoon—they were reading comic books together. I could understand why he feels so good today. He and mother have continued on friendly, understanding basis, and have advanced to point where he has convinced mother that part of growing up is having friends and sharing experiences with them as well as with mother and father. Indicated that father, too, has seemed more friendly. 'He gave me a nickel, then next day gave me a dime!' I thought it seemed that he had gone far in working out his problem. I knew he must feel good about it.

"Talked of going to movies on Saturday. Mother won't let him go to Ritz Theatre. Doesn't like him to cross Spring Avenue. 'She said I should go to the Greene, but I sneaked over to the Ritz. When I got home I told her I went to the Ritz but she wouldn't believe me. She said, "No, you didn't. You went to the Greene."' I thought he feels better telling things to mother now—that they seem to understand each other better. He found himself wanting to tell her he'd gone to the Ritz. He agreed.

"Talked of mother's treating him like a baby. 'So many things she won't let me do. She thinks I'm too little.' I knew he felt he is big enough to cross Spring Avenue alone and it hurts to have her feel he is not.

" 'It's funny thing. When I was little she always kept calling me her *big boy*—now when I'm big she treats me like a baby!' I knew that must be very hard to take. We discussed this business of growing—how hard it is to convince mother, other people, sometimes ourselves, too, that we are growing up—no longer a baby. We agreed again that there are times, too, when he wishes he were a baby.

"We discussed his feeling about talking with mother, re: his growing up; having responsibilities, like crossing Spring Ave. at traffic lights; like deciding for himself, perhaps with her help, which movie he would prefer. He thinks he would like to try. We discussed again the possibility of setbacks in relationships with parents. He feels so good now he wants to think about that later. Right now things are better than he ever thought they could be. Things in school are much better too. No fights in the last week. I could understand his wanting to enjoy fully this new feeling of understanding and of being understood."

"1/26/51. Teacher reports decided improvement in Alfred. He seems to be taking greater interest in class work, is more attentive, attitude less belligerent, fewer reports from safeties in charge, and from classmates concerning behavior."

"1/29/51. Alfred: Not so jubilant as last time, but feels that things continue satisfactorily. Talked of yesterday (Sunday) disappointing because of weather. He kept hoping and hoping for it to snow. Instead, it just kept raining. Couldn't go out. Nothing to do. Read comic books all day. I agreed it was a great disappointment to have such nasty weather for a Sunday. Seemed almost like wasting a perfectly good Sunday to have to spend it indoors doing nothing in particular. He smiled and agreed.

"Relationships at home continue good. Says he hasn't had a beating for a long time. 'Father says, "I won't hit you if you don't aggravate your mother." I said, "It's a deal." ' "

"I thought that he must be working awfully hard to have this new feeling of understanding between him and mother continue and develop as it seems to be doing. I thought that there must be times when mother does make him mad, and the deal with his dad must then be pretty hard to live up to. He agreed that there are such times but so far he's been able to handle them. 'I don't get as mad at her as I used to and she don't get as mad at me as she used to.'

"I indicated that I'd been talking with his teacher and that she feels things are better in school too. I wondered how he feels about school. He feels better about school, too. He was working on a composition on Brotherhood right before he came for interview. Asked if I'd like to see it when he gets it finished. I surely would, and thought Brotherhood sounds like an interesting but difficult subject on which to write. I wondered if he likes what he has written. 'Yes, I think it's pretty good. I like to write but I never know when to put periods. So I count five words, then put a period. Every five words I put a period.'

"I agreed that punctuation is a nuisance when you have ideas you want to put down on paper.

"He finds relationships with other children in school improved. (Though he is still paying penalty of being deprived of recess for last fight indulged in two weeks ago. Penalty ends tomorrow.) System he had devised now is as follows: If he sees a fight he walks away instead of taking sides and joining in as he used to do. I thought that must often be hard to do. If kids come after him, he walks away. If they follow him, then he has to fight them or they'll think he's scared to fight. But then his mother gets mad. I knew that was a hard choice to make—defending his pride by not refusing to fight or facing mother's anger if he does fight. However, since the last fight (above mentioned) he has not been required to make a decision on this issue. We agreed there seems to be real progress in his ability to handle situations as they arise."

"2/2/51. Alfred: Progress continues. He seemed at ease, pleased. Told of having talked with mother about things working out. She agrees, too, that things are more comfortable between them. Tells me they've each worked on keeping their part of the 'deal.' She hasn't hit him or reported him to father. I knew he must still feel awfully good to think his plan is continuing to work. Talked of going to aunt's house on Saturday for birthday party—little cousin was three years old. Boy friend had stopped over to ask him to go to movies. Had to tell him he couldn't go because he was going away. I thought he must have been glad and sorry. Glad to know he had something special to do, and therefore wasn't available for a movie. Sorry he couldn't be with his friend, who was sufficiently anxious to have his company for the afternoon to come to his house and ask him to go with him. Feels good to know that someone you like wants to be with you. He smiled and nodded.

"He feels good about school now. Teacher told him this morning his work has improved. He's allowed to go to recess now. Happy about that. No fights in the yard, no complaints in the room. I wondered how all this feels. Does he perhaps miss some of the excitement that went with breaking rules, getting into trouble? 'Yes, a little. I did skip steps this morning on the way up in line. Safety told me to stop it. I told her it hurt my legs to walk on every step.' I thought perhaps he just had to do something like that once in a while to prove to himself (and others) he still can if he wants to. He smiled and agreed.

"Told of being asked by mother to go to store today at noon. First said, 'Do I have to go now?' Then decided he might as well go or maybe she'd tell his father. We agreed that he seems to have arrived at a place where he thinks things through before making a decision—decides on basis of which way he prefers it in terms of consequences.

"Told again about mother and him talking things over. Says mother tells him teacher is trying to help him. Miss J. is trying to help him; she (mother) is trying to help him. I thought it seemed as if he, too, was doing a great deal of the helping. The biggest job has been his and I wondered if he didn't feel as if he'd gone a long way in the direction of straightening out his problem. He agreed that he has been working hard on it and is pleased with results."

Thus a counselor, in a period of about a month or so, helped Alfred to overcome what to him appeared to be impossible problems. The home situation, with tension among the members of the family—mother, father, and boy—was unbearable from a child's point of view. Remember that Alfred was only eight years old. Yet if this eight-year-old were not helped at this point, the chances are that, according to all the information we have on the subject of delinquency, the boy would have deteriorated, going from bad to worse, from Peck's bad boy to a potential killer. Perhaps this seems to be a long sweep, but we have enough case histories of little Alfreds who were *not* helped.

One little boy said solemnly, in parting with his counselor at the end of a period of work together, "You know, I didn't think much of this counseling business at first, but there is something to it, isn't there?"

One, a twelve-year-old girl, said, "Maybe if my mother had had a chance to talk with somebody when she was young, she wouldn't be having a nervous breakdown now."

Throughout the nation children by the thousands are awaiting admission to institutions for the mentally disturbed; yet adequate residential psychiatric facilities for children are practically nonexistent. Further, many juvenile courts have such a backlog of cases that several months elapse between the time of arrest and the courts' hearing of the cases. Probation officers carry such heavy loads that supervision is often an empty gesture, and probationers frequently realize that they can violate the conditions of probation with impunity.

Children and youths who are caught in today's tensions and instabilities, in their own home problems, are frequently brought into better perspective through individual counseling. Isn't it better that we help a child at the age of six with a period of counseling that may last from six months to a year than to wait until that child is sixteen and is brought before a judge to await life sentence for murder?

The teamwork approach is the best one. The work done in the Philadelphia school system by a team of counselors has paid off in dividends of better, happier, superior children—superior in the sense that they are able to make a better adjustment and do better school work. In 1942 the Philadelphia school system had 24 full-time counselors. By 1954 it had a staff of 251, of whom 117 served in the elementary schools. It is in the elementary schools that the children can be helped as they show the first signs of emotional disturbance, maladjustment, or incipient delinquency. The primary role of the school is a preventive role.

A good example of how juvenile delinquency has been reduced through a co-operative community project, spearheaded by the public school system, may be found in Passaic, New Jersey. For while juvenile delinquency is generally on a sharp rise throughout the country, Passaic has actually shown major decreases in its juvenile crime rate. This has been accomplished through courageous planning and sound community teamwork.

In 1937 the Passaic Board of Education established a lay committee known as the Children's Bureau. Its work was so successful that it was formally incorporated into the school board four years later.

The program worked out by the bureau called for co-operation of the schools, and other agencies in the community, including the Police Department. The Police Department itself had an office and worked directly out of the Board of Education headquarters.

Through the work of the Passaic Children's Bureau over the past seventeen years, the police and school have together attacked the problems of all children under eighteen. As a result, Passaic, an industrial community of 65,000 population, has developed a program that is so successful that it is looked upon as a model agency for the detection of the predelinquent as well as the treatment of the delinquent.

The Passaic Children's Bureau serves as a clearinghouse for all juvenile delinquency problems that may arise in the city. It is well equipped to handle the problems of the juvenile delinquent or predelinquent, and is concerned with all Passaic children from birth to the age of eighteen. The director in charge of the program has on his staff three plainclothes policemen, one policewoman, a social worker, a psychologist, a reading specialist, three attendance officers, and three secretaries. When a child is in trouble, for whatever reason, the combined talents of the bureau personnel are utilized to seek the reason for the trouble and to find a remedy.

There are many facets of the operation of the bureau that make it an intrinsic part of community life. Its functions include:

A continuing census of Passaic children, beginning with the registration of their birth in the Bureau of Vital Statistics and following through until they reach the age of eighteen, is maintained.

All working papers are issued and reports of violations of the child labor laws are made to the state Department of Labor.

Throughout the school year, private, parochial, and public schools are daily served by the attendance department.

Working closely with the Board of Health, school nurses, camp directors and parents, the bureau functions as a clearing-house for summer camp programs in the community.

The bureau director, serving also as the chief guidance counselor, works closely with the guidance counselors that are in each school. (The in-service training program is a continuing process and involves the full staff of the bureau and the guidance counselors.)

As a child-study and treatment agency, the bureau handles all juvenile offenders and disturbed children, as well as all "normal" children in Passaic.

Applicants for opportunity classes and the class for trainable children are screened and selected by members of the bureau staff, in co-operation with the school personnel. Home instruction, bedside teaching and assignment to special classes for the visually handicapped, deaf and hard of hearing, cerebral palsied, and those with cardiac involvement and orthopedic disabilities are also handled by the bureau.

Working through the bureau, a teacher group recently studied the gifted child. Known as the Committee for the Study of the Exceptional Child it reported on the practices and techniques in use in the Passaic schools, making an important contribution in this often-overlooked area of teaching.

Parent problems also become the concern of the bureau. Every attempt is made to solve unfortunate home conditions through conference, agency referral, and visitations, before resorting to court referral. Recognizing parental needs for guidance and treatment, a parents' clinic has been established. Both parents must voluntarily wish to co-operate. Enthusiastically supported, its results have been gratifying.

Visits by Children's Bureau personnel to homes continue to increase each year, from 2,724 in 1953 to 3,021 in 1954. Through co-operation with community groups such as the parent-teacher association, various presentations are made to explain the work of the bureau.

Many advantages are gained in the closely articulated setup of police and school personnel. Every complaint against a minor in the community, for instance, comes to the bureau. When a member of the regular police department picks up any youth for any violation, the case is referred directly to the bureau. This also includes minors cited in complaints made to police by the individuals in the community. This permits the child to benefit from bureau study and treatment before a court appearance, or as a substitute for one.

When the bureau was first established in 1937 most of the referrals to it came through the Police Department. Today with increased activity in the early detection of the predelinquent, most referrals come from the schools. In its first year of operation 96 per cent of the cases came from the police and 4 per cent from the school. Today the figures are reversed.

The police assigned to the bureau act as case workers or investigators, with emphasis on child study and treatment rather than on the apprehension and conviction of the youthful offender. In this scientifically planned program, the police serve in an unusual role. They are liaison officers between school, home bureau, and recreational or character-building agencies in the community.

All serious school behavior problems, truants, and failures are referred to the bureau for study and treatment. Thus, all children in the community have the resources of the bureau open to them for whatsoever reason they may have need of them.

Every child who is referred to the bureau by a parent, school, police, social agency, or individual, is first studied in an attempt to discover the *whys* of his misbehavior.

First, the school medical examiner gives the child a complete physical examination. If remedial defects are noted, or any treatment is indicated, this is obtained either privately or at the community clinics.

Second, a psychological evaluation is made by the bureau psychologist in an effort to determine the child's aptitudes, abilities, interests, and achievements, especially as they relate to the problem of the child's behavior.

Third, the home and neighborhood are visited and analyzed by the police worker or the social worker. These environmental factors are studied and family relationships evaluated as they affect the individual child. Through school personnel, a study is made of the child's school experiences.

The child is tested for his reading accomplishments. Through the bureau's Reading Center, remedial and corrective reading techniques are available to children that need them. It is well established that lack of reading achievement contributes to increasing failure in other areas of learning and leads to emotional and social ills.

The teamwork concept in Passaic really goes into action once all the data concerning an individual are collected. A conference is held. Such conferences usually involve the director, social worker, police worker, psychologist, and attendance officer, as well as the child's teacher, principal, or guidance counselor. Out of the conference usually develops a rather clear picture as to why the child behaves as he does. The resultant plan of adjustment utilizes various community agencies.

The bureau maintains its contact with the child, his parents and his school as well as with the other agencies dealing with him until his behavior reveals a satisfactory adjustment to his school and the community.

An evaluation of the work of Passaic Children's Bureau, through follow-up of more than three thousand cases, suggests that this approach to delinquency control and prevention can operate with a high degree of effectiveness. The year the Passaic Children's Bureau was started, there were 448 juvenile offenses; in 1953, there were 315, a decrease of 29.6 per cent. Each year shows improvement over the preceding year.

A recent study of the individual case records reveals the satisfactory adjustment of a large majority of the juveniles referred to the bureau: 56.4 per cent have not "repeated" after first referral for delinquent behavior; 18.6 per cent have repeated once; 8.7 per cent have repeated twice; 16.3 per cent have continued in the delinquent pattern.

This recent study shows an improved situation over a similar study made ten years ago, when 24 per cent continued in the delinquent pattern, 47 per cent had repeated, 10 per cent were referred back twice and 19 per cent repeated once after initial referral.

Nationally, it has been reported that 58 per cent of our adult criminals were known earlier as juvenile offenders. Records of adult arrests in the city of Passaic for the year 1953 indicate that only 5.2 per cent of adult offenders had been known to the Passaic Children's Bureau as juvenile offenders. Since the bureau's establishment a decrease has been recorded each year.

Dr. George C. Boone, assistant superintendent of schools and director of the Passaic Children's Bureau, summed up the Passaic program this way, "We aren't doing a dramatic job. It is a day-to-day, steady job, but it has brought results. The parents know that we are their friends. The children trust us. Of course, we still have juvenile delinquents. We probably always will. But we also know that we have helped hundreds of boys and girls straighten themselves out early in life. We hope that they will be better citizens when they grow up and take their place as members of our community."

For instance there was Katherine, who came to the attention of the bureau for truancy, stealing, and keeping bad company. Her mother had taken her on some of her dates with other men. Her father was impatient with her, accused her of being saucy, and frequently slapped her.

By the time she was twelve, it became impossible for her to remain in her home, and she was placed in a training school. There, the discipline was strict; she wrote her mother that she was unhappy and wanted to leave. Her teacher reported that Katherine "is not a very good student—reading is retarded about one year—and she is getting help."

After an investigation of several foster homes, it was decided that for the time being, she would return to the school, away from the community. The worker observed that "Katherine clings to her mother and needs to learn independence." The worker also reported that the two cannot live happily together and that it would be better for Katherine to be in a good home away from her mother.

Thereupon placement was arranged in a home with a girl just a year older than Katherine, who is now fifteen. It took four years to help Katherine so that she could become somewhat adjusted. The girl remained in the foster home and continued to make "great strides." Katherine has now graduated from high school and passed her qualifying examinations for a business course at a vocational school.

Here we find that from the age of eleven when the attention of the bureau was first focused on the girl, until eighteen when she was graduated from high school, the bureau took the responsibility of trying to salvage Katherine. It was a struggle but the bureau persisted—and not only Katherine herself, but society as a whole gains by this follow-through approach. For seven years the Passaic officials kept watch over Katherine—indeed as they do over thousands of individual boys and girls. Too often school systems take but a passing interest in troubled children. The bureau of child guidance in one large city found that a seven-year-old boy had schizophrenic tendencies and notified the parents that help was needed. When the mother refused to co-operate and would not allow the child to be treated, the bureau, in effect, shrugged its shoulders and did nothing more about it. But, ten years later, the boy committed a sadistic murder. Society was outraged. The Passaic approach is sound because it is preventive—and persistent.

This approach has paid dividends in terms of reduced delinquency in the area. The bureau, working with the police and every other agency in the community, is able to guide each child along the road of constructive living.

This is a far cry from the old grab-him-by-the-scruff-of-the-neck-

and-drag-him-to-school technique. In the first place, fewer children now play hookey than in the past. Passaic old-timers recall with a grin the time when they had a woman truant officer who used to chase truants on a bicycle. She would go up and down the sidewalk trying to track down the boys and girls who were staying away from school. Now the philosophy has changed.

When one child, a boy of twelve, did not go to school for three days and the truant officer came to see him, he looked up with great relief and said, "Oh, I knew you would come. I've been waiting for you." And then he unraveled the story of his unhappy life.

Another boy in Passaic refused to attend school, and began to "shake down" some of his classmates for money. He had come from a broken home, but that did not, in his case, seem to explain his behavior pattern. The bureau referred him to the hospital for a thorough physical examination, and it was found that he had a brain tumor. The tumor was removed successfully, and the child subsequently made a very notable adjustment.

Another boy stole money at every opportunity and with it he bought candy. A physical examination disclosed that he was a diabetic. He was treated for the ailment and straightened out quickly.

Instead of clapping the truant into a reform school, he is now sent to a doctor and then to a psychiatrist. A skilled social case worker follows through on each case.

A teacher complained that one boy fell asleep in class every morning. No matter how he had been scolded, no matter what the admonitions and threats, the boy simply could not stay awake in class. A social worker went to the home of the boy and in short order discovered the reason for his fatigue. He lived in a small three-room apartment with three younger brothers and sisters. The parents were alcoholic and stayed up late every night. They entertained rowdy friends, and the noise was such that the boy never got enough sleep.

"Ninety per cent of our delinquency problems can be traced back to home problems," Dr. Boone told me. "But it is not always the parents alone who cause them. Now often we must go back to the grandparents to find the explanation of a situation. We found out in one case of a delinquent boy, for instance, that the father was an alcoholic, and would not support his family. We checked and we found that the father's parents were both drunkards and had beaten up the father mercilessly when he was a child."

Because of the program that Passaic is successfully carrying out, in the last five years, through 1954, it has been necessary to send only one girl away to a state training school. A very few boys are sent away. For the most part the help that they secure right within their own community is sufficient to develop their mental, moral and spiritual standards to the point where they can adjust as normal members of society.

The schools must, regardless of initial cost, take the lead in helping the bewildered, emotionally disturbed, potential delinquent to develop into a normal, wholesome member of society. It certainly can be done. It has been done, not only in Philadelphia and Passaic but also in a number of other communities.

Mark C. Roser, of the public schools in Gary, Indiana, has been working for some time with a special clinic to help disturbed children. He seeks to prescribe the necessary course of action to put these children on the right track.

In Gary an experimental school has been set up, based on the following standards:

Classes do not exceed fifteen pupils for each teacher, in order to provide pupils with close and intimate relationships with their teachers.

Emphasis is placed on giving the pupils a feeling of some achievement each day.

Classes are held for half a day in order to give the children more freedom.

The centers at which the experimental school is held are conducted in as permissive an atmosphere as possible. For example, it is explained to the children that their attendance is not compulsory.

Children are given training in reading and writing, with

equal emphasis on free play, drawing, and related activities.

Case work counseling is provided for the parents, and efforts are made to modify existing negative attitudes in the home.

After two years of operation, truancy completely disappeared in this experimental school. The pupils' attendance bettered the city-wide average. Twenty-five per cent of the children gained over ten points in their intelligence quotient tests. The majority of the parents commented on the improved behavior of the children.

The cost of such a program per student did not exceed the cost of the average public school pupil in this country. The sense of freedom and the grouping of the pupils on levels of similar attainment tended to reduce feelings of hostility and rejection on the part of the children.

Sometimes individual schools set up their own guidance programs to help eliminate, reduce, or alleviate the problem of delinquency or potential delinquency. For example, in one of the junior high schools in New York City, the teachers agreed that they would pay special attention to the children who appeared to be in need of emotional reassurance or guidance. The program has had good results thus far.

In another New York City school program, poorly adjusted children are selected by the teacher in the kindergarten, and the first and second grades. Each child is studied by a clinic team. The parent is interviewed by the social worker. In groups of four or five, the children spend two hours a week in a playroom with the group teacher. The planning for the child then becomes a group responsibility that involves the group teacher, the class teacher, the principal, and the clinic team.

In a Brooklyn school, a guidance-class program was initiated. The school had sixteen hundred children in classes ranging from the kindergarten to the sixth grade. Although there was a wide intellectual range in the children, the economic status of their families was largely lower middle class.

The plans envisaged one special class for each of the six grades. Thus about one hundred of the most poorly adjusted children were to receive special guidance each year. Withdrawal of the children from their regular classes was done in such a way that their classmates would not be led to believe that the selected children were being segregated.

The children chosen included those who were withdrawn, submissive, of low vitality, hyperactive, or aggressive; those with phobias or with marked speech defects; those with notable physical disabilities, such as asthma and epilepsy; and those who were retarded academically. It was found that most of the students in these categories had more than one symptom. For example, most of them had a reading disability, as well as marked personality difficulties. All of the children were of average or superior intelligence.

The teachers for the special classes employ record cards, health histories, and standardized tests as well as conferences with parents, and—in some cases—the psychologist's classroom observations.

The curriculum for the child is determined by his needs and the special abilities of his teacher. Academic work is not overlooked although much of the school day is devoted to music, painting, ceramics, carpentry, block-building, housekeeping, and similar activities. At all times small classes are stressed. There is a maximum of twenty to a class, with fifteen as the eventual goal. The children have received the largest classrooms in the building. There are sizable corners for housekeeping and carpentry, space for rhythms and dancing.

According to the report on this project, gains for some of the children in these classes have been so marked that they have returned to regular classes after one year. Many need a longer stay. There are others who will need the guidance offered by the special classes beyond the sixth grade.

One problem with devising special programs in the schools has been the fact that the parents of disturbed children, themselves usually seriously troubled, are on the defensive. They have little insight into their children's problems. Frequently parents resist a special school grouping for their children; they consider it a reflection upon them as parents, and a threat to their children. However, the officials have discovered, to their surprise, that the parents' early violent resistance gradually recedes and is changed increasingly into greater co-operation. One school principal reports, "Many parents of these children have become more active in the parents' association. They initiate many stimulating questions at meetings. It has been interesting to see the shift in the direction of their questions from those dealing previously with school situations to those involving the home."

Although the findings are still nebulous, they are very suggestive. The greatest improvement in the various personality traits has apparently been shown in self-confidence. Of sixty children studied in the Brooklyn school program, twenty-four changed from "lack of confidence" or "needs frequent encouragement" to "usually works with confidence." Although the children were of average intelligence, with very few exceptions, they were retarded one or more years when they entered the guidance classes. This indicates that emotional disturbance affects the intellectual work of youngsters. The second greatest improvement was in aggressiveness. Twenty-one children changed from "does not assert himself" or "overaggressive, fights frequently" to "moderately aggressive." Other traits such as responsibility, leadership, social adjustment, and work habits all received improved ratings.

These brief excerpts from the records are illustrations:

"Marion has a history of shyness and poor academic work. One day, she surprised her mother and the Sunday School teacher by volunteering to sing "Fling Out the Banner" as a solo in the church auditorium. At the end of the school year, Marion returned to the regular classes."

"Harry was unusually aggressive and destructive from the beginning of his school career. After a year and a half in the guidance classes he has become more socially adjusted and able to participate in group activities. There is less evidence of chronic hyperactivity. He is particularly proud of his ability to handle a primer."

In an interview with the psychologist, another child explained:

"First I'm scared of school and then I got used to it. When I was in the second grade I was scared of reading. Then in the third grade

I wasn't scared. I didn't feel like reading when I was scared. When I got used to reading, I said, 'Why can't I have more reading?' and the teacher said, 'No, it would be too much.' So, I went to the desk and read by myself. I used to be scared to read to children. I'm still bashful to get up and tell the children what I did yesterday and other days. I'm not scared to play now. I talk to other kids. I read out loud. Many times I know the right answer, but sometimes I'm scared to say it. It's true I'm scared I'm wrong and I don't want to say the answer and get into trouble. I'm not so sure I'm right. I am scared again and then I get happy again. When I was in the third grade I became happy all the time. I had another book and I felt scared. Then I got happy and I wasn't scared of the book. Then I went to the other teacher and I'm still happy."

We know now that many of these children would not have continued school, would not have found reading to be a pleasure instead of a frightful nightmare if it had not been for the help and guidance they received.

The schools can do a better job when there is co-operation with other community agencies as there is in Passaic. The United States Department of Health, Education and Welfare, in its report "Helping Children in Trouble," describes another excellent experiment conducted in St. Paul, Minnesota.

The St. Paul project was limited to a particular area of the city so that the staff could become personally acquainted with the community and the people serving it. The plan was to work with all groups in this area, but difficulties in obtaining personnel and differences in the organization of the various groups serving children caused the service to develop faster in some fields than in others. Because there was special interest in the treatment of delinqency through administrative rather than authoritarian measures, a staff member was assigned to work closely with the police. A social worker appointed in the schools to work closely with the project staff also established an effective channel between the schools and the project. The project staff, which included case workers, a psychologist, and a psychiatrist, were able to handle a great deal of the treatment themselves, but called on other agencies in the community for specialized services.

With a limited staff, it was impossible to assign a special worker to each group in the community and, as a result, the contacts with health officers, recreation workers, clergymen, and others in a position to identify children with problems, did not develop as quickly as the contacts with the schools and the law-enforcing agencies. All these professions co-operated in the treatment of children who had been brought to the attention of the project staff, but most of the children brought to the project were brought by the schools or the law-enforcing agencies. As the work coming from these two sources made greater and greater demands on the staff, less and less time was available for developing contacts with other sources.

The services available in the area also played a part in determining the project's development. Where there was little understanding of children's needs, time had to be taken to develop understanding; where vital services were lacking or inadequate, help had to be given in developing them. When strong resistance to the project was offered, the flexibility of the program and the resourcefulness of the workers usually overcame it.

In order to get better identification of children needing service, members of the project staff met with local groups and discussed children's problems, pointing out what kinds of behavior should be considered questionable at different ages. At first the cases brought to the attention of the project were behavior problems of long standing for which little could be done, or less serious problems that were more annoying than harmful. There was a tendency to consider only behavior that disturbed others as needing treatment, and a lack of recognition of the types of behavior injurious to the child himself. However, the project staff worked on these cases, keeping all who had an interest in them informed of the developments. This accomplished what no amount of talks or lectures could do. The experience of taking part in the study and treatment of one child's behavior difficulties proved a telling argument for the need of identifying and treating all children with problems. In this way, the irreparable damage done to the child and the community by failure to recognize the early symptoms of difficulty was seen, and the need for an early identification of problems assumed its rightful importance. In most instances sensitivity to children's problems increased in direct proportion to the amount of instruction and interpretation given by the staff.

A study of the records shows that in most cases a personality problem in the child or in his family played an important role in causing his difficulty. Health, intelligence, education, and economic conditions were less frequent causes. But only in 10 per cent of the cases was the psychiatrist used in direct treatment. In 90 per cent of the cases other staff workers carried the major responsibility for treatment. Of the cases on which there was enough information to base a judgment, 18 per cent showed major improvement after treatment.

The project found that minor and incipient problem behavior in children can be identified by the community and that, if adequate community services are effectively used, much of this problem behavior can be corrected or, if not receptive to correction, prevented from developing into more serious forms. But in order to do this, the child must be seen as a whole and his problems treated as a unit, regardless of their number or the areas of his life in which they appear. Not only the social agencies primarily concerned with the neglected, dependent, and delinquent child, or the child in need of special care, but also agencies established to serve all children, such as the group work agencies, the recreational agencies, the health agencies and the schools, must work together to accomplish this end. The principle that the child must be treated as a whole, and its corollary, the inclusion of all services affecting children in any way, is of primary importance in a program designed to prevent the development of problem behavior in children and to identify and treat such behavior if it does appear.

It has been accepted as doctrine that the early detection and treatment of emotional disturbances in a child should not be left to chance. Any community, by working with its schools, can help to develop a co-ordinated program for such early detection and treatment if it has patience and adequate instruction. Thus the community can make important contributions to the reduction of juvenile delinquency.

One of the most fruitful projects, and one from which other communities can learn, is in operation in one of New York's five boroughs, the Bronx. With the aid of the New York City Youth Board, an organization that co-ordinates and finances antidelinquency programs in the city, a co-operative venture with the Board of Education was set up in one section of Bronx County in 1945. The project, known as the Three Schools Project, is a planned effort to evaluate the effects of intensive social and psychiatric treatment services in the school setting. The board selected an elementary, a junior high school and a senior high school on the basis of the apparent high incidence of emotionally disturbed children and high delinquency rates among the school population and the surrounding community. The pupils represent a cross-section of the many national and racial groups living in the area.

A clinic unit was established in each of the three schools, consisting of a supervisor, two part-time psychiatrists, two clinical psychologists, three psychiatric social workers, and three stenographers. In addition a vocational guidance counselor was included in the junior high school unit, and a vocational guidance counselor and a job placement counselor were included in the high school unit.

With the units located right in the school buildings, the staff has been able to reach larger numbers of children at an earlier age than might otherwise be possible. In addition, clinical workers and teachers have brought about a closer relationship, permitting better interpretation of the clinics' services on a day-to-day basis. Sometimes the teacher is resentful and suspicious. But the experience of the Three Schools Project proves that the technician and the teacher can work on the basis of mutual understanding and respect.

In each of the three schools the initial screening is done by the social workers. These workers assume major treatment responsibility for some cases. They interview the youngsters, evaluate their potentialities, assist in determining which professional service might offer the child the most help. Those children who are seriously disturbed are referred back to the psychiatrist for treatment.

It was found that the children seen at the clinic show a great range of problems, varying from relatively simple maladjustment to full-grown psychosis. Problems include hostility to other children and to teachers, truancy, stealing, lethargic or apathetic behavior, severe depressions or anxieties, as well as the need for vocational guidance or job placements.

The New York City Youth Board reports that a multilateral service is offered by the Three Schools Project. Work with parents is an accepted responsibility of the clinical unit. The level of the relationship with a parent varies from occasional contact to a sustained treatment, depending upon the need and the parent's readiness to work with the clinic.

"The whole field of social-clinic relationships of the type developed in the Three Schools Project is relatively uncharted," the Youth Board reports.

"More experience and close study of that experience is called for. Careful research and continuing self-appraisal and examination may help throw light on such significant matters as the amount and type of clinic services needed for a given school population; methods of developing more effective teamwork between the educator and the clinicians; the implications for curriculum planning; new approaches for handling groups of children with problems within the school's setting."

How has the project worked out in practice? The teachers are divided as to the effectiveness of the program, but on the whole they are thoroughly convinced that it is of great value.

Here are some of the comments they made to me about it:

"Children who needed individual help have been greatly benefited."

"The Youth Board has had a stabilizing influence on the school."

"The school and home were brought together."

"Youth Board workers are friendly, warm and pleasant."

"It has given the teacher a feeling of support."

"In the cases of several boys, the Youth Board supplied information to me which stopped me from butting my head against a stone wall."

"Many of our boys are neglected at home. When the Youth Board has taken an interest in them, it has helped the boy to realize his own worth. The Youth Board has been able to make inquiries which the teacher by herself is unable to make."

On the other hand, some teachers feel that the program still must be refined considerably before it functions properly. Some of their comments were:

"Not enough time is allotted for conferences."

"The duties of the teachers were increased."

"No recommendations are made to me directly; generalizations are directed to the faculty as a whole."

In general, however, the faculties agree that the clinic in the school setting has been one of the most effective remedies for the detection and treatment of juvenile delinquency yet devised. A survey of one of the graduating classes of the high school showed that 41 per cent of the graduates had received some type of service from the clinic unit.

That the program has been successful is borne out by the many case studies that have been made by the Three Schools Project. How many of these young boys or girls might have become delinquent if they had not received this early help is difficult to say. Again, how many of these boys may later become delinquent, despite the help that they receive, is also difficult to guess. But it is not difficult to see that the early help that the program is giving these children has become a valuable part of the program of these particular schools. It is to be hoped that a vast majority of these children can retain and build on the gains in adjustment that they have made.

Let's look at the Three Schools Project from the point of view of a few of these children.

"Paul M. is a maladjusted six-year-old. He is the oldest child of a conglomerate family grouping of four adults and five children who live in a grimy, dirty, disorderly five-room apartment furnished with a minimum of dilapidated furniture.

"The central figure in this family grouping is Paul's maternal grandmother, 69. The other members of the household include

Paul's mother, aged 35, Paul's sister, 3, a brother, 2, born out of wedlock, Paul's maternal aunt and her two preschool children. The grandfather, suffering from an arteriosclerotic heart condition and a hernia, is the ninth member of the group.

"Both Paul's mother and his aunt are separated from their husbands. Paul was conceived while his father was in the army; his parents separated shortly after the father's discharge, so that John has never had any continuing relationship with his father, who is now hospitalized for tuberculosis. The family is supported by the Department of Welfare, which supplements Mrs. M.'s occasional earnings as an office worker. One year ago Mrs. M. gave her newly delivered out-of-wedlock child to a friend for formal adoption. She has epileptoid "attacks" which have been established as psychogenic.

"The grandmother is the controlling link in the total setup, but there is a minimum of cohesiveness in the family: They rarely eat together; the usual procedure is eating in shifts, with the grandfather always eating alone. He is unable to tolerate the constant noise and squabbling of the children and other adults and has removed himself—except physically—from the family; he is a bystander rather than a participant in family activities. An attempt at one point to see the grandfather was unsuccessful; the grandmother refused to agree to any such arrangement, insisting that her husband was in and out of the house and had almost nothing to do with Paul.

"The grandmother has major responsibility for the care of Paul and the other children, though his mother usually puts Paul to bed and cares for him on weekends. All the children seem well fed and are well dressed. When visited on a number of occasions, the apartment was always noisy with the children crying or quarreling among themselves. The grandmother varies between ignoring the children's antics or handling them by yelling and slapping. Among all the children she expresses a preference for Paul, whom she describes as 'so quiet . . . except when he gets too rough with the other children.' She did not see Paul as any particular problem, but a number of observers have been struck by Paul's extreme tenseness and withdrawal.

"Paul was referred to the clinical unit by the school. It was noted that he was a persistent thumb-sucker and made an inordinate number of trips to the toilet. He was shy, nonassertive, lethargic, although he did show some responses to extra attention from the teacher and seemed stimulated by being grouped with the brighter children; he seems to be of at least average intelligence and may well be brighter than that.

"Paul's mother was seen by the unit about a Play School application for Paul. She expressed interest in continuing with the unit but failed three successive scheduled appointments. The Play School reports described Paul as 'a fussy, slow eater . . . very quiet, halting and hesitant, who could relate only to extremely withdrawn children.'

"Paul's mother came to the unit once more for discussion of Paul's 'shyness.' She repeated her interest in help for him about this and an appointment was made for a home visit. Mrs. M. then wrote in saying the home visit was not necessary and she would come to the office; she did not do so. A home visit found no one in.

"In response to another approach Mrs. M. said it was 'not necessary' for the clinic to see the child. When interviewed personally in the street she refused permission for Paul to be seen by one of the clinic psychiatrists and insisted she would not discuss the matter further. An earlier effort to administer psychological tests to the boy was met by his flat refusal to accompany the worker, despite the assurance of classmates who had been tested that it was 'fun.'

"In the interim Paul's sister was admitted to school and has shown many similar behavior traits.

"More recently, the unit's efforts have been limited to interpretative contact with Paul's teacher. She reports some slow response to considerable personal attention. The unit can now do little beyond maintaining teacher contact; it continues watchful waiting in the anticipation of a development which may make Mrs. M. more accepting of service."

Unless some way of reaching Mrs. M. is found—and this neither the school nor the school clinic has been able to do—then all the work that the clinic itself might do with Paul will go undone.

Here, surely, is a case that proves that if we are to develop normal children, we must find some way to deal with abnormal parents.

Then there is the story of Helen. Helen, sixteen, is the second youngest in a family of three girls. Helen's relationship with her siblings appears competitive. Her father is a lawyer, her mother is a housewife.

"Initially Helen came in to the unit and spoke of feeling 'closed in' as if 'somebody was on top of me when I get in an argument' and she 'tells them off.' The intake worker described her as 'not too bright, aggressive, ready to fight, projects all her difficulties, not interested in understanding herself but only in getting what she feels is her due.' She rejected counseling and apparently was not ready for help. About nine months later Helen was referred to the clinic by the school doctor because her complaints were nonorganic in origin.

"Helen indicated she felt confused about herself and her abilities. She was interested in determining vocational goals but doubted her ability to do anything. She described her feelings of 'going around in circles.' She appeared less aggressive and apparently more ready for counseling than she had been nine months earlier.

"Helen's typing teacher, upon noting that Helen had made contact with the unit, volunteered some of her observations about the girl. The teacher reported that Helen was experiencing difficulty socially as well as in her classwork. 'She wants to attract attention from boys, but does not know how to handle it.' In the classroom 'she talks a lot—she has a tendency to rush ahead, without waiting for instructions, makes mistakes constantly and then feels she is stupid.' The teacher also commented on the unusual type of brassiere Helen wore and her tendency to wear only sheer nylon blouses.

"Helen is in a general course, although taking commercial subjects approved by her school counselor, and her work has been barely passing. Her cumulative school record revealed consistent evidence of ability within low average range. In the psychological testing situation, although she related easily, she was anxious, continually sought reassurance and verbalized comments reflecting concept of herself as an inferior, intellectually inadequate individual. She made derogatory remarks about herself such as, 'I can't work with my hands—I can't even work with my brains.'

"Psychological examination ruled out the possibility of prepsychotic functioning.

"Test findings revealed maximum potentials were within high average, but marked variation in her performance suggested severe emotional disturbance. Personality findings gave a diagnostic impression of a neurotic personality, showing anxiety, strong feelings of inadequacy, with depressive and anxiety features. A tendency toward hysterical manifestations was dominant in her pattern. While emphasis was placed upon excessive control and rigidity, there was a tendency toward acting out in interpersonal situations.

"Her primary ideas of difficulty appeared as trouble with authority, with the concept of self (inadequate and worthless), and with interpersonal relationships with the opposite sex. Although she was rejecting of self, emphasized externals, and regarded relationships with others as competitive and hostile (particularly with men), she evidenced a tendency to test out between what was real and what was fantasy. She sought to overcome feelings of rejection and self-contempt by pointing out that she loves herself because she knows nobody else will.

"Therapeutic contacts began in 1952 and have continued to date [1954]. During this period, there were periodic conferences with the psychiatrist, employment counselor, school doctor, school counselor and several teachers.

"This dated the beginning of real therapeutic contact. There were reported episodes of stealing, indiscriminate petting, associations with peers that were apt to foster this acting-out behavior, and fears about pregnancy.

"Helen appeared heavily weighted down by her own self-contempt, referred to herself as the 'black sheep of my family.' Although unable to move toward boys on any but a sexual basis, she reacted with self-contempt and also contempt for them.

"During the first four months of contact she continually spoke of herself, her experiences, her vocational plans in a manner which vacillated from a concept of self as repulsive, lowly, to that of fantasy about self as angelic and noble. This would appear alternately as talk about taking a job as 'barmaid' contrasting with talk about 'working with the poor,' as a nurse. She enjoyed relating experiences which might shock others, and repeatedly told of aggressive, noisy behavior at dances, or at Times Square, where she and her friends were regarded as 'real crazy.'

"Her initial reports of stealing were accompanied with no real evidence of underlying sense of values. She was predominantly guided by concern of being apprehended (no formal charges were ever made) rather than by a concept of right and wrong. She seemed cold and detached about kissing and petting.

"She did everything to attract attention to her large high bust, and then reacted with aggressive insults and rebuttals to the boys in school who made the comments. She was insulting to authoritive figures such as policemen, but not to teachers or her parents. She enjoyed viewing herself as a very complicated, unpredictable individual, and expressed the hope (before each weekend) that 'nothing would happen,' thus placing the blame on an uncontrollable environment rather than on impulses from within.

"She met many boys: none of these relationships lasted beyond a few dates. She enjoyed exciting males sexually and then laughed at them, expressing her hostility with little awareness of her behavior.

"After six months contact, Helen began to express interest in employment and demonstrated sufficient inner strength to look for a job on her own, successfully. Recommendations for educational courses in keeping with her interests were accomplished. Gradually she appeared to be developing a growing recognition of her role in relating to others, particularly boys. She showed evidence of becoming somewhat more critical of self in a constructive way. The changes were subtle, and her overt behavior did not seem to undergo much change.

"After nine months of contact, Helen showed evidence of more growth, particularly in concept of self and of others. She met a boy, John, who was different from former boy friends. Here was someone who accepted her for herself, rather than only for what she described as 'my body.' She was able to appreciate that this was the first time she had been aware of the fact that there were people like John. Repercussions of this growth were also evidenced in her relationships with her family; at long last they, too, accepted her friend.

"By the end of June, 1953, Helen had dropped her 'old crowd,' had begun making new friends, and had developed a growing, wholesome relationship with John. And she was impressed with her own awareness of a changed self.

"This was also reflected in her feelings about sex. As she exclaimed, 'I don't feel dirty—I don't see it as dirty or horrible . . . I never felt like this before.'

"One other manifestation of stealing appeared, in keeping with her need to prove to other girls that she was not a 'jerk' (inadequate or inferior). This provided further opportunity for Helen to examine herself in terms of her new insight, and for the first time enabled her to formulate a concept of right and wrong.

"Gradually symptoms of acting-out have appeared to subside, in proportion to the noticeable growth in her manner of relating to others. Prognosis for continued growth is favorable."

What would have happened if Helen had not received the help she got at a crucial stage in her adolescence? The training schools —and the streets—are full of other Helens who were unfortunate enough not to have access to the help and guidance provided by the Three Schools Project or a similar service.

Many types of services may be developed by the school. It is quite unlikely that all schools should develop the same programs for assisting delinquent youth. The nature of the programs should depend to a large extent upon the cultural characteristics of the community itself. In many rural areas special school personnel simply are not available. In other areas of scattered population there is a limited need for such personnel, most of whom should be utilized on a county-wide basis. On the other hand, large urban school systems now frequently do provide visiting teachers, who teach children in their homes if they are sick or have to stay away from school for other reasons, and psychological, or even psychiatric, services, together with special programs for severely maladjusted children.

At all times teamwork must be considered the key to an effective program for finding and treating seriously maladjusted children.

A case in point is the setup in Des Moines, Iowa. The Department of Pupil Adjustment there includes the services of visiting teachers and psychologists. Children who have problems of maladjustment are usually referred by principals or counselors to visiting teachers who may employ the diagnostic advisory service of the psychologists. However, psychologists are also regularly assigned to the various schools, where their services may be given directly to teachers and counselors.

The following, selected from the October, 1953, issue of the *Research Bulletin* of the National Education Association, show what is being done in some other typical communities:

In Birmingham, Alabama, within the past ten years the number of visiting teachers has been increased from three to eleven to cope with increased enrollment. Special class placements are made and, if necessary, the pupils are referred to a mental hygiene clinic. In serious behavior cases the Attendance Department uses the services of the juvenile court, the Department of Public Welfare, and the Children's Aid Society.

In Cleveland, public schools have a counseling service of 32 people in the Bureau of Attendance; 123 junior and senior high school principals, assistant principals, and counselors; 5 special classes of visiting teachers; 2 adult education teachers; 31 elementary school supervisors; 7 psychologists; and one psychiatric case worker. For serious cases of problem behavior, the Bureau of Attendance has a counselor for boys, a counselor for girls, and one social worker, two part-time physicians, and one nurse. In addition, the bureau may use the facilities of the psychological clinic, the Health Services Division, and the service of the Board of Education psychiatric consultant.

In Hartford, Connecticut, the Attendance Department, Guidance Department, Psychological Department, and thirteen school social workers are grouped in the Bureau of Guidance and Pupil Adjustment. The bureau also has the services of a psychiatrist for one day of the week. Having all these special services in a single bureau promotes co-ordination of efforts when working with problem cases.

In Long Beach, California, the schools provide several services that are intended to promote better adjustment of pupils. Each school has counselors. Some special classes are provided. An adjustment class of twelve children in one elementary school is designed to help those who are quite severely disturbed. The psychological service consists of three psychologists, three psychiatric social workers, and one psychological tester, all of whom work with the children on both the diagnostic and therapeutic levels. Special services are offered by the mental hygiene clinic, Family Service Association, Catholic Welfare Bureau, Long Beach Jewish Community Council, County Probation Department, and the Long Beach Juvenile Bureau.

In Richmond, Virginia, the public schools regard juvenile delinquency as a problem for the community as a whole. Parent education is attempted through PTA programs covering such subjects as children's emotional problems and child rearing practices. Seven special classes are available for the mentally retarded. A special school for about seventy-five boys is designed to care for those unable to adjust to the regular program. Services and procedures available to the regular classroom teacher in problem behavior cases include curriculum adjustment, individual tests, the advice of a clinical psychologist, and the help of visiting teachers and of the attendance workers.

In San Diego, California, the Guidance Department attempts to co-ordinate its efforts in helping school children with those of other community agencies. The department works closely with the county probation office, city police department, community chest agencies, and church groups. The Guidance Department is composed of twenty-four visiting teachers, nine psychologists, a psychiatric clinic, a vocational guidance section, and a speech therapy section. Seventy-five classes are maintained for moderately mentally retarded pupils.

Thirty-six adjustment classes are maintained for children who have emotional problems which impede their school progress.

This summary of what some of the communities are doing to explore—and also to prevent—the problem of juvenile delinquency suggests strongly the vital role played by the school, together with the home and community in the lives of our youth. Several schools have demonstrated that substantial progress can be made in reducing truancy. However, the various types of misbehavior and maladjustment still found among our children suggest that not enough is being done as yet.

The National Education Association concludes, "Schools need more specialized personnel than they now have to care for the problems that have been encountered. It is recognized that budget and legal provisions will play a part in sharing individualized services. To provide a better co-ordinated approach to pupil problems, reports from schools indicate a tendency to place all pupil personnel services in a single division. Also, school authorities will want to encourage public support of other community agencies that make specialized facilities available to school children."

What is needed is a new approach in our schools to the handling of the emotional life of the child. We can safely leave the religious life of a child to the home and the church. However, there is no place except the school to which we can entrust the emotional and mental development of the child if his home does not answer his needs—or, indeed, if it poisons him.

New horizons, new techniques to deal with our thirty million children in school are necessary. In the words of Abraham Lincoln, "The dogmas of the quiet past are inadequate to the stormy present. We must disenthrall ourselves."

We have seen that many of the larger school districts have set up special schools or classes to meet the problems of the maladjusted youth who may develop into delinquents. In some instances, it may be necessary to have special diagnostic and guidance personnel in order to develop a worth-while program. In other instances the services may be made available by the school's pupil guidance unit. In schools in which these services are offered, the educational program is usually considered to be part of a comprehensive treatment plan in which the psychiatrist, psychologist, and social worker play important roles.

Special schools or classes for delinquents and maladjusted youth offer these opportunities:

Opportunity to deal informally with the individual pupils, according to their specific needs and interests.

Teachers who are selected on the basis of their interest in maladjusted youth and their ability to deal effectively with children's emotional problems.

Relaxed environment in which the opportunities for personal and social adjustment are considered to be of major importance.

A concentration of supplementary services, including a psychiatric, psychological, and/or social work program.

The removal of pupils with special problems from regular classrooms in which their behavior has been distracting to other pupils and in which their teachers have neither the time nor the facilities to help them.

In summary, it is my suggestion that the following steps be taken in an effort to reduce juvenile delinquency through our schools:

1. Double the amount of money that we now spend for our schools. We spend approximately 2 per cent or seven billion dollars ($7,000,-000,000) of our national income for public elementary and secondary schools. Let us spend about 4 per cent, or fourteen billion dollars ($14,000,000,000) of our national income, an amount that is far less than the costs of crime. It costs from $1,200 to $3,000 annually to keep a child in a public training school. The average cost of educating a child in a public school is approximately only $250 a year.

2. Improve the teachers' training standards. It is not enough to give teachers an outmoded, nineteenth-century training program.

3. Give the teachers smaller classes. This will result in a better rapport between parent, teacher, and pupil. It will also facilitate earlier recognition by teachers of a pupil's unusual problems.

4. Provision must be made to meet individual differences of pupils. Assistance for pupils with special problems must be pro-

vided. Moreover, the curriculum should be made adaptable so that all types of children may fully profit from it in accordance with their own potentialities.

5. Provide adequate psychological services.

A survey, sponsored by the Association of Psychologists in the New York public schools, to determine the extent of psychological aid available in the public schools of the United States brought out some shocking figures. The association studied 144 school systems in 35 states. It found a total of only 351 psychologists employed, with 38 per cent of the cities lacking psychological services for children altogether.

The association considered a ratio of one psychologist to 3,000 school children to be desirable. In New York City the ratio was found to be 1 to 17,000, while in Chicago, it was 1 to 5,576. Some of the smaller cities had better service, and in some communities where psychologists were not employed in the school system, state health department clinics for mental hygiene provided limited service.

Personnel standards in the employment of school psychologists were generally very low. Of the cities reporting, only three required a doctorate, while fifty-eight employed psychologists with only master's degrees, and twelve required merely a bachelor's degree.

Salaries were in general excessively low for a highly trained professional. They ranged from an initial $1,900 to $4,800 up to a maximum of $2,550 to $6,250.

6. Meetings between parents, teachers, counselors, and pupils, for the consideration of individual problems, should be arranged by schools whenever possible.

It behooves all of us to help to develop within the schools an attitude that will consider the so-called deviates, the maladjusted, the emotionally disturbed children as our particular charges. The schools can and must call for extended social services from the community and for better understanding from all its citizens.

When this is accomplished, we will find that the school is truly the first line of defense in our fight against juvenile delinquency. A sound school system, adequately staffed, competently adminis- tered, is essential in the campaign the nation is now undertaking to stamp out juvenile delinquency. When the citizens of this nation recognize the role that the schools must take in helping our youth become good citizens and good voters, then the necessary funds will be forthcoming. The importance of a sound school system can not be overestimated.

10. The Community

"At that time Mrs. A. responded to the worker's warmth . . ."

When a sergeant of the air force is walking through a city park in the heart of New York City and is set upon by four teen-agers and stabbed twenty-three times, a problem is presented not only for the police, the courts, the schools, and the parents, but for the whole community.

When a fourteen-year-old boy is sentenced to a state training school, and his mother tells sympathetic neighbors, "Oh, he was such a good boy, he was such a good boy—everything that he stole he brought right home to me," that too is a community problem.

How can the community solve this problem? In addition to co-operating with the schools, there are several other obvious answers. One of them literally hits us in the eye—the need for slum clearance.

Low-rent housing projects, whether they are made possible through federal or municipal aid, certainly provide a more health-ful physical and social environment for growing children than the slums. Public Housing Commissioner Charles E. Slusser says this: "By eliminating overcrowding and providing space for athletics and other recreation, public housing offers slum-bred children an escape from alley gangs where prestige goes to the one who can outsmart the cops. A decent home and a place to play may not offer a guarantee against delinquency, but it is significant that the adult crime at the end of the delinquency road has been reduced greatly by public housing projects wherever they have been built."

This position is well accepted in the field. Many cities have learned that slums are the place where delinquency begins, that the

208

elimination of them cuts the delinquency rate. For example, the city of Louisville, Kentucky, shows that a public housing project actually saved the city money since the families who moved in required fewer services than they did when they lived elsewhere in slums. A study of public services and blighted areas in Louisville, conducted in 1951 by the Planning and Zoning commissions, with the assistance of other city and county agencies, showed that a standard residential area or a public housing project required less than half as many public agency services as a substandard slum area.

Louisville Police Chief Carl Heustis said, "In the Police Department we have referred to these areas before slum clearance as hot-beats, where the need was urged for twenty-four-hour constant patrol. The problem in such communities has been changed as if by magic."

Assistant Commonwealth's Attorney Carl Ousely reported that three men are arrested in the slum areas for every one in the standard (public housing) areas. The proportion of arrests for women in the slum areas is even greater. It is significant that 76 per cent of those arrested who have previous felony records are from the slum areas and only 24 per cent are from the standard areas.

The Louisville study also showed that the slum areas required twice as many ambulance and patrol car visits as did the standard areas, burdened the criminal courts with more than three times as many cases, and required more than four times as many visits by welfare and relief agency personnel. *The slum area* required 13.5 times as much help for dependent children and *sent three times as many cases to juvenile court.*

Not only do cities find that slums contribute to juvenile delinquency, but small towns like Marietta, Georgia—a town of twenty thousand—also report that their substandard areas have been a heavy drain on the treasury, the community chest, and the community well-being. Marietta found that its areas of bad housing and rates of high truancy—and consequent delinquent rates—coincided.

The local Housing Authority report from Pittsburgh is also enlightening. The children of the Miller Public School, which is near a housing project, were asked to appraise life in a housing project. Applause was not always in order. One child wrote:

"Things I like about Terrace Village. I like Terrace Village for its nice lawns, its laundries and the nice places to play. There are places to go at night, recreation halls to play in, instead of playing in the streets at night. The way the houses are made, so that no kind of bugs or rats can get in.

"Things I don't like about Terrace Village. I don't like Terrace Village for these reasons: nebbey people, walls are too hard to clean, too many people act bosses, too many fights, people write all over the walls."

The Housing Authority is not quite sure what nebbey people are, but on general principles it does not care for them much either.

Other youngsters liked the heating system of the project, which meant they no longer had to get up early in the morning to light a fire in a tenement stove.

Teachers from the schools near public housing projects reported that children from these low-rent communities are happier, healthier, and cleaner than they were before they moved into them. Improvement in social behavior was noticed; truancy has become rare; gang feuds have gradually disappeared; ideas of sportsmanship are more commonly accepted; the tendency to destroy and deface public property has diminished.

But even in the newer houses, despite all their physical advantages, the community must not relax its vigilance about the emotional health of both children and parents. Some communities report that vandalism continues even though housing is improved.

The Housing Authority of Savannah, Georgia, handled vandalism in one project in an enlightened way. In this instance, the management had to replace 180 broken windowpanes a month. On the average of once every four hours, there was the tinkle of shattered glass somewhere in the project. The cause was usually the same—stones thrown by boys. Today the loss has been cut to twenty-five panes a month, and very few of these may be charged to vandalism.

"We solved the problem," the manager explained, "by organizing a troop of Boy Scouts and equipping a playground. We had to haul away twenty-seven loads of trash from the playground site, but now the Scouts keep it clean. It's a funny thing: if a window is broken now, I know all about it in thirty minutes. They get hold of the culprit right away and let me know that the situation is in hand."

One of the leading scouts is a boy who was formerly known as an expert rock-thrower, specializing in street lights. He could talk out of the side of his mouth as skillfully as any movie gangster. One evening he appropriated the manager's car for some pleasure driving. The police stepped in and the youngster was put on parole. Which way his career would turn was a toss up.

The manager had an idea. First he got the boy interested in scouting; then he gave the boy a job in the project's maintenance shop. The youngster changed completely. When several of his pals made the mistake of twitting him about his good conduct, they were invited to step back into the pine woods for a lesson that changed their ways of thinking. Before long they, too, were in the scout troop.

Police Chief William H. Hall of Savannah recalls that Yamacraw, once an infamous slum area, now transformed into a housing project that the city can be proud of, used to be one of the Police Department's worst headaches.

"We haven't had one tenth of the trouble we had before," the police chief said. "We don't get the cutting and shooting scrapes we used to. Before Yamacraw Village was built, 19 per cent of Savannah's crime originated in that area. Now the figure is less than one per cent. People tend to be like their environment. These new public housing buildings are really nice, something the city should be proud of. I hope we can build more like them to replace our other slum districts. This Police Department is short twenty-five men now, and it sure helps to have Yamacraw the way it is."

Improving the external environment means more than building houses. It is important that the community plan to provide its new developments with adequate recreational facilities. Too often this is not done, and that is when trouble begins—just as it did when the same families were living in the slums. Not long ago the American Association for Health, Physical Education and Recreation said that there is a definite relationship between insufficient physical activity and the alarming delinquency problem. In its yearbook, the Association pointed out that children need from two to four hours of vigorous activity each day for normal growth. Without this amount of regular and vigorous activity, young bodies will not develop and maintain the necessary muscular strength, physical fitness, and health.

The report went on to say, "A sound program of physical education not only develops muscular fitness but also provides a healthy outlet for the tensions of modern living, which otherwise may be expended in antisocial behavior. A well-planned, well-conducted activity program is essential for children in the formative period of their development. It should begin with the nursery school, and kindergarten, and continue through college."

Various recreation programs have been initiated throughout the nation. For example, the recreation department of the school system in Canton, Ohio, has operated on the theory that a busy child does not have the time to become a delinquent. Many community agencies co-operate to provide recreational services for the school children of Canton. The Police Department sponsors a police boys' club in which over four hundred boys meet during the week. A manufacturing company provides extensive recreational facilities for children of its employees. The community service clubs all add their efforts toward the welfare of the youth in their community.

The National Recreation Association, through leadership training and consultation services, offers organizations and communities assistance in developing sound recreation programs. The executive director, Joseph Prendergast, in referring to the role of recreation in juvenile delinquency prevention, notes, "Recreation operates in a positive way in its relation to delinquency by building in the boy or girl interest, skill, and resources which crowd out the call of the gang. There is no doubt that, if a youngster is busy enjoying leisure time activities, he does not have the time—nor is he likely—to be getting into trouble."

There is some danger, however, in overemphasizing the importance of recreation. How can recreation help a boy who is caught in a web of family tensions and disturbance? We must recognize that the physical existence of a recreation center of itself is meaningless. We must add trained leadership and dynamic programs that will attract and benefit all of the children in the neighborhood, not only those who normally would conform and normally would not get into trouble anyway.

Our problem, then, is something like that of the preacher who beseeches his parishioners to attend church regularly. Unfortunately, as a preacher is so wont to say, he is trying to reach the sinners but he is preaching to those who are already saved. In the same way, many children who are delinquents or potential delinquents, do not take advantage of the facilities offered by community services. Various studies in this field show that the aggressive and exciting pattern of group behavior that gangs engage in makes it difficult for gang members to accept the traditional recreational pattern offered by community agencies. In this connection, it is important that the agencies make their programs so attractive and worthwhile to potential or actual gang members that they will want to participate in them.

The study made during a project conducted by New York University between 1927 and 1931 indicates the limitations of traditional recreation programs.

The Boys Club of New York University was set up to serve as many as four thousand boys at a time. The club appealed more to boys fourteen and older than to younger boys, though many of the members were from seven to thirteen years of age. Membership reached a total of 12,450 boys. Most of them were potential delinquents as judged by low social and economic status, educational achievement, and emotional instability.

Did the club help reduce delinquency by co-operating and working with potential delinquent boys? The answer is no. Only 18 per cent of the delinquent acts committed by members occurred before the boys joined the club. Twenty-eight per cent were committed after some participation in club activities. And 61 per cent were committed during a period in which the boys were actively affiliated with the club. In addition, the percentage of members engaging in delinquency or truancy that brought them to the attention of courts increased rather than declined as the boys continued in membership in the club. The explanation seems to be that as the boys increased in age, the likelihood of their committing delinquent acts increased.

Case studies of sixty problem boys suggest why the club was not more successful in curbing delinquency. The conclusions drawn from these studies were published in "The Boys Club and Juvenile Delinquency" in the *American Journal of Sociology* in 1936. They are of interest today.

The acute behavior problems in those cases, the findings noted, were precipitated by various combinations of family disorganization, dire poverty, school maladjustments, gang activities, association with older hoodlums and underworld characters, demoralizing experiences on the streets, in institutions of commercialized amusement and at neighborhood hang-outs. These influences for the most part were beyond the power of the Boys Club to neutralize, particularly in the limited time each week which the average Boys Club member spent in club activities involving, as they did, little real guidance from the club personnel.

Although the disturbed child may not always respond to group activities, it is quite likely that he may have a wholesome response to what in a sense is modified group therapy. For example, the probation officer of Ramsey County, Minnesota, presents this illustration of how the social direction of the potentially delinquent young child can be changed, in this case through the movement of the Boy Scouts.

The officer reports: "There were the Terrible Tigers, a group of nine-year-olds whose activities included shoplifting and crapshooting, and whose main objective seemed to be the harassing of teachers and police. After a brief indoctrination, they were introduced to the Cub movement and emerged a fine Cub Pack. I am happy to say that most of them are still in scouting, in one of the troops in downtown St. Paul."

Another gang had as its objective the rifling of boxcars. Through the co-operation of the railroad and the Boy Scouts, a troop was organized within two blocks of their rendezvous. With a year-round program in school and at scout camp, the energies of the gang were diverted into wholesome channels.

From another across-the-tracks area, the Scouts organized a troop to change the complexion of a gang that was fast becoming delinquent. Their interest in outdoor activity was channeled into camping. Their wanderlust was solved by scout hikes. Their skill in shoplifting was sublimated so that they became adept in various scout crafts.

The gang *can* be converted into a wholesome feature of our society. One of the most effective and progressive efforts is being made by the New York City Youth Board, which was established in 1948. The growing seriousness of lawless juvenile gangs, together with the fact that we still do not have adequate rehabilitation machinery, has accentuated the need for a new approach.

And that is what the New York City Youth Board, headed by Judge Nathaniel Kaplan, has evolved. Rather than depend on the police to break up the gangs forcibly, or on providing limited recreation as did the Boys Club, the Youth Board has a more direct method. Organized on a neighborhood level, it stresses grass-roots participation of local residents and utilizes and strengthens the adult leadership of the community. This area approach has given evidence of being the most productive way to handle the teen-age gang problem.

The board sends workers into the streets to locate the gangs and their hide-outs. Once contact is established, the workers seek to gain the gang's acceptance. Then they are personally in a position to rechannel the boys' misdirected energies into socially acceptable outlets.

These principles are enunciated by the Youth Board as a basis for work with street gangs:

Participation in a street gang or club, like participation in any natural group, is a part of the growing-up process of adolescents. Such primary group associations possess potentialities for positive growth and development. Through such a group, the individual can gain security and develop positive ways of living with other individuals. Within the structure of his group the individual can develop such characteristics as loyalty, leadership, and community responsibility.

Some street clubs or gangs, as a result of more fundamental factors such as family disorganization, economic insecurity, racial and religious discrimination, poor housing, lack of recreational and educational facilities, emotional maladjustments of their leaders and members, etc., have developed patterns of anti-social behavior, the most widely known of which is street fighting. This type of teen-age gang warfare over the past decade has produced an annual toll of innumerable injuries and several deaths.

While the protection of the community at times necessitates the use of repressive measures in dealing with the antisocial street clubs or gangs, these methods do not bring about basic changes in attitudes or behavior.

Street club members can be reached and will respond to sympathy, acceptance, affection, and understanding when approached by adults who possess those characteristics and reach out to them on their own level.

The positive relationship that is developed between an adult worker and a street club can serve as a catalytic agent for modifying antisocial attitudes and behavior. This relationship can also be used to help the individual member meet his needs in more positive ways.

To be effective, the work of these adults must be co-ordinated, unified and applied on a saturation basis.

Because of the close relationship that is necessary for workers to develop with club members, and because of such factors as group loyalty, distrust, and fear of other clubs, it is imperative that each worker be assigned to only one street club.

On the basis of these assumptions, the following goals were formulated by the Youth Board:

Reduction of antisocial behavior, particularly street fighting.

Friendly relationships with other street gangs.

Increased democratic participation within the gang.

Broadened social horizons.

Responsibility for self-direction.

Improved personal and social adjustment of the individual. Improved community relations.

Looking to the future and considering the work of the project, it is important to remember that street club work is not a panacea for all of the problems presented by street gangs and their members, that street club work is not an isolated, particularistic approach to the problem of gang delinquency, and that while much has been learned about how to work with street clubs and their members, there is still much more to be learned.

Workers on this project are not able to modify directly such causative factors of gang delinquency as broken homes, distorted values, poor housing, discrimination, and other social and economic inequities. However, they concentrate on the latent potentialities of the young persons affected by these conditions and with whom they work in seeking new avenues toward a solution of the problems.

Summarizing his work with a gang, one of the Youth Board workers pointed out that there has been some reduction in intergang warfare in his area, with only one major conflict occurring since the worker has been with the gang. There has also been considerable reduction in the use of narcotics. At the beginning of the worker's contact with the gang, nearly all the members used narcotics at least occasionally. At present there are only four members who still do. The autocratic leadership and chaotic club organization that existed at the beginning of the year have been to a large extent replaced by the development of democratic participation and election of leadership. Participation by gang members in socially desirable athletics and in cultural and social activities has been tremendously increased, and the range of these activities has been greatly broadened.

With the reduction of intergang conflicts and other antisocial activities, there has been a corresponding development of a more positive social code of behavior by both the large majority of individual members and also by the gang as a whole.

It is still too early to know what lasting effect this Youth Board program may have. But we do have evidence that on many levels the reaching-out approach has lowered delinquency rates in those areas where the program has been in effect for any period of time.

It will be some years before we will know definitely whether this approach is to be more effective than any other.

Another municipal program that has had considerable success is a community project in Chicago. In a committee report, this point was brought out: "The social life of a child in his neighborhood brings him inevitably into contact with the older children who have already acquired the know-how or the experience and the sophistication required to turn an extra penny by use of their wits.

"Here we have a combination of environment and family life, that lends itself toward delinquency. Yet it was found that most delinquent boys and girls in these deteriorated neighborhoods are socially but not emotionally maladjusted. Only a few actually need psychiatric treatment. For the others, human relations may be the answer."

The Chicago report states that it is important to give the predelinquent or the delinquent boy an opportunity to form an attachment to, or come under the influence of, a person or persons from whom he will receive recognition for conforming to the conventional standard of conduct. In a sense this becomes a matter of substituting for the delinquent boy's leaders, law-abiding men and women who can come, in time, to mean as much to him as his previous leaders. Where the community has co-operated in advancing this type of leadership program in Chicago, there is definitely a falling off in the delinquency rate.

But not all children are receptive to the friendship of those adults who would like to help them. It takes more than a "good brother" to keep boys from becoming delinquent if they do not have the proper home, school, and community environment to complement one good relationship. The Big Brother Movement, based on the idea that children benefit by having adult sponsors who will take an active interest in them, is valuable, as is any agency or organization that plays an active role in helping children in trouble. Yet this movement by itself cannot be expected to work miracles.

The results of the Cambridge-Somerville (Massachusetts) Youth Study, published by the Columbia University Press in 1951 as a report on *An Experiment in the Prevention of Delinquency,* supports this conclusion. Dr. Richard Cabot, an eminent doctor at

Harvard, wondered whether "delinquent and potentially delinquent boys would develop into youths of upright character if they were provided with the continued friendship and wise counsel of adults who were deeply interested in them." According to his original plan, the boys chosen for study would be youngsters about seven years old who seemed to be headed for delinquency. However, teachers and others seemed unwilling, or perhaps unable, to identify such children. The criterion for selection was therefore changed to boys presenting difficulties in school or elsewhere.

A committee was set up to select matched pairs of boys. One group was to receive guidance and other assistance, and the other act as a control group. Each group had 325 boys, most of whom were nine to eleven years old. Staffed by nine counselors, a supervisor, and an executive, the project's service program worked with the boys in the chosen group and had no contact with those in the control group until about seven years later.

Instead of waiting for individuals to apply or to be referred for help, the boys and their families were sought out and urged to accept the agency's services. Each boy received continuous help until late adolescence. Instead of a case work relationship, a friendship program was instituted. The counselors frequently took the boys on trips and engaged in various other recreational activities with them, securing needed psychological and medical service, and providing tutoring.

The counselors found that with minor exceptions, families cooperated. Yet in spite of the friendly relations with the boys and with the families, the services had little effect on the boys' behavior patterns. A study made after the project was concluded showed that the friendship approach just did not work for the majority of the boys involved.

Twenty-one per cent of the boys were definitely helped, 10 per cent were only slightly helped, 6 per cent had temporary benefit, and for 9 per cent little was accomplished. In 37 per cent of the cases, the help was clearly ineffectual, and in 17 per cent no help was needed. The police and court records of the treatment and control groups were compared at the end of the study. It was found that the two groups had nearly identical records.

The final report of the study, written by Edwin Powers and Helen L. Witmer, made these observations:

"We conclude, then, that there are identifiable types of boys with which efforts of the Study type are likely to be successful and types with which they are likely to fail. . . .

"The counselors were chiefly successful in working with boys who were socially, physically, or mentally handicapped, but who were relatively healthy in personality and whose parents were either emotionally healthy or somewhat dependent and immature. . . .

"Given the proper type of problem (that is, the kind of boy and home situation that usually proves amenable to Study efforts) it was necessary that proper treatment methods be employed. With some fairly well-adjusted boys from socially and emotionally adequate homes the method that proved helpful consisted of removing some specific handicap that stood in the way of wholly adequate functioning. . . . With most boys, the effective treatment method was one that, in one way or another, offset parental inadequacies. A few somewhat neurotic boys were aided by service through which good parent-child relations were established. . . . In most cases, however, little was accomplished in the way of changing parents' attitudes . . . and attempts to work with parents to the exclusion, or the relative ignoring, of the boy proved ineffectual or actually detrimental. The chief method, then, by which good results were achieved was that of giving most attention to the boy and subordinating work with the family to that requirement, the aim of this boy-centered work being to offset parental inadequacies. . . .

"If the boy was seriously emotionally maladjusted and yet was the type that sought the friendship of adults and so was likely to be amenable to treatment, it was especially necessary that contact with him be both long sustained and sensitively attuned to his needs, and that nothing be permitted to arouse in him the sense of being let down or rejected. . . .

"All in all, success in the Study work was dependent on the boy's being of the requisite personality make-up and having some desire to be aided in dealing with his difficulties, and on the counselor's being able to ascertain where the trouble lay and to direct his efforts accordingly."

We have seen that any program is more effective when there is co-operation with the home. It is important that the family help agencies participate in any community's attack on the disease of delinquency. Again, the New York City Youth Board is an example of the effectiveness of a many-sided approach. For in addition to working productively with juvenile gangs, the Youth Board provides all forms of services for parents and children who either are in trouble already, or who are approaching it.

The board reaches children and young persons with behavior problems and emotional disturbances who are not being served through the customary community services for youth. Frequently a mother will throw up her hands in horror at the mere suggestion that perhaps her child is unhappy and needs some kind of help. Being neurotic herself, the mother will not recognize the neurotic symptoms in her own child. She feels, of course, that she is normal, and therefore the child is normal if the child follows in her own pattern. All too frequently those families that need the most help are the most reluctant to seek it out. Indeed, they aggressively reject such help. Families are not ashamed to seek relief when in physical need, or at any rate will not permit their children to starve for lack of food. However, when families are in desperate need of emotional help, guidance, or remedial assistance, they maintain a hands-off attitude.

The average family agency in most communities is not equipped to do an adequate job. We must recognize that because we have a family service agency in the community, we can not smugly assume that we have an adequate antidelinquency program. The reports from many communities and various agencies stress the fact that if we are to have a good antidelinquency program, we must build it upon the co-operation of the entire community, utilizing the facilities—or creating them if necessary—of psychiatric and mental health clinics, juvenile courts, school counselors, etc., in addition to the family service agencies. We must also assume a community responsibility to combat delinquency in the home, even if the parents themselves may be reluctant to co-operate; we must recognize that the child is a member of society, as well as of his family.

The case of William illustrates the importance of a constructive,

almost aggressive but sympathetic, approach on the part of the community in some instances. William is the second boy in a low-income
family of four children. This youngster, of average intelligence, came
to the attention of the New York Youth Board through the school
because of his very disruptive behavior. Although his mother indicated an interest in remedial services to the referral worker, she did
not respond to an appointment made with her. The Youth Board
adds:

"We, therefore, visited the home. Mrs. A. blamed the school for
William's trouble, indicating that she was doing her best by severely
punishing him and thus could be expected to do no more. It was
obvious that, in spite of her denial of the problem, she needed help.
The worker was encouraged when Mrs. A. accepted our offer of
again getting in touch with the school to evaluate the situation currently in the light of what Mrs. A. herself had said.

"At the second home visit, we reported that the school would have
to suspend the boy unless there was some sort of a change in his
behavior. At that point Mrs. A. could allow herself to take a more
positive attitude. She admitted that the severe punishment she had
used had not worked, and then vacillated between feeling that her
husband was too strict and that the child was to blame. Still, she
tended to minimize her own part in the situation, and sought a solution in a psychiatric examination of William.

"We could tell her then that the school psychologist who had already examined the boy had felt that family tensions were the root
of William's behavior problems. Still, Mrs. A. did not keep an office
appointment, and we made a third home visit. At that time Mrs. A.
responded to the worker's warmth and her desire to help by telling
of her marital difficulty in the home. Mrs. A. went further, and encouraged her husband to come to the office. After a period of inde-
cision, Mr. A. requested help with his own personal problem.

"Both Mr. and Mrs. A. have been working with us since that time
on the relationships within their family. They could now frankly
discuss behavior problems of the other children, too, and get some
sense of the dynamics of the total family situation. While there are

still some broken appointments, they follow through more and more responsively.

"Progress is slow and there is a heavy investment of agency time. From a long range point of view, however, this preventive work can be a sound investment for the community."

This case is indicative of the difficulties often found in trying to get the family to co-operate. It also highlights the vast amount of time that must be put into each case. Even so, the community will pay far less in the end than would be necessary if William had to be sent away to a training school at a cost to the state of from $1,200 to $3,000 a year, and at a cost to society of a lost boy.

As the New York City Youth Board said in its study, "Reaching Teen-Agers," issued in 1954, "Our young people will be the adult members of tomorrow's community and they are now becoming the kind of adults they will eventually be. Therefore, if agencies are to meet their responsibilities to youth and accept the challenge and privilege of helping them grow into mature citizens, agencies must constantly be seeking new and creative ways to work with youth. Only thus will they be able to establish and maintain a dynamic, forward-moving partnership with youth. If they find themselves in the position of either trying to catch up with, or hold back young people, they will not be able to share significantly in young people's experience as they cross the threshold to adult living."

A Delaware County juvenile court in Pennsylvania has explored the uses that a clinic may have in dealing with cases of delinquency. In some instances the judge in the juvenile court refers the child and his parent to the clinic before he makes his final disposition of the case. In other instances the child is placed on probation, with attendance at the clinic made a condition of the probation.

Educators have found that both of these methods help the child and the parent to recognize the seriousness of the problem. Since the child and the parent realize that the court has continuing jurisdiction, they are more likely to co-operate in attending the clinic. The court also provides moral support for both the child and the parent.

During the course of this Pennsylvania program, it has been found that, although the psychiatrist may often at first be confronted with hostility and rebellion, the child is exposed to a positive relationship. Once that relationship takes root, the deep-seated fears, hostility, hate, and anger that fill the child begin to come to the surface and can be treated.

As Dr. George Gardner, director of the Judge Baker Guidance Center in Boston, said before the Senate subcommittee investigating delinquency: "Psychiatric treatment, particularly as it concerns juvenile delinquents, is an attempt on the part of expertly trained people to get at the needs, the motivations, the motives and drives that cause an individual to act in a certain way.

"Specifically, it is done in a relationship between a trained physician and the patient. In this situation the physician is able not only to know the conscious meaning of the child's acts, but the unconscious meaning of them as well."

Dr. Gardner was asked how to find out what treatment the child needs. And the psychiatrist replied, "You try to find out by trying to determine what basic needs the child has. These needs may be several, and the psychiatrist has to take them all in consideration. They may be external needs. He may need a new home, a new overcoat, or a new school, or a new tutor.

"Also, he may need the elements of security and friendship in a relationship with another human being.

"In other words, the delinquent that we see has entirely different concepts of the world from those of the child who is not a delinquent. Maybe he has been kicked around. Certainly he has had very little love or spiritual love. His concept of an individual human being is quite different from that of the next child, who is not a delinquent.

"So the psychiatrist has to do what he can to supply those needs, both spiritual and emotional, in order that the child may [develop] a different attitude toward himself and toward other human beings in the world in which he resides."

It is the opinion of Dr. Raymond W. Waggoner, director of the University of Michigan's Neuropsychiatric Institute, that psychotherapy can accomplish the social reorientation of youthful gangsters in many cases.

Dr. Waggoner said that plans are being developed to submit to the state legislature a recommendation to convert the present 35-bed children's unit of the institute for the reception of fifteen-to-nineteen-year-olds. Younger children will be studied and treated in the 75-bed psychiatric hospital now under construction.

"It is quite evident that jailing these young offenders provides no solution to the problem," Dr. Waggoner declared. "While some may be behavior problems, others show signs of definite mental illness.

"This group is completely indifferent to the results of their lawless acts, both as they affect others and may affect themselves. A policy of 'toughness,' announced by the police and courts, makes no impression on them.

"We can do much for the youngster who is mentally ill, but so far as I can learn, there is not one facility in the United States devoted to the diagnosis and treatment of this class of offender.

"The causes of delinquency are so many and varied that a rare opportunity would be presented for instituting valuable studies. These should certainly include the relationship of the delinquent to his parents and to his home environment."

Although some of the emotionally disturbed boys who become hoodlums and gangsters probably cannot be readjusted, he believes that a great majority of juvenile law-violators could be helped through intensive hospitalization followed by a period of out-patient treatment.

Here we find an emphasis on a particular approach to the problem of how to develop a program that will eliminate, if possible, but in any event at least reduce, the incidence of delinquency.

Services available for psychiatric care in most communities are extremely inadequate. Dr. Wexberg of the Mental Health Division of the Department of Health of Washington, D.C., made this observation, which typifies the situation existing in most other localities: "To give an idea of how inadequate our services are, in view of the demand, let me quote that we have at the present time on our waiting list 124 children. That means that a child who applies for help or whose parents applied in December [1953] . . . has a fair chance of being taken on for treatment in August or September, 1954. . . . Diagnostic work can usually be done within five or six weeks. However, treatment is the one thing that counts and that can only be done according to the waiting list, with the exception of emergency cases. We have to be pretty strict in qualifying a case as an emergency because otherwise soon there wouldn't be any emergencies; there would be another waiting list for emergencies again."

We know that not every delinquent or potential delinquent requires psychiatric examination and treatment, but they should be available for the child who does need it. For, as was pointed out during the hearings before the Senate subcommittee, the annual cost for a child at an industrial home school for boys is $2,025; the annual cost for a child at a receiving home is $3,109. On the other hand, the annual cost of service per child at a guidance clinic is $100. From the standpoint of finances, entirely apart from the effect in salvaging human lives, no community can afford the false economy of being without a guidance clinic, with all its implications in the prevention and cure of juvenile delinquency.

What is the community's answer to the problem of juvenile delinquency? I believe that it lies in the teamwork approach that is essential today. We know by this time that no single aspect of our life, of our society, is the prime and only cause of delinquency, not even the home, although it is the key factor. Because the contributing causes are many, the solution to the problem demands the best work of several different agencies.

Two recent studies indicate the role the community can play in helping to prevent delinquency from developing into a more serious problem.

Edward Flynn of the Washington Criminal Justice Association made a study of typical cases coming to the attention of the juvenile court. Richard Heaney of the Bureau of Prisons in the nation's capital made a somewhat similar study of one hundred cases from the District of Columbia in the National Training School for Boys. Their findings point up clearly that there are many times in the life of a potential delinquent when the community, with a little effort and at relatively small cost, can take steps to prevent delinquency, with its resulting enormous cost to the community. The studies proved that, with community co-operation, the delinquent-to-be could have been detected and treated at an early age; through co-ordinated community activities, he could have been helped to develop a more wholesome personality.

Unfortunately, the various agencies in a community do not always co-operate with each other. There is frequently some unexpressed, often unconscious rivalry among them. Sometimes the private organizations want to usurp the field, or the public agency may not be in sympathy with the work done by private agencies. For instance, the testimony at the subcommittee hearings indicated that in Washington, D.C.—and this exists elsewhere too—there exists among the agencies a serious lack of co-operation. That testimony shows that the park police are handling juvenile delinquent children on an informal basis without sharing their information automatically with the metropolitan police. The juvenile court does not make available to the police or to school officials information needed by these officials if they are to carry out their duties effectively. The subcommittee believes that the necessary information can be released from one agency to another involved, under proper safeguards to prevent unnecessary and undesirable publicity for the juvenile concerned.

The juvenile court has not developed effective procedures for making information about support payments available to the Department of Public Welfare. The department must have such information from the court, and must have it promptly. If it is not received, the department is often forced to operate in the dark, with resulting injustice both to the recipient and to the taxpayers.

The juvenile court does not utilize all available information concerning the juveniles coming before the court. Specifically, in a vast majority of the cases, the information which the police, school, and welfare departments already have about the children in question is not secured by the court; very often, therefore, pertinent data cannot be taken into consideration in deciding the disposition of the cases.

Similarly, the Welfare Department and the National Training School for Boys do not give the police information concerning parolees and escapees promptly enough for effective police action and protection. Also, the Office of the United States Marshal does not execute promptly the attachments for juveniles issued by the juvenile court.

Washington is cited merely as one community in which there is a lack of effective co-operation among the various agencies attempting to cope with the problem of delinquency. As long as the agencies involved do not co-ordinate their activities effectively, it is obvious that the entire program for combating juvenile delinquency will suffer.

It behooves the community to utilize all its resources—the schools and the churches, the psychological clinic and the Mental Health Association, the Boy and Girl Scout program and the Police Athletic League, and all the others—in developing its antidelinquency program. Further, it is essential that each community allocate sufficient funds to finance the best possible preventive and remedial program.

It is not enough to blame the slums even though the slums may be involved. It is not enough to blame the so-called breakdown in schools, or to blame "progressive" education, even though the schools may have lost some of their disciplinary hold over their pupils. It is not enough to blame the police, or lax courts, or inadequate training facilities. What is most important is to strengthen, and co-operate with, those institutions that are working to help eliminate delinquency, and to create new ones that may be needed.

Both the local and national service groups, such as the Rotary Club, Kiwanis, The Lions, The Masons, or the Knights of Columbus, play a very important part in helping our youth.

The Young Women's Christian Association attempts to provide youth with experiences which will help them to build healthy personalities, to become aware of democracy as a formula, not only in politics but also in human relations. It helps girls grow in understanding, cutting across racial, religious, and cultural lines. It also helps them to learn skills that lead to the creative planning and carrying through of leisure time activities.

The Scouts want their youngsters to understand and assume the responsibilities and privileges which begin at home and stretch to include the whole world.

The Young Men's Christian Association has as its chief characteristic a group work program. The youth group and other Y clubs of various sorts are self-governing bodies in which the youngsters determine their own program, with the help of a sympathetic, understanding adult.

The Allied Youth is an organization of nonsectarian, nonpolitical persons interested in the field of educating youth concerning the problem of alcohol in the light of available scientific data and the analysis of its effects upon social behavior. It works in thirty-nine states through Allied Youth posts in 260 high schools.

The Boys Club of America stresses that parents' efforts must be supplemented by opportunities for wholesome activities under trained leadership and guidance. When these opportunities are not present, influences of home, church, and school may be undermined. The Boys Club attempts to provide those supplementary opportunities, and offers guidance for boys between the ages of eighteen and twenty who reside in less privileged neighborhoods. The organization has 375 clubs, with a total membership of 360,000.

A community program must work closely with the school. The professional workers in the community must help teachers learn how to detect at the earliest possible stage the pupils who need special help. The community must also establish better ways through which the schools can refer serious cases to outside agencies. It is a community disgrace, a community scandal, when a great many school systems keep waiting lists as long as six months or a year before their emotionally disturbed children can receive the kind of special help they need—simply because there is no agency that is available or in a position to help the child.

The effect of the church is salutary in maintaining good community relationships. There is no question that it is desirable to encourage our youth, the teen-agers as well as those of all ages, to go to church with their parents. "Families who pray together, stay together," is a slogan based on sound common sense. Parents who do attend church regularly are less inclined to live in constant tension. Many of the churches maintain guidance clinics of their own. If these clinics were co-ordinated to a greater extent with the entire community program, with the schools, and with the various referral agencies, the church and the community as a whole would be in a stronger position to do a more satisfactory job.

The effort to prevent delinquency may often have to be extended beyond the community itself. In some cases it will be necessary to have the state take a part in the work, as has been done in New York State through the establishment of a State Youth Commission. The commission co-operates with local communities throughout the state and helps provide not only funds but leadership. The youth board includes judges, clergymen, businessmen, police officers, doctors, workers, and housewives. It may even be advisable to establish a national body supported by federal funds. Delinquency is not just an individual problem, nor is it merely a local problem. If we are to profit more fully from the research, the technical aid, and the treatment facilities the various private and public agencies can offer, it is essential that the attack on delinquency be co-ordinated on all levels—local, state, and national.

Specific antidelinquency proposals put forward by a Denver group of investigators appearing before the Senate subcommittee included the following:

Federal legislation should be amended to bring deserting fathers under the present federal Fugitive from Justice Act.

Crime and delinquency should be deglamorized by the public press, radio, and television, and the achievements of youngsters emphasized.

A Department of Morals should be organized in the federal government to police the mass media for the country and by so doing prevent the demoralization of the nation's youth through emphasis by mass media on crime, violence, and sex.

The federal income-tax law should be so amended to allow persons accepting foster children into their homes to claim exemption for their wards.

Slum clearance should be given priority as a national defense program to reduce juvenile delinquency.

During Senate hearings in Boston many other specific recommendations were made. Some of these could be carried out by local authorities, others would require state or federal action:

Federal statutes should be amended to permit the use of federal funds, now granted only to welfare departments, by other agencies such as the Youth Service Board.

A juvenile squad should be organized in all police departments, having in it trained men who can cope with the modern problems of juvenile delinquents.

Restrictions on recreation facilities in public housing developments should be eliminated and adequate recreational facilities and services should be developed.

A statewide juvenile court system should be created to enable juveniles to be handled uniformly and with benefit of trained and skilled probation and allied court services.

Action should be taken by the federal government to give more effective aid to the return of runaway children.

Methods should be worked out to insure that workers in the field of delinquency co-operate fully in utilizing limited services and facilities to maximum capacity.

Basic research on a sustained basis should be pursued into the causes and treatment of juvenile delinquency, with particular reference to mental health aspects.

At the 1954 National Conference on Juvenile Delinquency, the following principles were suggested as basic to local community action in coping with juvenile delinquency.

1. Citizens should have the responsibility of finding out what is happening to all the children in their community. They must know first hand what goes on in the courts, the police department, the detention homes, the training schools, and the mental hospitals.

2. Young people should be appointed to serve on all committees and commissions.

3. Professional people, whether judges, police, or probation officers, workers and community agencies, must feel the responsibility for doing more than just a good professional job. They must alert the community by effectively telling citizens about the unfilled needs of children in trouble.

4. Isolation of the professional expert and the layman must be bridged.

5. Each community must have an essential core of leadership that can spark action in behalf of youthful offenders. After all, there is no one pattern for successful community action.

6. Bold action must be taken. We have more children than we have ever before had at any other time in our history. Our efforts in their behalf have not been great enough. We must dramatize the problems and the methods of meeting the problems by utilizing all resources available, such as mass media, public relation specialists, advertising experts accustomed to selling an idea.

7. Bold steps must be supplemented by ceaseless work in every community, and a greater enlistment of volunteers must be made to work with young offenders.

We take steps to prevent polio, and we readily come to the support of physically crippled children and their families. It is just as essential that we take steps to prevent and try to cure emotional disorders that threaten our children, and so often lead to delinquency.

Only as a community working together, recognizing and diligently attempting to solve the problem, can we help to develop a nation in which the scourge of juvenile delinquency will be a thing of the past.

11. The Police

"Anybody that had anything to do with the law was my enemy."

Normally, the police are responsible for the protection of life and property, and for the maintenance of law and order. Obviously, this function must apply to dealing with juveniles as well as with adults. It is necessary, however, to recognize that juvenile offenders are not in the same class as adults. The problem for the police thus becomes one of finding ways to prevent young boys and girls from becoming habitual delinquents, of avoiding their development into adult criminals, and at the same time of safeguarding the community.

The evidence indicates that the police force today deals with more delinquent children than does any other community agency with the exception of the schools. In 1952, approximately 400,000 boys and girls came before the various juvenile courts, and 40,000 were sent to the training schools. And for every boy or girl who is brought to court, two or more come into contact with the police and are not even brought to court. For the most part, the child who is in trouble is picked up by the police for committing some specific act, or he is picked up "on suspicion." A small number of children may be called to the attention of the police by various agencies, by the schools, by parents, or even by neighbors.

Since the police come into contact with so many of our young people, it is necessary that the police adopt a sound philosophy. What attitude should the police take toward the delinquent child? Should a policeman who catches a boy of twelve who has just turned in a false fire-alarm hit the child over the head with his club?

Of course, the answer to such a question is no. However, in

the case of a sixteen-year-old who has committed assault and battery, the answer is not so simple.

Basically, the job of the police is to enforce the law, to apprehend its violators. However, where children are concerned, there must be some variation from this accepted pattern.

The attitude of the police officer to the juvenile can often determine whether or not he will become a good citizen. Frequently the police officer can show a child in trouble that he is the child's friend and wants to help him. If, on the other hand, as is the case more often than it should be, the policeman takes a night-stick approach, he can bring about fear and hatred, as well as distrust, in the juvenile.

Here is an example:

"That night I was picked up for being in the hallway by the project cops, me and another. It seemed that I hit a boy with a pipe in an argument over a girl. The girl was his sister. So me and a few others was brought down. At first nobody would tell who did it so the detectives took my friend in some room and beat him. Still nobody talked. So they gave him another beating. He came out looking so pitiful that I told them I was the one. They took me in a room and beat me with a night stick. One of them kicked me in the balls. I started to throw up so he put a blackjack in my mouth and said if I throw up he'll knock my teeth out.

"That's when I started to get worst. I didn't have no faith in nobody after that. Anybody that had anything to do with the law was my enemy. When I went to see my probation officer everything he said went in one ear and out the other."

Although the brutality revealed in this case may not be typical, it is significant to note that in 1954 only about half of both the boys at the Jamesburg training school and the girls at Hudson felt that the police had given them a fair break. In 1937, 80 per cent of the boys at Jamesburg said that the police had been fair.

In spite of these figures, there has been a recent change in the concept of the role of the police who are in contact with children. It is now generally accepted that, if the police officer uses a humane approach, even though it must be firm, the effect on the child is likely to be salutary. This is not to suggest that police officers must coddle a defiant and aggressive delinquent. But it is in keeping with our knowledge that a child in trouble needs a friendly, firm hand rather than a rough slap across the face.

We now come to the question of how to organize and train police officers to work with young people. In times gone by this was no problem—not because there were no juvenile delinquents, but because police departments did not recognize the difference between misdeeds of a child and those of an adult. It was a general practice to punish a child severely if he violated a law. We now recognize the fact that juveniles should not be treated on the same basis as adults. In the first place juveniles cannot have the same degree of understanding of, and responsibility for, their acts. Secondly, juveniles are unable to control their own environment.

In view of this, the police dealing with youth today must have special skills and training. Yet we find that in about 50 per cent of the communities in the country there are no special police officers whose training is geared to working with juveniles. Cities with a population of a half-million or more often do have juvenile specialists on their police forces. But only 28 per cent of the communities with a population of less than 10,000 have special officers assigned to deal with problems of youth.

Some communities have worked out a program of training that has proved successful. Occasionally, if a city is near a college or university, a special program may be set up. Schools of police administration, schools of social work, may prove to be valuable in giving assistance. Some people feel that the police departments should recruit juvenile officers from among the best qualified men and women within the community. Others believe that the juvenile officers should be drawn from the existing personnel in the police departments and should be given special training. It must be stressed that not every officer on the police force is suitable in temperament or personality to work with young boys and girls.

In the study, "Helping Delinquent Children," the federal Children's Bureau listed these suggestions as a guide to police officers dealing with children:

DO THIS

Treat the juvenile with consideration. Remember that what he thinks of you and your conduct may influence his future attitude to be in favor of, or opposed to, social and legal requirements.

Be friendly. Many juveniles feel that the world is against them. Do not let your conduct further the development of an antisocial attitude in the child. Many juveniles are discouraged. They believe they are failures, although they have not had time to be. You would not expect a half-completed airplane to fly. You cannot expect an undeveloped child to function as an adult.

Be firm. Appeal to his intelligence, his reason, his sense of fairness.

Discover the child's problems if you can. His problems are as important to him as yours are to you. If you know his problems, you may be able to help him.

Try to gain his confidence and respect. In attempting to determine the child's guilt or innocence with respect to any overt act, your chances are far better if he believes in you.

Remember that the child of today is the man of tomorrow. A boy who hates a police officer because of the officer's abusive attitude will, as a man, have little respect for him.

Be positive in your attitude. Show the benefits that come from an attitude of conformity with lawful requirements rather than dwelling on the harmful effects of antisocial behavior.

DON'T DO THIS

Don't resort to vulgarity, profanity or obscenity. The use of such language by a police officer is especially reprehensible and should not be tolerated under any circumstances.

Don't "brand" the juvenile. Epithets such as "thief," "liar," "burglar," or "forger," etc., should never be used toward juveniles whether in custody or not; nor should such terms be used in reference to juveniles in their presence or in the presence of their parents or relatives, or of any other person not a member of the police department—nothing is to be gained by it, and there is definite indication that it is very injurious to the child. Such epithets give rise to justified complaints. They are rightfully resented by the parents. The use of such epithets toward juveniles is a reflection upon the character and intelligence of the officer using them.

Don't lose your temper. To do so is an admission of mental inferiority to the person being interrogated.

In a survey made of twenty typical communities with a population of 100,000 or more, I found the new police approach toward the handling of delinquent youth to be one of humane consideration. John W. Polcyn, Chief of Police in Milwaukee, said, "The old methods of so-called stern justice and discipline have failed. The old police insistence on a pound of flesh for juvenile misconduct has not accomplished any favorable results. Rather it has developed fear and hatred toward the police among youth, and has, indeed, tended to increase juvenile crime."

James B. Nolan, Deputy Police Commissioner of New York City, has pointed out that police departments traditionally have concerned themselves with crime suppression rather than crime prevention. The transition from the traditional philosophy of crime control to the new philosophy of preventing crime is taking place in police departments throughout the country. Often the great opponents of crime prevention efforts by the police are the police themselves.

However, police generally now agree that prevention is an important part of their work. How much the police can do and how much they should be expected to do, are still open questions. There is no question that a police officer has an important responsibility. Sometimes he has a vital decision to make—a decision whether to dismiss a child with a warning or to bring the young offender into court. If the police officer makes the correct decision, it may mean the difference between the child's becoming a problem or not. The police officer must decide whether he is being confronted with an occasional delinquent—the boy who steals a watermelon from a neighbor's farm, or a candy bar from a store—or with a dangerous delinquent who needs psychiatric help.

The federal study "Police Services for Juveniles" states that the following information should be obtained by an officer making a thorough investigation: (1) details of the offense, including all data necessary to sustain a petition in court; (2) the record of any previous court or social agency action; (3) attitudes of the child, his parents, and the complainant in the offense toward the misdeed; (4) the adjustment of the child in the home, school, and community; (5) record of any previous police action.

Here are some of the approaches that police departments have found to be effective when they talk with young people in trouble:

All necessary information should be obtained with tact and patience. The child should be encouraged to tell his own story. It is always wise for the police officer to obtain as much information as he can about the offense prior to the interview.

The officer should put his questions into simple language, being sure that the child understands clearly what is being asked.

After the facts about the particular offense have been cleared up, an encouraging reminder that it is best to clean the slate for a new start may lead the child to tell about other offenses he may have committed.

When the police officer feels that a more inclusive investigation is called for, he should attempt to make the youngster feel that he really wants to help him.

It is wise to remember that the child who gets into trouble with the police usually is in trouble at home too. Perhaps he has never before had an opportunity to discuss his problems with anyone. For the first time, he may find that he has the attention of someone in authority who is willing to listen to him and who is ready to encourage him to talk.

When should a delinquent be referred to a court?

Again, common sense should be used by the police. If the offender has committed a serious crime, and if the police know that he is a chronic offender, referral to the juvenile court should follow almost as a matter of course. But if the child is an occasional offender,

and if the offense is not too serious, a warning by itself may be sufficient to keep the child from committing any further anti-social acts.

At the invitation of the federal Children's Bureau and the International Association of Chiefs of Police, fifty leading police officials
and other representative workers held a conference in 1953 in East
Lansing, Michigan. The following were set up as criteria for referring young offenders to the juvenile court:

The particular offense committed by the child is of a serious
nature.

The child is known or has, in the past. been known to the
juvenile court.

The child has a record of repeated delinquency extending over
a period of time.

The child and his parents have shown themselves unable or
unwilling to co-operate with agencies of a nonauthoritative
character.

Case work with the child by a nonauthoritative agency has
failed in the past.

Treatment services needed by the child can be obtained only
through the court and its probation department.

The child denies the offense and the officer believes judicial
determination is called for, and there is sufficient evidence to
warrant referral, or the officer believes that the child and his
family are in need of aid.

There is apparent need for treatment.

On the other hand, when should the child in trouble be released
into the custody of his parents or guardians without referral to
another agency or to a juvenile court? We know, of course, that the
home is the best place for the child unless the circumstances are
such that the home itself is emotionally tense and disturbed. Before
the police officer releases the child, he might want to look into the
family's ability to meet the particular problems involved and to provide adequate home life for the child.

The conferees at East Lansing listed the following criteria for
referring the child back to his parents or guardians:

The offense is minor in nature, and there is no apparent
need for treatment.

The child shows no habitual delinquency pattern.

The family situation is stable.

The relationship between the child and his parents is good.

The parents seem aware of the child's problems and able to cope with them.

Adequate help is being given by a public or voluntary agency in the community.

Typical of what is being done by police forces is the program carried on by the Crime Prevention Division in Houston, Texas. Before an appointment is made to this division, an officer must have successfully completed thirteen weeks of training under the direction of the local university and the police department. The division is staffed by detectives, policemen, and policewomen. All cases concerning juveniles are investigated by those staff members. All juvenile delinquent girls are handled exclusively by policewomen. Each member of the staff of the division is carefully chosen for his understanding of juvenile problems. Before appointment he must express a desire to work with juveniles, and he must show ability in this field.

In Texas boys under the age of seventeen and girls under the age of eighteen are considered juveniles. Older persons are subject to the regular criminal laws of the state.

According to L. D. Morrison, Chief of Police of Houston, the program operates as follows after a juvenile offender has been apprehended: One or more members of the Crime Prevention Division are assigned to make a complete investigation to determine the guilt or innocence of the accused juvenile. After the investigation has been completed, the case is handled in one of the two following ways:

The juvenile is released directly to his parents or nearest relative, in the event that his offense is not a serious one and if he is a first offender. The officer working on the case will counsel the parents of the child and help them to work out a program to solve his problem.

Should the case be a serious one, or should the offender be a repeater, then the offender may be released to his parents and referred to the probation department; or he may be taken directly to the probation department and placed in the juvenile detention ward while his case is being further considered.

A special kind of problem that police officers must frequently deal with are cases of neglect. An officer may be called in by a neighbor who pities a child who is hungry or beaten or neglected. The officer is placed in the position of being both a prosecutor and a judge. He must determine whether or not the neglect is real or whether the parents are striving within the limitations of their economic and mental ability to provide a decent home for the child. Unless help is extended to a neglected child, he may become delinquent. The decision of the officer is thus very important and must be made carefully, with the prevention of delinquency in mind.

The parents of neglected children can be brought into court by the police; this often happens. But even when the parents appear in court on neglect charges and promise to take better care of their children, parents usually do not keep these promises either because they don't care or because they have little control over their own environments.

Where, then, shall the neglected child be sent if he is to be taken from his home? Too often our communities do not provide adequate facilities for housing for these neglected children. It is unjust and unreasonable to place them in detention homes for delinquents, or in jail, simply because their homes are not fit for them to live in.

The police officers may refer neglect cases or delinquents in their custody to various other agencies besides the court, agencies that may be far better equipped to deal with them, particularly in the early stages of their development. These agencies may include the child guidance clinic, the family service bureau, the mental hygiene clinic, public agencies serving families and children, visiting teacher services, church groups, and other organizations. The proper referral of a young offender or neglected child to one of these groups, made in time, may well reduce the chances of his ultimately appearing in court. It is important to remember that it is the job of the police to help secure treatment for the delinquent or predelinquent child, as well as to protect the community from his antisocial acts.

A good working relationship between the police department and other community agencies, public and private, is essential. For example, the police officers in the juvenile department must co-operate, not only with the juvenile court, but also with the probation department, with case work agencies, with the schools, with recreation agencies, with health agencies, with business and civic groups, with state agencies, and with the press.

Because of the close relationship between police work with juveniles and the programs of other agencies in the community, and because of the great interest of many laymen in problems affecting youth and children, the United States Office of Education points out that a police department might do well to secure the appointment of a citizens' advisory committee to assist police executives in planning a program on behalf of juveniles.

In testifying before the Senate subcommittee investigating juvenile delinquency, Leroy E. Wike, executive secretary of the International Association of Chiefs of Police, said that the growing number of police departments that are setting up programs directed toward juvenile areas of their community is a welcome sign.

Mr. Wike listed the following activities that forward-looking police departments are including in their programs:

Boys' detail. These officers co-operate generally with juvenile courts, investigating cases and giving opinions as to a program best suited to rehabilitation of a delinquent.

Predelinquent detail. These officers generally operate as a plain-clothes detail, cruising their districts to discover children who are in danger of becoming delinquent and to discover and eliminate moral hazards affecting the youth of the community. Character-building programs are at times suggested when the facts justify them, but the action taken is left entirely to the discretion of parents.

Sports detail. These officers co-operate with recreational departments in the city and sponsor sporting events and award trophies to winning teams.

Summer camps. Some departments operate summer camps for underprivileged children, with YMCA officials, officials of the

Boy Scouts or similar youth organizations, and police juvenile officers supervising the camp activities.

City mothers' bureau. This bureau is generally staffed by policewomen, giving aid and counsel to elderly people and to youngsters who are too old for the jurisdiction of juvenile courts.

Women's probation department. A woman probation officer and a policewoman co-operate in investigating applications for probation and parole of women who have been convicted in court.

Men's probation department. This detail performs functions for men similar to those performed for women by the women's probation department.

Juvenile jail. One crime prevention division has its own juvenile jail for boys between sixteen and seventeen years of age. The boys are held until the court subsequently orders a transfer to the county jail or custodial release to parents or to a social agency.

Boy Scouts sponsorship. Police departments frequently sponsor Boy Scout troops.

Boys' clubs. Some departments have organized nonsectarian boys' clubs. Athletic supplies are furnished, a summer camp is operated, a medical and dental clinic are available, and various activities are sponsored which will appeal to juveniles. Such clubs are most frequently financed by contributions of interested citizens and by means of an annual campaign for funds.

Other programs. Many other programs have been developed, some more intensively than others, such as Big Brother bureaus, Big Sister bureaus, juvenile aid divisions, junior police patrols, police scouts, junior legions of honor, junior sheriff's clubs, sponsorship of youth centers, and delinquent parents' court.

In each instance the aim is to deter activities leading to juvenile crime. The program is administered through the police department by officers who have either special training in the field or special aptitude for the work. Community participation is encouraged.

Many police departments have established special divisions, often called juvenile police bureaus, that deal solely with children and adolescent boys and girls under sixteen, or in some localities, seventeen or eighteen years of age. What does the juvenile police bureau do? Some of the duties that have been suggested as appropriate for such a unit include the following:

Processing to disposition juvenile cases investigated by other units, with the possible exception of traffic cases.

Special patrolling of known juvenile hang-outs, where conditions harmful to the welfare of children are known or suspected.

Maintenance of records on juvenile cases.

Planning a delinquency prevention program, as well as co-operating with other community agencies in implementing the program.

Patrolling juvenile hang-outs is one of the oldest preventive methods used by police. Some of these places include the following: (1) the poolroom or bowling alley where children loiter late at night, where the youngsters are allowed to buy cigarettes, beer, or even hard liquor, where they can receive their first lessons in gambling; (2) the dance hall, bar, or cabaret in which young girls not only drink but may also solicit for immoral purposes; (3) the candy store and other establishments that may sell pornographic literature to youngsters; (4) the various entertainment places, like movie houses, that attract children during school hours and thereby encourage truancy.

For the most part, the police are aware of the existence of these places. Sometimes they are allowed to prosper through corruption, and in many cases, because of an inadequate police staff or lack of community co-operation, very little can be done about them.

Sponsoring recreation programs is a more positive approach taken by police to reduce delinquency. It is certain, first of all, that youngsters develop a far more favorable attitude toward the law when they know law-enforcement officers through a recreation program, in addition to recognizing them as the guys with badges and night sticks. About 50 per cent of the police departments of the country now plan recreation programs for the youth in their areas.

Not enough is being done, however, because there are often too few police officers for each community, too few available recreational facilities. In cases where such programs are undertaken by the police, they should of course be co-ordinated with the rest of the community work program.

In Cleveland, the Police Department maintains a Juvenile Bureau consisting of a captain, a lieutenant, a sergeant, and twenty-five patrolmen. Members of the bureau do not wear police uniforms, nor do they drive cars bearing police markings.

Bureau members do not receive any special training in working with juveniles; they participate in the established program of training for all Cleveland police. Assignment to the bureau is made by the captain in charge; he selects men in the Police Department who indicate a desire to work with juveniles.

The bureau attempts to reduce delinquency to a minimum in four different ways:

The bureau arranges for mass youth attendance at professional sports events. It has helped more than 200,000 boys and girls to attend baseball games of the Cleveland Indians each year, and about 50,000 children to watch the football team of the Cleveland Browns in action.

The bureau organizes recreational activities among adolescent boys. It organizes baseball leagues in various areas of the city; these leagues are handled by the officers of the bureau.

The bureau counsels parents and children in informal hearings. These hearings are conducted by the captain in charge of the bureau at various points throughout the city. They usually concern some minor violation deemed by the bureau not to be serious enough to warrant referral of the offender to the juvenile court.

The bureau sponsors a Juvenile Protective Council, composed of industrial plant personnel, clergy, and businessmen. The purpose of this council is to consider mutual problems, such as vandalism, as well as legislation pertaining to juvenile activity.

Chief Probation Officer John J. Mayar of the juvenile court of Cleveland observes that there are as many different types of police units dealing with juveniles as there are police departments in the country. Usually it is the local situation that determines the type of service the police should give. If the community has a well developed social welfare program and an active, well-integrated recreational division, for example, the need for the police to supply leadership in such areas is minimized, or perhaps completely eliminated.

The Cleveland Police Department operates on the principle that the basic responsibility of the department is law enforcement. It has been unanimously agreed in various committee deliberations in Cleveland that nothing should interfere with this primary function of law enforcement and that all resources of the Juvenile Bureau should be utilized to help make this part of the department's over-all work as effective as possible.

The bureau may sometimes have to go beyond the limitation of what is generally accepted to be law enforcement. This would include such measures as warning children who are getting into difficulty, rather than arresting them immediately for infractions; co-operating with playgrounds, neighborhood clubs and other organizations in maintaining general decorum in the local community. However, Mr. Mayar points out that this type of activity by the Juvenile Bureau should be subordinate to the primary function of law enforcement.

He further suggests that the responsibility for recreational activities, such as athletic leagues and boys' clubs, should be transferred to the Cleveland Recreation Commission. Mr. Mayar also recommends that there should be a closer working relationship between the Juvenile Bureau and welfare agencies. The bureau would then be in a position to refer more cases to the agencies, which are generally better qualified to give the appropriate service.

The relationships between the Juvenile Bureau, the juvenile court, and the school system are excellent in Cleveland. This has been largely responsible for effective control of juvenile delinquency in the area.

Milwaukee offers another good illustration of how a Youth Aid Bureau established by a police department can help to develop programs to reduce juvenile delinquency. The Milwaukee Youth

Aid Bureau was established in 1946 to deal with the problems of youth. Since that time there has been a definite reduction in the number of delinquent acts committed in the city.

The following are the duties of the Youth Aid Bureau, as defined by the Milwaukee Police Department:

To plan and to put into operation whatever measures that may be deemed appropriate for the prevention of juvenile delinquency.

To establish contact and deal personally with the parents of all predelinquents and complainants in such cases.

To establish and maintain contact with social agencies interested in delinquency and assist in working out a program of mutual assistance and co-operation.

To investigate school and other environmental conditions of each predelinquent.

To investigate and attempt to settle neighborhood complaints involving juveniles before court action becomes necessary.

To establish and maintain contact with the Attendance Division of the School Board.

To maintain contact with probation officers and co-operate in all cases of juvenile complaints and juveniles placed on probation.

To avoid, whenever possible, duplication and overlapping of work devolving upon probation and attendance officers in connection with their duties.

To help secure adequate social interests for juveniles, such as clubhouse facilities, playground facilities, etc.

To carry out systematic patrol and investigation of problem areas to ascertain individuals contributing to delinquency.

To be vigilant in the suppression of juvenile delinquency.

To attempt to break up so-called gangs of juveniles and direct them into proper pursuits.

To be observant of children out at unreasonably late hours of the night without proper supervision.

To investigate and report any conditions that may lead to

delinquency, such as improperly supervised dance halls, cabarets, pool and billiard rooms, bowling alleys, and places where delinquency is likely to occur.

Because the problem is so enormous, and because so many criminal careers begin at an early age, crime prevention work in the Milwaukee Police Department now centers around the delinquent and predelinquent child. The Youth Aid Bureau, as a crime prevention unit of the department, seeks to emphasize this point of view—prevention in its approach to delinquency and its treatment.

The program has proved effective in reducing delinquency. Let us look at the records of some of the girls and boys whom the Milwaukee Youth Aid Bureau has been able to help.

One policewoman tells this story: A girl of fourteen was referred to the bureau by her stepfather. The girl had rebelled against her stepfather because of his strict discipline, which was forced upon her against the wishes of her mother. Her misconduct had been a direct result of the conflict between her parents. She did not hesitate to show her dislike for her stepfather openly.

Following a long interview and a discussion with the parents, the policewoman was able to convince the parents, especially the stepfather, that a more understanding attitude toward the girl would bring results. With excellent co-operation from the parents, plus the faith and confidence the girl had in the officer, the girl has now developed a much better behavior pattern. The home is more harmonious because a better understanding exists between the parents and the child.

In another case, involving a group of ten youngsters, the same policewoman discovered that the cause of their misbehavior was a lack of scholastic progress and a real dislike for school. She formed a study club at the Milwaukee Urban League, which met every Saturday morning to assist these children in mathematics, textbook studies, and several other subjects with which they were having difficulty. On several Saturdays these children were taken on outdoor hikes and were encouraged to participate in the many activities provided at the Lapham Park Social Center. From their teachers, it has been learned that this group of children is now progressing favorably. No further complaints about their behavior have come to the attention of the Youth Aid Bureau.

A Milwaukee patrolman reports the case of two brothers, aged thirteen and fourteen, who were wards of the County Home for Dependent Children because divorce had broken up their home. After the mother remarried, she obtained a release for the boys and brought them to their new home. Now the boys were allowed to roam wherever they pleased. Finally they were referred to the Youth Aid Bureau for keeping late hours and for smoking.

The officer made a personal contact with the mother and the boys. After a lengthy discussion, a program was worked out for a better relationship between the boys and their parents. Paper routes were obtained for both boys by the officer. He also interested the boys in joining the Boy Scout troop at their own church.

The boys now attend church services regularly, assist their mother with housework, get to bed early, have refrained from smoking, and turn over the funds from their paper routes and odd jobs they do around the neighborhood to their mother. The parents are co-operating fully and are well pleased with the results of the bureau's services.

The pattern is simple. Someone took a humane interest in the young boys. And this interest was enough to change potential delinquents into normal boys.

In reporting on a group of twenty-five boys who were continually getting into trouble, another Milwaukee officer said, "I contacted this group after several referral cards were turned in by the officer on the beat. One of the boys, seventeen years old, had run away from home in company with another seventeen-year-old boy and their whereabouts were unknown to their parents or to the police. I could not obtain any information about them from the other boys, but I felt they knew where they were and could reach them by mail.

"I put a proposition to them about organizing an athletic club for the purpose of getting a team together to play in the PAL's [Police Athletic League] baseball program, which was to start in the summer. They informed me that one of their best players was one of the runaway boys. After some persuasion the boys agreed to write to this boy to inform him of the new club and program.

"The boy returned home immediately, and I had a good talk with him and with his mother. She thought the program was an excellent one, and to show her appreciation she gave the boys permission to set up their club headquarters in the garage behind her sweet shop.

"The boys acquired the necessary furniture, and are enjoying many group activities. They are orderly and quiet, and no more complaints have been received from this area. They co-operate with the playground director by assisting him in keeping the children busy and maintaining order.

"The father of two of the boys in this gang assisted as coach of the baseball team, and transported the entire team to the many games they played. The team finished in second place in the PAL's North Section League," the Milwaukee police officer notes with justifiable pride.

During the fall and winter the gang made up a football team, three basketball teams, and are now enrolled in the PAL's boxing program. The patrolman says that, since contacting this gang of boys, their attitude toward the Police Department has changed from wisecracks and ridicule to friendliness and co-operation.

Another officer of the Milwaukee Youth Aid Bureau reported on a boy who was a habitual runaway and truant. He would start out for school in the morning and in many instances would never get there, or he would leave school at recess or noontime and stay away from home until late at night.

The officer talked to the boy and the mother. He succeeded in making a friend of the boy by gaining his confidence and instilled in him a sense of loyalty and trust and a better realization of his duties and responsibilities to his parents, his school, and himself. The officer visited the boy frequently; on each visit the boy showed a marked improvement. The mother co-operated very well; she happily reports that the boy has not missed a day at school since the officer's visits began. The mother is grateful to the bureau and to the police officer for the remarkable improvement in her son's behavior.

These cases are typical, and can be duplicated in cities elsewhere in the United States. They illustrate what can be accomplished through the efforts of a well-organized juvenile unit in a police department.

It is necessary to remember, however, that the police by themselves can do no more than a superficial job. But the police force is certainly in an excellent position to help a community discover where the problems lie and to develop the type of co-ordinated program that will attack the delinquency problem effectively.

The Youth Bureau of Chicago is another agency that illustrates the importance of a trained police unit to deal with the problems of youth. In 1946 the police division of the Chicago Park District set up its Youth Bureau. The bureau's job is to work with the predelinquent and the delinquent child. In every case referred to the bureau, a home visit is made, and the parents are interviewed by an officer of the bureau. In this manner both social and police information are accumulated for the juvenile case-history report. The compilation of this data is essential in determining whether or not referral is necessary to some other agency that would assist in bringing about the child's adjustment. Relations have been established with all other agencies that might be interested in co-operating in the program. The bureau's ambition is wide in scope, and allows for research and study of the problem in a realistic manner as well as immediate action.

In order to insure co-operation of the entire police force, the Chicago Police Training Academy established a course for training of police personnel in the field of juvenile delinquency prevention and treatment. All members of the Police Department attended the course.

During 1953 there were 2,821 cases involving children that were referred to the Chicago Youth Bureau for investigation, disposition, and adjustment. In the preceding year, 2,498 cases were similarly processed by the bureau. In other words, an increase of 323 cases, or 13 per cent was shown for the year of 1953 over the year of 1952. It was found that the greatest proportionate increase was in the number of cases involving children from ten to twelve years of age.

Here are some typical cases that the Chicago Youth Bureau tried to help, and in many instances did help, in its program.

After a complaint had been presented to the police by an irate and aroused community group, an intensive investigation was begun at one of the neighborhood parks. The complaint alleged aggravated social misconduct by teen-agers late in the evening. Most offensive was the vulgar and obscene language boisterously rolling from the darkened confines of the park area. In the months preceding the time of the complaint, both the number of the gang of offending youngsters and the amount of bold, daring, promiscuous activities had increased.

Soon after the complaint was received, the police arrested part of the group, six young men and four juveniles; three of the children were girls and one a boy. In the subsequent interview held in the office of the Youth Bureau with the mothers and the juveniles present, a solid front of protestations and denials were made by all concerned. The actual offenders apparently had departed posthaste with the advent of the police.

After acquainting the parents with the serious allegations charged, the bureau requested them to co-operate by determining who the other members of the group were. The parents refused; the mothers were willing to forego the counseling their children needed so badly.

For weeks after the police action, the tranquility of the night remained undisturbed in the park. Then, toward the end of the month, one of the girls in the group was found in a drunken stupor, lying in the park. Through interrogation, and with the help of a now very co-operative parent, the details of this escapade were brought to light.

The girl revealed that a party had been held in a girl's home in the absence of her parents. It was an all-girl gathering of a group who had formed a club called The Robins. Through various kinds of subterfuge the girls had connived to get away from their own homes, assuring their parents that they would be in good company for the evening. Some of them used the dodge of attending their high-school dance. Others said they were going to the movies. Liquor was procured by telephoning and having it delivered to the home; the mother was supposedly indisposed in another room of the house. Several of the girls had dated their boy friends and were to meet them later in the park. Among these was the girl who was found intoxicated.

When all those involved were brought into the family court, they were apparently repentant. Subsequently, after the judge advanced the possibility of commitment to the state training school, both juveniles and their parents had their eyes opened fully.

Law enforcement and preventive delinquency action can only be as effective as the people of a community desire. Without a total integration of effort, no one agency can hope to succeed fully in any endeavor. In this case, had not an aroused citizenry taken action in policing their own community, a decidedly bad situation might have grown much worse. On the other side of the ledger, had others in that community co-operated with the police in the beginning, when their own children were accused of improper behavior, the later developments might well have been avoided.

Another case handled in Chicago involves a juvenile named Daisy. While walking past an interviewing room at the family court, one of the Youth Bureau officers overheard Daisy mention a park in his district. He asked for, and received permission to interrogate the girl. Startling and electrifying information was forthcoming, which resulted in a cleanup of a distasteful and dangerous situation.

Daisy told of having met a group of girls from her high school about a year ago. They talked of exciting happenings which involved a number of young men, most of whom were between eighteen and twenty. After a period of time, stimulated by a curiosity to see for herself the affairs occurring in the locale of the whispered events, she, too, began to frequent the park.

There were about twenty boys and ten girls in the group, which congregated nightly in the same part of the park. Beer drinking and outrageous petting were the end result of these gatherings. As Daisy associated more and more with the group, she soon learned that the boys played for keeps. On one occasion, seated in the rear seat of an automobile parked in the neighborhood, Daisy reported that she was forced to submit to the desires of one young man. Later, she claimed, she was again subjected to sexual molestings, but said she was dazed by a drug put into a drink. The other girls also were involved in the same kind of thing.

Plying naive girls with intoxicating liquors and portraying themselves as men of the world, the young men in the group had succeeded in creating false impressions of sophistication and grandeur. Daisy spoke of the many times one or another young man would produce a gun. Accompanying this display were excitement-laden tales of criminal derring-do. Every now and then, the young men would show wads of money which they said they had taken from victims of their escapades. Many of the youths had automobiles, but Daisy was only familiar with a few in her immediate clique. Almost to a man, those involved in crime had their own "molls" among the teen-aged girls. Daisy hadn't been "spoken for," and so remained a toy for all.

Heated arguments developed between Daisy and her foster parents because of her nightly excursions to the park and elsewhere in the company of these young hoodlums. Daisy's own parents had separated years before. She had been shunted from one foster family to another during her early life. Realization and shame for her actions and the accompanying frictions at home finally prompted the girl to run away, which subsequently resulted in her apprehension and detention by the Chicago Youth Bureau.

When the identities of the group members had been obtained from Daisy, the police started to round them up. Finally all who were connected with the group were detained. Among the group were several male juveniles, one of whom acted as the gunman whenever armed robberies were the night's activity.

The Youth Bureau officer, while interrogating one of the juveniles, obtained a complete confession of the numerous crimes committed by the adult male members of the group. As a result it was possible to clear from police record-books complaints of ten armed robberies, four auto larcenies, and two burglaries.

Five men, along with one juvenile, were indicted by the grand jury. With the exception of Daisy, the other girls were placed under the supervision of the family court. Daisy continued to be detained, pending a plan to enroll her at an out-of-state school.

Precocious youths can become a greater problem to themselves than to their parents or society, especially when the development of the body exceeds that of the mind. In essence that is the story of Marilyn, another girl who came to the attention of the Chicago Youth Bureau. Here is the bureau's report on Marilyn:

"Marilyn first came to our attention about sixteen months ago when she was observed playing truant from school, wandering quite alone through the halls of a museum. Her fourteenth birthday had occurred only a short time before, and she was completing the first semester of high school. Original investigation disclosed she was a good student in school, but disposed to periods of moody daydreaming. Recently she had taken to absenting herself from school without permission.

"Marilyn's parents were divorced three years after her birth, shortly after her only brother was born. Both children were placed in the hands of aged, maternal grandparents, while the mother worked. After several years, the mother remarried and again took up the full time task of rearing her children. This marriage was never a particularly happy one, there being almost constant strife about money and the amount needed to raise the children. A move was made in which the family obtained an apartment in the same building as the grandparents, where once again they could attend to the children. With that, the mother went to work.

"Family affairs continued inharmonious, however. When Marilyn was twelve, her mother had divorced her second husband.

"For years the grandmother had been unable to administer more than token discipline to the children. Marilyn and her brother never enjoyed the love and attention so necessary to growing youngsters. And grow Marilyn did.

"When first we knew her, she weighed 165 pounds and was over average height. Because of this, she appeared much older than her years. During her first year in school she bore the brunt of many ill-natured jibes by her classmates. Her escape was to associate with girls years older and, in many instances, years wiser than she was. To keep up the masquerade of belonging and being wanted, she entered into the spirit and doings of these older girls, most of whom were out of school.

"Within a short period of time her academic work had suffered to such an extent that she was transferred to a social adjustment school. Also during this time she had again come to our attention, but now as a sex delinquent, necessitating referral to the family court.

"Prior to this, the Youth Bureau officer had attempted to stimulate the mother into a constructive program for her daughter. It was obvious that Marilyn would profit from having an interested and affectionate parent, and from losing her excess weight. The mother promised to co-operate, and to place her daughter under a physician's care. The mother did not keep her promise since she was too interested in pursuing a new affair of her own.

"Nevertheless, Marilyn's mother, as well as her grandmother, came to rely heavily upon the Youth Bureau officer's ability to cope with their problems. Every other week, for a time, one or the other would come to us with a new problem, or a new angle on an old one. In addition, Marilyn would tell her side of the story, for she said the officer was about the only one who would listen to her.

"Then, for an eight-month period, while the girl and her mother were under the supervision of a family court worker, the Youth Bureau did not hear from them. And then once more a referral was made to the Youth Bureau, this time in another part of the city. The officer assigned to the case, by checking with headquarters, knew that Marilyn's case had been handled previously, and received some background on the case.

"A lengthy talk in the presence of a sympathetic policewoman revealed the mental tortures Marilyn was suffering due to her excessive weight. A plan was subsequently evolved whereby Marilyn would join a weight-reduction class. She was also enrolled in an art course.

"At the last report Marilyn was pursuing both courses industriously. With both body and mind actively occupied, we can only hope a partial answer to her needs is being supplied."

Even a partial answer is worth attaining. The help that the police are giving Marilyn—and the hundreds of others in similar difficulties—is of tremendous value. Again, we see that the police officers are not attacking the problem with a punishment philosophy.

William J. Szarat, Chicago police captain and director of the Chicago Park District's Youth Bureau, points out that, while the bureau is not directly connected with the Chicago public school system, it has developed a close working relationship with the principals, adjustment teachers, and truant officers. In all cases that have school-connected problems, the police staff of the bureau works with the school personnel in an effort to bring about a satisfactory adjustment.

Captain Szarat told me that each member of the bureau's staff receives special training in its Youth Bureau Institute, with respect to the sociological, psychological, legal, and practical aspects of the problem. In addition to this training, all these police officers have taken a number of courses in schools of social studies at local universities. The balance of the Police Department has received some training through the medium of the In-service Police Training Academy.

"The philosophy of the bureau is to use the courts only as a last resort, only after we have exhausted every other community resource," Captain Szarat said. "The exception occurs in the most aggravated cases, where we have no alternative but to refer to the court for formal disposition.

"I like to refer to this approach as the social police approach to the problem. In every case referred to the bureau for investigation, one of the bureau officers goes directly into the home of the offender for an interview with the parents or guardians. He gathers social information for the purpose of trying to determine some of the unmet needs of the family that might be encouraging the development of antisocial behavior. In many instances it is necessary for us to have professional diagnosis made to help us in this determination. Once it is made, then the bureau makes a referral to an agency in the community that is best equipped to cope with the child and his problem."

"In the majority of instances," continued Captain Szarat, "referral to appropriate agencies for therapy has been very effective in helping the child to adjust satisfactorily."

Detroit is another city that has developed an excellent Youth Bureau program in connection with its Police Department. It co-operates with Wayne University, under the direction of Professor William W. Wattenberg, in the university's research alliance with the Child Study Clinic of the Wayne County Juvenile Court. Twice a month the group has a luncheon at which it considers the developments in the field of juvenile delinquency.

The Detroit Police Department Youth Bureau was founded in 1950. It incorporated the Boys' Juvenile Bureau, the Crime Prevention Bureau, the School Safety Section, and a part of the Woman's Division which had dealt principally with delinquency.

The Youth Bureau is primarily concerned with behavior problems, street traffic safety, and the protection and personal safety of children. In order to carry out these objectives, the bureau is divided into four sub-divisions; the Boys' Behavior Section, the Girls' Behavior Section, the School Safety Section, and the Statistical and Research Section.

The Boys' Behavior Section is composed of fifty uniformed patrolmen. Three men are assigned to each of the fifteen police precincts, where offices and records pertaining to their work are kept. These men receive complaints and information relating to juvenile offenders.

They make necessary investigations of crimes committed by juveniles in their precincts and make the necessary dispositions of the boys involved. According to Inspector Ralph Baker, Commanding Officer, Youth Bureau, of the Detroit Police Department, every effort is made to determine the cause of a child's misbehavior, and every effort is made to eliminate the cause, if possible.

The officers of the Youth Bureau screen out minor offenders and try to deal with them at a precinct level by means of parental co-operation or referral to some agency within the city which is equipped to deal with their particular problems.

In serious offenses, children may be sent to the detention home, where they are held during investigation of their cases. These cases are often taken to the juvenile court, where responsibility for re-habilitation and correction becomes a court function.

The precinct officers are also concerned with the problems of children who are not involved in infractions of the law. In the interest of forestalling delinquency, they solicit the aid of community organizations to carry on active programs for youth. The officers are thus able to direct unaffiliated youth from a street corner to wholesome activities in the neighborhood.

In connection with the educational aspect of the Detroit program, the Youth Bureau has two officers who devote their full time to the intermediate and secondary schools. The Board of Education has co-operated in making it possible for these officers to go through entire schools, giving two-hour talks to groups of thirty-five to forty children at a time. These talks are designed to teach good citizenship to the children by showing them the relationship of law, courts, police department, and their own responsibility in the total community picture.

The Girls' Behavior Section of the Detroit Youth Bureau is composed of eleven policewomen and a policewoman sergeant. They have the responsibility of investigating all cases of misbehavior on the part of juvenile girls. At present they work out of the central office. They deal with the girls in the same manner as the male officers deal with the boys. When the policewomen are not actually engaged in investigation work, they spend their time on patrol and visit places where youth congregates. They are constantly on the lookout for those circumstances which tend to cause young people to become delinquent.

The School Safety Section is responsible for the street safety of all school children in Detroit. Officers train and supervise the work of the safety patrol boys. They make checks and surveys of school crossings and make recommendations for the placement of traffic control devices. Their program also includes talks to school assemblies to teach the children safe walking and playing habits.

The annual report for 1953 of the Detroit Youth Bureau states that 36,249 juvenile boys and girls were contacted by the behavior sections of the bureau. A total of 2,991 girls were in trouble, as compared with 20,126 boys. Another 13,132 boys and girls were not involved in any offenses but met with officers to obtain advice or assistance with their plans or problems.

As the report points out, youth work on the part of police officers entails skill in the investigation of crime; it requires knowledge of the social problems of a community; and perhaps most important it requires the knowledge, the ability, and the desire to take a course of action that will be most beneficial to the future of young Americans.

The work to be done by the police departments throughout the United States in combating juvenile delinquency is still far from complete. Indeed, many of our communities do not yet have any type of juvenile delinquency program in their police departments.

The Michigan State Police does not have a juvenile delinquency bureau. The officers are merely trained in the routine police training of a nine-week period in all phases of police work although they do work closely with the county probate judges who handle juvenile cases. In addition, officers give talks at rural schools, show motion pictures, and take part in other related activities in co-operation with the parent-teacher groups.

Commenting on this limited activity, Police Captain C. K. Dymond said of the Michigan State Police, "We do not have a follow-up method to determine the effectiveness of these activities other than our yearly records, which might indicate a trend one way or the other as to the juvenile cases."

At best, it is doubtful that delinquency will be reduced by occasional lectures given to school children by police officers. Far greater concentration on the problem is needed to bring about effective results.

The average, decent police officer with a love for children is without a doubt doing a good job in patrolling his beat. But that officer alone can hardly do the necessary job that is important in today's ever-growing problem of treating juvenile delinquents. There are obstacles in the way of securing better juvenile police. These obstacles include low salary scales, high turnover, and lack

of training facilities. It is not always the fault of the police departments when punitive methods are used. In many communities the
police officers are overtaxed and overextended in the type of work
they already do. They simply do not have the time, the personnel,
or the budgetary provisions necessary for engaging in an effective
program.

Training of officers, education of the public, and the closest possible working relationships with all community agencies in the
juvenile delinquency field must be stressed in every police force.
This is doubly important because the police department itself is in
an extremely strategic position for pulling together and stimulating
all community efforts relating to delinquency prevention and
control. Police Superintendent Thomas R. Jones of Minneapolis
lists the following essential characteristics of sound police services
for children, which will undoubtedly be accepted by police officials,
as well as by informed educators and laymen, everywhere:

*Proper recognition by police officials of the importance of the
problem in their particular jurisdictions.* One of the requisites
of arriving at a true picture of the juvenile problem is to have
accurate and factual statistical data relating to delinquency. The
lack of such data is one of the great weaknesses of many communities in evaluating their own problems. The fact that over
40 per cent of all major crime in the United States is committed
by persons who are twenty-one years old or younger should
be sufficient to rouse people everywhere to recognize the importance of collecting data on conditions in their own communities.

*Sufficient police personnel to cope with the problem in each
particular jurisdiction.* The larger communities should have
separate divisions for juvenile work, composed of personnel
who have had training in this highly specialized field. In smaller
communities regular police personnel may have to assume these
duties. In either the small or large community, however, nothing can take the place of sufficient officers for patrolling the
streets, parks, theaters, and other places where children are
found.

Proper training and instruction for all police officers having contact with juveniles. It is especially essential that police officers assigned to specialized juvenile units be equipped to recognize the causative factors of delinquency, and to utilize the facilities of available community agencies.

Adequate detention facilities. The lack of proper detention facilities results in many evils. Foremost among these is the holding of children in jails with adult offenders or in quarters that would tend to add to their antisocial tendencies.

Maintenance of complete records and files on all juvenile services. In view of the startling statistics on crimes committed by juveniles and the all-too-prevalent fact that today's delinquent too often becomes tomorrow's adult criminal, no unnecessary obstacles should be created which will prevent the police from carrying out their primary obligations to the whole community.

Complete co-operation with all available community agencies. It is absolutely necessary that the police maintain the highest degree of co-operation with all other agencies in the community. The number and scope of the available agencies are directly related to the duties and responsibilities which must be assumed by police departments. In large communities, where there are a number of agencies concerning themselves with case work, recreational programs, social problems, and other related fields, the police may assist themselves and the community greatly by referring cases to the proper agency for investigation and treatment.

At all times we must remember that there is no such thing as a bad boy or a bad girl. We must look beyond the act itself into the personality of the actor. Only when we approach the problem on the level of treating the cause of the delinquent act rather than the child's act itself, will we begin to make any substantial progress in reducing delinquency.

The role of the police department in this momentous task is a serious and important one. Today, with the increasing attention being given to the juvenile bureaus of our police departments, we can justifiably hope that the departments will play their parts effectively.

12. Delinquency: Only a Legal Term

". . . we haven't sorted out the children."

In the early 1800's in England and elsewhere children of eleven or twelve were sometimes condemned to death for stealing. This is what one reporter wrote in verse to describe the scene when a twelve-year-old child was condemned to death for stealing in London:

> *When he was sentenced at the bar,*
> *The court was drowned in tears*
> *To see a child so soon cut off*
> *All in his tender years.*

Since the lad had committed what was a crime in the eyes of the law, he had to hang from the same gallows used for the execution of hardened criminals.

Why did the twelve-year-old child in London steal? Was it because he was hungry? Was it because he had no parents to guide him? Was it because he was emotionally sick? The judge did not ask; evidently he was not concerned with that. It is important that our courts be concerned with these questions now. It is important that our courts define "juvenile delinquency" in order to find a cure.

Dr. Sophia M. Robison, Professor Emeritus of Social Work Research at the New York School of Social Work, indicated three main categories of delinquency. In the first are "troublesome, disruptive juveniles, whose healthy, active spirits have not been properly channeled." Children in the second group are those who are "try-

263

ing to work out relationships with their parents, who may themselves be emotionally upset." Such children may steal to "get even" with parents whom they feel do not love them enough. The third group comprises the emotionally disturbed children who need psychiatric treatment for their violently aggressive and destructive tendencies.

Dr. Robison makes a highly justified criticism of our law courts when she says, "We have made no progress with the problem because we haven't sorted out the children. We treat all the children who come to the courts the same—we call them delinquent." It is the legal sense of "delinquency" and "delinquent" that is under discussion. Dr. Robison gives an apt illustration of the inconsistency of laws relating to juvenile delinquency when she points out that "a boy who steals a watermelon in the country is a prankster, while a boy who steals a banana in the city is a juvenile delinquent."

There is inconsistency from one community to another. One community may be more lenient than another. Even one area within one community may be more lenient than another area. We may find more apprehended delinquents in some areas, for example, because the police are more alert to them, with the result that a boy may take a car without permission of the owner in an underprivileged area and be apprehended immediately, whereas four blocks west, in an upper-economic-class neighborhood, the owner of a "borrowed" car may not press charges, and the incident will be written off merely as a symptom of understandable growing pains of the boy. One culprit thus may become a juvenile delinquent statistic; the other may go unnoticed.

A report on juvenile delinquency in the schools, prepared in 1951 by the New York City Board of Education, made this point: "The child who steals and is apprehended is legally a delinquent; *the one who steals without being apprehended is not* [my italics]. The boy who breaks a store window and whose parents refuse, or are unable, to pay for it is a delinquent; the one whose parents pay for it is not. The boy from a culturally deprived home who is involved in sex difficulties is frequently labeled delinquent; the one from a home better able to care for him is not."

We must not indiscriminately label all boys and girls who get into trouble. One boy with whom I spoke at a public training school said to me, hatred and frustration in his voice, "You want to know how I got here? Well, I'll tell you. Me and my buddy went over to the other side of the block—you know, the high-class one. We met up with some guys there, and we decided to cop a car. The four of us drove away, but we got caught. Sure, we went before the judge. Me and my buddy got sent here for eighteen months, but the fancy guys got a fancy lawyer and got nothing. So now I'm bad. They was just as bad as me. I'm mad as hell about it."

Four boys committed the crime. From now on the records will show that two of them are delinquent, and two are not. Delinquency? Only a legal term.

Before further examination of legal notions of juvenile delinquency, let us consider for a moment the meaning of the term in another sense. In its ordinary usage, "delinquency" carries with it the suggestive significance of criminality, bad character, chronic misbehavior of a serious nature. No one but a puritanical and dyspeptic judge would consider a boy who steals a banana to be a juvenile delinquent. Let us suppose, however, that this boy is a persistent pilferer of fruit stands, candy counters and ten-cent stores, that he has been warned time and again, that his thefts have been reported to his parents and to his teachers, that he has been punished, that threats have been made to send him away. Nevertheless, though he may have promised countless times "never to do it again," he continues to steal, and he continues to be caught at it. Whether or not he ever suffers the stigma of "adjudicated delinquent," he is unquestionably a child in trouble. Not only the child but also his parents deserve the attention of the psychiatrist and the social worker.

In the absence of such a behavior pattern of chronic antisocial activity, can the commission of a single act convert an otherwise well-behaved child into a delinquent? Psychiatrists and social workers would consider such a circumstance unlikely. They would expect to find a syndrome, that is, a collection of symptoms or danger signals which, to an observant parent or teacher, would serve as a warning of possible trouble ahead. The law, however, typically takes the point of view that the courts can concern themselves only with the proximate causes. *The act, not the actor, is considered of first importance.* Both adults and children are tried for the commission of overt acts which infringe statutes and criminal codes. A single act committed by a child which, if it were committed by an adult and were to constitute a crime, is sufficient to warrant placing a child in an institution, the court may feel. And whatever its contrary pretensions, in 90 per cent of the cases, the function of that institution will be to hold the child in custody rather than to provide the type of remedial treatment that will prevent his becoming a criminal.

Legal concepts as to what constitutes delinquency vary from state to state. In the recent subway gang-vandalism case in New York it was possible for the courts to try a sixteen-year-old ringleader as an adult. In Massachusetts or Michigan, where the upper age limit of juvenility is seventeen, if the ringleader had been found guilty, he would have been dealt with as a juvenile delinquent. There are many paradoxes in the laws of the several states and certain deplorable inconsistencies.

The Senate subcommittee pointed out that "dispositions by juvenile courts oftentimes are more restrictive and penalizing than would have resulted through criminal court action. A youngster found delinquent for shoplifting, for example, may, under minority commitment to a training school, be institutionalized for several years. An adult, convicted for the same offense in many jurisdictions, could not be given a sentence of more than a year." It was, in fact, pointed out to the subcommittee that in certain jurisdictions juveniles preferred to be treated as adults because they felt they would get off easier before a criminal court.

Dr. Milton L. Barron of Cornell University, points out in his book on *The Juvenile in Delinquent Society:* "The laws generally agree in defining a delinquent child as one who is over seven years of age, and under sixteen to under twenty-one years of age, and who violates any law of the state or commits any act that, if committed by a person above this age group, would be an offense punishable other than by death or life imprisonment; or who is habitually truant from school, incorrigible, ungovernable, habitually disobedient and beyond the control of his parents or other persons in custodial charge of him. In short, the laws generally cover not only most violations for which adults are held responsible, but they also burden children with the responsibility for the avoidance of a number of ambiguous and indefinite acts, conditions, and behavior problems presumably peculiar to children and representing no violation of law if committed by adults."

The list of "other acts or conditions" that may bring a child within the jurisdiction of the juvenile court—aside from the common denominator of incorrigibility, ungovernability, and habitual disobedience—includes "immoral and indecent conduct, immoral conduct at school, knowing association with vicious or immoral persons, growing up in idleness or crime, knowing entrance and visit of a house of ill repute, patronizing a policy-slip or gaming place, patronizing public poolrooms, wandering about railroad yards or tracks, jumping a train or entering a car or engine without authority, habitually using obscene or vulgar language in public places, loitering and sleeping in alleys, using intoxicating liquors, comporting oneself so as to injure oneself or others, smoking cigarettes, being in an occupation or situation dangerous to oneself or others, begging or receiving alms, or being in the street for the purpose thereof . . ." etc.

Dr. Barron adds that, in its definition of delinquent behavior, no state includes all of these items, but that various state laws have an average of eight or nine of them in addition to violations of already enacted laws.

So we can see that even the question of what constitutes a delinquent act is an open one.

There is also the question of the difference between the varying legal definitions of juvenile delinquency as compared with the definitions of child behavior given by sociology and psychiatry. The intelligent trends today, fortunately, are toward a more humane conception of delinquency, with greater attention paid to the possibility of rehabilitating the child as a potentially useful member of society. Unfortunately, as we have discussed, because of the current increase in juvenile crime, there may also be a trend in the opposite direction, a merely punitive trend that is clearly motivated by fear and anger.

Except in the eyes of the law there is no real hard and fast distinction between the delinquent—that is, the 400,000 "legally delinquent" children, who have broken the laws and have then been referred to the juvenile courts—and nondelinquent children. These adjudged delinquents represent approximately 2 per cent of all children in the ten-to-seventeen age group.

The problem before us is not only how we are to deal with the 2 per cent of our children who are adjudged delinquent, but how we are to deal with children generally.

How do we judge a person to be delinquent? As Abraham G. Novick, superintendent of the New York State Training School for Girls at Hudson, New York, said, "The word delinquency is a legal term. In some areas there is no difference between a delinquent and a nondelinquent. It is only a difference of degree." Dr. Novick points out that, after the period in which aggressive, destructive behavior is normal, around the ages of two to four, the average child gives up some of this pleasurable behavior; as you may recall, to a two-year-old, aggressive, destructive behavior is pleasurable. But through affection, love, and healthy attention to him as a person, through discipline, his control widens and he slowly gives up habits that later are known as antisocial.

Thus in the early stages all of us could be considered delinquent. One difference between delinquency and nondelinquency, then, is the age level. Many of us remain children emotionally. We just have not grown up.

The important consideration is what motivates the boy or girl at eight years and over to commit the act that we glibly label "delinquent." When we recognize the difference between the act itself and the boy or girl behind the act, we will be better able to find the answer and to treat the individual. This requires calm, reasonable judgment. Delinquency may be only a legal term, but it has a highly charged emotional content. We must find out why youth escapes into antisocial sets—and how to prevent this from happening. And we must find it out without hysteria. In a speech made January 11, 1955, to the New Jersey Legislature, Governor Robert B. Meyner made this plea for a firmly grounded approach:

"I now turn to the ever-present problem of juvenile delinquency.

Upon a state level, we have commissions and committees which are engaged in a study of this situation. Additionally, many public-spirited groups and organizations are giving their attention to this problem. Here and throughout the country, there is a tendency to pass what can be properly termed stopgap legislation.

"We should not, in any event, minimize the seriousness of this situation or despair of its solution, but, on the other hand, we should not be unwisely led into the passage of unreasonable or unworkable legislation."

13. The Courts

"It is as though an ambivalent society created a new institution and then, not being sure about what it had wrought, provided so few new resources that the institution could not flourish."

Jimmy had been at the training school for ten months when I paid my visit on Friday morning. He was listed to go home on Sunday. A dark-haired eleven-year-old, he stood close to the director of the school, almost leaning on him, looking to him for some approbation, some show of affection.

"Going home Sunday, Jimmy?" I asked.

"I—don't think so," he said.

I saw a tear coming into his eyes. "I think my mom has moved. She didn't know my address."

Then he brightened up. "I made four belts," he said, "one for my mother, one for my father, one for my sister and one for my younger brother."

"Why are you here?" I asked.

"I was getting in trouble," he said. "I was going away from school. I took money to buy candy from a store, but I won't do that any more.

"The worst thing about it here is that you can't go to see your mother and father," he added. "I could have seen her last Christmas, but I didn't get an answer from my mother and I didn't get an answer on Easter, either. I haven't got no letter from my mother in eight months. The first one I got from my father was six months ago. I ain't gotten one since, but I write twice a month anyway.

"Maybe I have the wrong address. Mom don't seem to get my

270

letters. I was in camp last week. I wrote three letters from camp. I'm anxious to get back home."

He stopped.

"Come back a bit later, Jimmy," the superintendent said. "Maybe you want to go out now and take your lunch."

"What's the story?" I asked.

"The father is alcoholic," he said. "He pays little attention to the boy. He is financially unstable. He is reluctant to accept the child. He heads an unstable family. Jimmy's mother has rejected him for whatever reason, I don't know. Yet the boy will not accept that. He keeps asking for his mother. He keeps asking, 'When will my mother write me?' Guess we'll have to place him in a foster home. I mentioned that to the parents and they seemed only too glad to get rid of him."

I looked up the record. It was curt, brief, as such records are: ". . . while playing in the neighbor's home with their son, subject entered the bedroom and stole their wallet. The subject appeared in juvenile court and was charged with larceny. Age of child, 9."

At the age of nine, Jimmy had become a common criminal. The report went on: "It might be stated here that the county judge was reluctant to commit subject and probably would not have done so had it not been for the complete disrespect shown the court by subject when the judge attempted to counsel him to some degree. In discussion with the subject, the judge asked him what he would do if he, the judge, left his wallet on the desk and went out of the room. Subject's immediate answer was that he would steal it. The judge didn't have to leave the room, he would steal it anyhow."

What is behind this case history?

The family lives in a second-floor five-room apartment which they rent for fifty dollars a month. They are behind in their rent by one month. They live in a middle-class residential area where the delinquency rate is comparatively low.

Let's go a bit further. The father, James, Sr., is now waiting entrance to a general hospital as a disabled veteran. However, the father, because of excessive drinking, is a disturbing influence at home.

"This is a very tense and almost explosive family situation

since the family at this immediate point is terrifically financially pressed. The father has been unemployed for quite some time and when he is able to do work, it must be a specialized type because of his severe nervous condition. The family has received three grants from the Welfare Department of $25 each."

The tension at the home is intense. Go back to the boy. At the age of four he was sent to an orphanage where he remained until he was eight. According to his mother he had been a constant source of trouble to her. His main diversion was that of smashing his toys. He didn't belong to any clubs because they wouldn't have him. The boy then built up an "I don't care" attitude. The family situation is poor financially and the boy's coming back will not help it. The boy has not received any Christmas gifts from his family and they resented having him visit home.

"Come in, Jimmy, come in. Have a good lunch?"

"Oh, yes."

He came in.

"What happened, Jimmy?" I asked, as he sat down with me, a smile on his face. He had been tense until this time.

"I was bad in school," Jimmy began. "I took money out of the store, the delicatessen store. The man wasn't there, but the police caught me. Once I was playing with my boy friend. I took five dollars from his home. The boy told my mother. She hollered at me and spanked me. The other boy's mother called the police. They took me to the police headquarters. The police said I'd be sent away. They locked me up, asked me why I took it, and I said I wanted the money, I wanted to get some candy and a water pistol. I wanted to get a cap pistol and a magic sword. I want to be a magic man when I grow up." He looked at me with a smile.

"A magician?" I asked.

"Yes, you know, like pulling rabbits out of a hat and things like that. Mother never had time for me. She had to take care of my baby brother. I was just like a regular boy around the house, I mean somebody who didn't belong in the house. I like to be with my mother. She buys me games for Christmas and on my birthday. She had a big birthday party for me once. Two boys came."

"Who were they?" I asked.

"One was my little brother and one was my big brother.

"When I get bad," he added, "I get spanked and sent to bed without anything to eat. My father likes my baby brother. He brings him candy, and sometimes games and a surprise for him in his lunchbox, but he never brings me anything. That's because I'm not little any more. I'm going to save some money, though. I want to buy some flowers for Mother's Day. I wasn't home for Mother's Day this year. I made a potholder for her. I'm keeping it here. I'll give it to her. I'll give her the potholder and a bracelet, belt, a pair of earrings, and a big pin."

He looked up at me.

"Do you want to see them?"

"Oh, yes, I'd love to."

He brought them out a few minutes later. "Here they are," and he showed me the little trinkets which he had made under the guidance of the workshop instructor.

"I'm going to give her a hug and a kiss because that's all I want. I want nothing from my mother. I want to help her pay the bills. I don't have to get lots of stuff from my mother. I want to give her things to make her feel happy. I'm going to work and get some money.

"She likes flowers. She likes violets. I'm going to buy her some violets. I want to ask them for the address of my mother. I want to see where my mother moved to. I want to see what's going on. I'm going to write to my probation officer. I'm going to say, 'Will you please see if my mother moved; if not, what's wrong with her? Is she sick? Why can't she write?' I'd like a letter from my mother. Everybody else here gets letters. Why can't I get just one letter from my mother? That's all I want."

Tears came to his eyes.

"Will you see if you can find where my mother moved to?" Jimmy asked hesitantly. "Just so that I could write to her so that she would get my letter? That's all I want. Goodbye. See you some other day."

He suddenly became cheerful again, walked out of the room.

What is to be done? To return the boy to his home would be tempting fate. The boy is apparently well steeped in delinquency.

Would he do better in a foster home, away from a highly nervous father and a terrifically overburdened mother?

"Since he will not be twelve years old until the end of 1955, is there not some possible way that supervision could be transferred back to the social service bureau in view of the sordid home conditions to which he will have to return otherwise?" the social worker asks in the report. The report goes on: "The parole officer considers his home emotionally inadequate and believes the parents incapable of effective supervision. The mother does not want the boy to come back home. The mother asked that the boy be placed in a foster home. There is both an emotional and financial instability in the home of this child."

What is society's responsibility toward this boy?

In 1899 the state of Illinois passed a law that has since become a milestone in the history of social legislation. The Chicago Bar Association Committee had successfully fought for the passage of the first juvenile court law in this country. "The fundamental idea of the law," the Chicago Bar Association said, "is that the state must step in and exercise guardianship over a child found under such adverse social or individual conditions" that crime is encouraged. "It proposes a plan whereby he may be treated, not as a criminal, or legally charged with crime, but as a ward of the state, to receive practically the care, custody and discipline that are accorded the neglected and dependent child. . . ."

Since the passage of that law in Illinois many other states throughout the country have tried to introduce a legal philosophy that considers neglected and delinquent children of the state as individuals who can be helped to grow into useful, constructive members of the community.

There is a growing trend throughout the country to set up specialized courts dealing solely with children, commonly known as children's courts. In a study made by the federal Children's Bureau, in co-operation with the National Probation and Parole Association and the National Council of Juvenile Court Judges, a new approach to the subject of juvenile courts is suggested. In the bureau's publication, "Standards for Specialized Courts Dealing with Children," issued in 1954, the philosophy behind the courts is clearly outlined. Among the criteria set up for a good court is the objective that the legal constitutional rights of both parents and children should be protected.

The question of the proper balance between what is the right of the child or the parents and what is the responsibility of the court is one that has never been fully resolved. On the one hand, some authorities favor a court that has complete freedom on the steps to be taken on behalf of a juvenile offender. This is predicated on the point of view that "to save a child from becoming a criminal the Legislature surely may provide for the salvation of such a child . . . by bringing it into one of the courts of the State without any process at all. . . . The act is but an exercise by the State of its supreme power over the welfare of its children, under which it can take a child from its father and let it go where it will . . . if the welfare of the child . . . can be thus best promoted."

There is a tendency for this point of view to be adopted less frequently. However, we do not take the position of adopting the extreme opposite point of view, which is based on the principle that the child and the parent must remain free of any judicial interference in their lives, beyond meting out punishment for committing infractions of the law.

On this score there has been a great deal of progress during the past fifty years. Now the principle that a child who is involved in delinquency is in need of, and has a right to receive, treatment is more widely accepted than it was a half-century ago. Indeed, juvenile courts have been set up on the basis of providing children with a better outlook on life and of equipping judges with the facilities necessary for the recognition of children in trouble so that offenders may receive help, rather than the birch rod.

In writing in Pauline V. Young's book on *Social Treatment in Probation and Delinquency*, Roscoe Pound suggests the importance of a flexible, as well as a humane approach in the children's courts. The great jurist said, "The powers of the Star Chamber were a trifle in comparison with those of our Juvenile Courts and Courts of Domestic Relations. . . . It is well known that too often the placing of a child in a home, or even in an institution, is done casually or perfunctorily, or even arbitrarily. . . . Even with the most superior personnel, these tribunals call for legal checks."

Proceedings in the children's court must be based on the assumption that the welfare of the children themselves is the first consideration. It is a tremendous emotional shock for a child to be torn away from his home, even if that home may be upset by dissension, distrust, disturbance, and unhappiness. Proof of this is found in the fact that, when a child is asked if he wants to leave home, he almost invariably answers no. Further, he is even likely to say, "I love my parents," even though in reality his love may have long since been turned into hate—conscious or unconscious. I have spoken to hundreds of children in training schools, reform schools, and foster homes. When I asked them, "Would you want to return home?" almost without exception, the answer has been, "I can hardly wait to get back."

The solution, then, is not to seek the line of least resistance in dealing with delinquents who come from unfavorable home situations; in other words, not to have courts that will dispose perfunctorily of cases by having young offenders committed to institutions or to foster homes. The solution is rather to equip the courts to co-operate with the child and his own family in eliminating the factors that have brought about an emotionally disturbed, maladjusted child.

A court does have the legal right to send a child away from his home temporarily, or even to take a child away from his parents completely and place him in a foster home. But there are certain principles that should guide court action in these cases. These principles are listed in "Standards for Specialized Courts Dealing with Children," as follows:

> The conditions under which the State is empowered to intervene in the upbringing of a child should be specifically and clearly delineated in the statutes. Whenever the State seeks to intervene, it should be required to show that those conditions do in fact exist with respect to a child or the community, or both. The State should not be able to interfere with the rights of the parents with respect to their child and assume jurisdiction

over such child on the generalized assumption that the child is in need of the care or protection of the State, or merely because it disagrees with the parent as to the "best course to pursue in rearing a child."

Both the child and his parents are entitled to know the bases on which the State seeks to intervene and on which it predicates its plan for the care and treatment of the child. They are equally entitled to rebut these bases either directly by questioning witnesses, or indirectly by presenting facts to the contrary.

The statutes should authorize the court to take specific actions in relation to certain causes rather than allow it unlimited discretion to make any disposition, or to order any treatment that it may think advisable.

There should be certain procedural safeguards established for the protection of the rights of parents and children. Although parties in these proceedings may seldom make use of such safeguards, their existence is, nonetheless, important.

According to the report, if these principles are observed, the rights of society will be protected; at the same time the child and his parents will be treated fairly in such fashion that the family unit will be preserved and the child's welfare promoted.

When the state does assume authority, or partial authority over the child, by reason of his delinquency or because of his parents' neglect, the problem is one of deciding on the best steps to be taken to bring about a solution that is beneficial to the community, as well as to the individual concerned. Before final action is taken in any case, there should certainly be a thorough investigation of the offender himself, as well as his family situation.

Such an investigation may well furnish the basis on which the judge is to make a decision on the case. It may help in answering such questions as these: What is behind the delinquent act? Are the parents doing the necessary job? Is there evidence that the child is being neglected or rejected by his family? Is this his first offense? Is there a history of delinquency on the part of his parents, as well as on the part of the child?

After the judge has received the answers to these and other questions through reports of workers in other agencies, he is likely to be in a better position to reach a just decision on the case. He should bear in mind one of the cardinal principles in child care, as stated by Katherine F. Lenroot, in the foreword to "Juvenile Court Standards," "There should be a presumption in favor of keeping the child in his own home and his own community, except where adequate investigation shows this not to be in the best interest of the child."

Undoubtedly the most important single factor in the entire program of our juvenile courts consists of the qualifications of the judge. Needless to say, the judge should be a member of the bar in his or her own state, and he should have experience in the practice of law. In addition, it is essential that he be (1) deeply concerned about the rights of people, (2) keenly interested in the problems of children and families, (3) sufficiently aware of the findings and processes of modern psychology, psychiatry, and social work to enable him to give due weight to the findings of these sciences and professions, (4) able to evaluate evidence and situations objectively, uninfluenced by his own personal concepts of child care, (5) eager to learn, (6) competent as an administrator, and able to delegate administrative responsibility, (7) able to conduct hearings in a kindly manner and to talk to children and adults sympathetically and on their level of understanding, without loss of the essential dignity of the court.

It is essential that politics be kept out of the judge's chambers at all times. In the children's court, more than in any other court, the judge should not be subjected to the whims of local politicians, whose endorsement and support may depend upon whether or not the judge has "played ball."

In appearing before the Senate subcommittee hearing on delinquency, William B. McKesson, judge of the Superior Court of California, and judge of the juvenile court of Los Angeles County, suggested how great a gap there is between what children's courts can do and what they actually do. He related that he was on the bench for only a few months when a committee of judges came to him and suggested that he be placed in the children's court.

He went on to say, "I explained to this committee several reasons why I should not be assigned to the juvenile court. With these reasons I thought I had an adequate answer, until they finally said, 'After all, Bill, you are the newest judge in the court, so you haven't any choice in the matter anyhow.'

"That is the way I got into the juvenile court field. That is, unfortunately, the way many judges get into juvenile courts—not because of prior training or experience they have had, qualifying them to sit in what I consider to be the most delicate court we have today. If I make a mistake in the trial of a civil case, there are higher courts to set me right on errors of law. But even if they make an error, and some adult has to pay some money to some other adult, we human beings get over these things fast. But as I sit during the day and look at the faces of twenty-five boys and girls who are in court with their parents, I constantly say to myself, 'If I make a mistake in the trial of this case today, I won't know tomorrow.' The next year, or five years from now, perhaps we will know whether the answer was right or wrong.

"It is an extremely heavy responsibility, therefore, that one who sits in juvenile court has," the California judge said, "because he is dealing with the future life of a boy or girl. 84,419 boys and girls in my State last year came in contact with police officers. Now, far be it from a Californian to admit there is anything we can't overcome, but we can't overcome the loss of 84,000 kids a year. No state can afford to lose its boys and girls. We have to do something to rehabilitate the boy and girl who get into difficulty," Judge McKesson concluded.

It is also essential that highly accredited men and women be enlisted for the probation staff. Their educational background should certainly include a college degree, with a great deal of work in the social sciences, and experience of at least one year in case work under professional supervision.

In the report of the United States Office of Education it is recommended that the qualifications of a probation officer include: emotional maturity, a sense of integrity, sensitivity, good health, willingness to abide by the court's policy, and ability to deal effectively with the public while working under pressure. It is especially important that the probation officer possess the ability to exercise authority, without becoming an authoritarian.

According to "Standards for Specialized Courts Dealing with Children," it is proposed that "the probation staff should not be required to perform duties not requiring social work skill, such as routine collection of support payments, record-keeping of a mechanical nature that can be done by a clerk, routine transportation of persons not requiring a personal relationship, and serving routine notices and summons on witnesses."

The work of the probation officer is equally as important as the work of the judge in the children's court. When a probation officer recommends that a juvenile offender be placed on probation—and this is often done, it is essential that there be a well-organized program under which the officer will have the time and funds to do an adequate job in guiding the rehabilitation of the child. Too often such a program is not in operation; frequently being on probation merely means that a child must report at stipulated intervals to his probation officer.

Probation has not worked out successfully in the majority of these cases. We do not have a sufficient number of trained probation officers plus clinical facilities to do an adequate job of rehabilitation during the probationary period. The present survey suggests that there must be a change in our system.

In 1954, 75 per cent of the boys at Jamesburg and 59 per cent of the girls at Hudson said that they had been on probation before they were sent to the training schools. In 1937, 67 per cent of the Jamesburg boys said that they had been on probation before they were institutionalized. A number were on probation from two to four or more times. If the probationary services had been more adequate, there might have been fewer recidivists among the probationers and fewer final commitments to the training schools.

In "Standards for Specialized Courts Dealing with Children," it is proposed that the number of cases handled by workers dealing with children on probation should be limited to fifty. Sometimes these workers are put in a position where they have to carry a case load of as many as five hundred children. Even the smaller number recommended should be reduced if the social worker is making studies and carrying on other assignments in addition to handling cases.

It is proposed that probation be ended when the child has received as much benefit as he can from the service. Special studies and periodic checkups must be made in each case in order to determine when that point has been reached. This, too, is often not feasible because the courts may have an insufficient number of social workers and probation officers, and because those who *are* assigned to cases may have inadequate training.

The children's courts should have effective clinical personnel in order to do an adequate job. They should have ready access to the services of a psychiatrist, physician, and psychologist, as important members of the team devoted to the prevention and cure of delinquency.

It became apparent some time ago, when various persons asked that more help be given to our children in court, that the children's courts are *not* doing an adequate job. This point is illustrated by Dr. Alfred J. Kahn in *A Court for Children,* who showed that there are many weaknesses in the setup of the children's court in New York City. Similar failings undoubtedly exist elsewhere too. It was concluded that only a minority of the thousands of children who appeared before the court each year have been served with both kindness and skill; that the majority of the children receive service that "does not reflect the juvenile court movement's aspirations."

Dr. Kahn's report went on to say that for some children the court represents a well-intentioned, but inadequately prepared pressure group of individuals who cannot achieve what they strive to do. For many others it is the insensitive instrument of an indifferent or hostile social world.

Dr. Kahn states that in most instances the New York children's court fails to act as a good parent or a skilled counselor. Far too often it does not even appear to the children to be a kind friend.

The following are some of the findings on the New York children's court, as summarized in the report by Dr. Kahn:

Some judges are outstanding, but "other judges seem to be insensitive, punishing, unconcerned, or too harassed to care."

The probation department is overworked and understaffed, having a lack of trained personnel; suffers from excessive turnover (25 per cent in 1952) because of low salaries; and consequently delivers adequate service in only a small percentage of its cases.

The Bureau of Adjustment, which seeks informal disposition of the less serious cases, gives "very poor" service in a third of its cases, and "good or very good" service in only a tenth of its cases.

Almost half of the court attendants perform their jobs in an unkind and indifferent manner and confuse and frighten the children and their parents.

Most of the facilities are old and dismal, tending to inspire fear and create tension instead of creating a calm, reassuring and healthy atmosphere.

Some of the basic services and facilities on which the court should depend are completely lacking.

Yet New York City's presiding justice of the domestic relations court John Warren Hill, head of the judges of the children's courts, has said, "There are some who refer to our work with children as that of reclamation. Our purpose is not mere reclamation. We want to build character." Here, surely, is a paradox compounded of noble purpose and poor performance.

We know that half of the juveniles who are considered delinquents by the juvenile courts later develop into adult criminals. Is it not possible that, if the children's court had acted effectively in giving counsel at a crucial time in the life of the bewildered and confused youngster, there might well have been a substantial reduction in the number of children who have become repeaters—and then adult criminals?

A child who is brought to the hospital with a broken leg receives immediate treatment. He does not have to undergo a lengthy lecture first on the inadvisability of climbing trees. If the same child is brought into court on a delinquency charge, as a result of an emotional maladjustment, he is often not even offered the help of a splint built of understanding of his basic problem, either when he is in court or on probation.

In the case of probation in the New York children's court, as Dr. Kahn points out in his excellent study, the officers are frequently not qualified to do the job they are asked to do; they may be mediocre or, at best, not superior men and women of the community. Unfortunately, in almost every city in the country, little is done to attract superior personnel to this important field— salaries are low; advancement is slow; and working conditions are unsatisfactory.

Dr. Kahn reports that in 1952 New York City's sixty-seven probation officers had seven thousand investigations to make and four thousand children on probation to supervise. This was an impossible job for them to do effectively, even if they had been top-notch people for their jobs. Partially as a result of this situation, 25 per cent of the staff left the court service during the year, meaning that there was a turnover of one out of every four officers.

Under such circumstances, what happens to the juvenile offenders? As Dr. Kahn says, "The court labors mightily to bring children to a point where they are to be placed on probation, but probation usually proves to be a feeble attempt to police their activities, or an inept introduction to a community resource."

Since the probation workers are unable to give adequate attention or time to their work, for the most part they merely check up on the children. If everything appears to be "in good order," that is all the probation officer wants to know. He does not have the time to find out whether the young offender in question is making a better or worse adjustment as a member of his family, his school, his community, or society at large.

Not only do the children's courts lack good probation officers, but also psychologists, social workers, and clinical assistants. An important reason for this situation is that they are inadequately financed.

In a sense, the community has set up a children's court by statute and then said, "Well, go ahead and do what you can. There is nothing further that we will do for you." In the words of Dr. Kahn, "It is as though an ambivalent society created a new institution and then, not being sure about what it had wrought, provided so few new resources that the institution could not flourish." Obviously, this is not the way in which to develop an adequate court program to combat juvenile delinquency. Indeed, few courts even function effectively in co-operating with the various agencies available in their communities, no less carry out proper investigative and follow-up techniques that should be part of their job.

As the federal Children's Bureau notes, "Some of our communities have so few resources—if any—that many times juvenile court judges have to dismiss cases against delinquent boys and girls because there is nothing better that can be done for them. Most judges are reluctant to send a boy or girl away from home to be treated, particularly in those states where the training schools are not what they should be. The judge, therefore, takes the risk of releasing the child and hoping that some kind fate will keep him out of further trouble."

On the other hand, what happens when a juvenile is taken into custody?

The lack of adequate facilities for the detention of delinquents has disturbed many judges, police officials, as well as others who are interested in the welfare of our youth. Needless to say, juveniles—particularly those who are first offenders—should not be kept in jail with hardened criminals. Yet few communities actually provide separate detention quarters; where they are provided, they are inadequate. What can the police or the courts do? When it is found that a child cannot remain at home, or when the offense is of such a nature that he must be placed in custody, jail may be the only place in which the offender can be detained pending further action on his case.

In New York City, domestic relations justices are given a report each morning on whether there is room in Youth House to commit delinquent boys. Youth House is the only temporary detention shelter open to the children's court. It was originally built to house 120 children, and is now used to shelter 165 children.

"We're in a vise," said former justice J. Irwin Shapiro, now commissioner of New York State's investigations commission. "We hand down decisions not on the basis of what is right but on the basis of the space available to us at Youth House."

He cited the case of three fifteen-year-olds who chained a boy to a post, stomped on his legs, and tried to extort five dollars from him. "A few days in detention would have shown them we mean business, but the Youth House officers told me they were full up. So, I had to parole them to their parents. Now they go back to their neighborhood and spread the word that 'Children's Court is soft.' "

Just recently, a little boy of seven spent several weeks (including the Christmas holidays) in a city jail on the grounds of lewdness and immorality because he had put his hand under a five-year-old girl's skirt. If this boy was guilty only of innocent exploration normal in a child of his age (and this was probably the case), what sort of reaction will he have after spending weeks in a jail for common criminals?

Each year a hundred thousand children from seven to seventeen are detained in county jails and police lockups because there are no special facilities in which they can stay until their cases come up in court or final disposition is made of them. Many of these jails are substandard, even for adults. This is true in more than twenty-five hundred counties in the country, which are not large enough to build special detention homes for children.

Sherwood Norman, director of detention services of the National Probation and Parole Association, reports that thousands of children are held in basement cells or behind bars in detention homes which offer nothing more than the cold storage of physical care and custody. The pity of it is that so many of these cases have really done nothing to merit this kind of disgraceful treatment.

A detention home is a specialized type of institution. It is not a training school as such. It can, however, serve a useful purpose in giving a child an opportunity to get adjusted before he is remanded to the proper training school.

To remedy the present lack of proper detention facilities, district lines must be broken down. Twenty-five hundred counties obviously do not have the resources or the need to maintain individual detention homes for juveniles. Yet even as our schools have "consolidated" in the interests of providing a more efficient educational system, so can the counties with small populations and little need for individual detention houses maintain a common detention house that will serve the needs of an entire area.

Dr. Norman proposes that a state agency should take these steps in connection with improving the detention home setup throughout the country:

Set standards for detention care, provide detention consulting services, inspect detention homes, and publish reports on them.

Provide state subsidies to county detention homes meeting basic recommended standards.

Encourage the development of a joint detention home owned by one county, but serving other counties on a per diem basis, by providing a state subsidy for construction.

Construct and operate district detention homes for the use of geographically related counties, each too small to justify constructing and maintaining its own building.

To quote Dr. Norman: "The detention period is a crucial experience for a child. His relationship to adults, to authority, is twisted. The type and training of detention personnel and the type of detention program may reinforce his hostile attitude toward society—or may lead him to the conviction that authority works on behalf of his best interests. If the detention experience does not help the child to reinterpret authority he may strike back at society—gun in hand."

This is a tragic situation—once again born of old-fashioned philosophy and a lack of adequate facilities or trained personnel. It is a situation that prevents even the most enlightened judges from doing a job equal to the tremendous responsibilities of the court. For the decisions of the juvenile courts are vital to the future of our youth. A judge should not have to worry about the inadequacy of the means for rehabilitating offenders when making such decisions. Unless the detention homes, and the training schools too, back up the courts by providing needed services, the courts cannot do their job. We must put into action improvements all along the line.

In order to develop better children's courts, the federal Children's Bureau has suggested various standards on which the courts should operate. William H. Sheridan, consultant on juvenile delinquency to the Children's Bureau, has indicated that the application of the new standards may lead to revisions in the practices of juvenile courts and in legal statutes.

Some of the major standards suggested by the Children's Bureau are as follows:

Due process of law is as applicable to procedures in Children's Courts as in any other court. The right of a child to live with his own family and the rights of parents to the care, custody, and control of their children are paramount and should be limited only through due process of law under clearly defined conditions. In observing due process of law, specialized courts dealing with children must keep procedures flexible, and maintain the basic philosophy of the court, which is to treat, not punish, the child.

The powers of the court should not be drastically limited or removed. If the court does not have power to dispose of cases, the alternative is to give this power to an administrative tribunal or panel, such as a clinic or a committee of experts and lay citizens.

Unlimited discretion should not be placed in any judicial officer to do as he sees fit with any child. Such discretion is not allowed in many statutes which, in outlining the powers of disposition, permit the judge to "order such other care or treatment as the court may deem best." Statutes should specify a number of types of disposition that may be used by the court and permit flexibility in their use.

All parties coming before the court have a right to know the facts on which the court makes its decision. The public also has a right to know about the general operation of such a court; however, such information should not be disclosed at the expense of the privacy of the individual child and his family.

The parent and child have a right to legal counsel in proceedings in the specialized court and, under certain conditions, counsel for the child or the parent should be appointed by the court.

An administrative agency should be able to take some action with respect to a child placed in its custody without recourse to further court order. For example, commitment is not now clearly defined in some statutes—as to the rights retained by the parents, the extent to which their rights are limited and placed in an administrative agency, and the degree of power that is still held by the court. There must be a more precise definition of the rights, duties, and responsibilities of all parties to an action involving a child, including the child himself, his parents, the agency, and the court.

Not long ago Judge Paul W. Alexander of the juvenile court of Toledo, Ohio, said, "We need a basic philosophy on juvenile courts and probation services." He termed the juvenile court as a treatment agency concerned with returning a healthy child to society. He added that, in moving forward to curb juvenile delinquency, we must recognize that the juvenile court is not primarily a preventive agency, but that it can and does do much to prevent children from becoming chronic criminals.

What is needed today is a greater recognition of that preventive function of the juvenile court. Only when we actively recognize the fact that we are going far beyond the danger point by withholding the support needed by our courts, our probation officers, our clinical workers, our psychiatrists—indeed the entire team working with the judges—can we expect to meet the problem that confronts us and continues to grow more ominous.

Attempts have been made in various parts of the country to lessen the gap between old methods of the courts and their proper role in relation to juvenile delinquency. A juvenile court judge in Louisville, Kentucky, has hit upon a new idea. Judge Louis H. Jull established a youth advisory committee. The idea for the committee grew out of the judge's experiences in handling the flood of cases through the juvenile court. The group, which was originally composed of nine members, expanded to include fifteen youths by August of 1954. Three of the members have been before the court on delinquency charges.

At their first meeting with Judge Jull, the nine original members surprisingly agreed that the court was generally too lenient. Juvenile delinquents—and nondelinquents, too—"don't have the fear of the court they should have," said seventeen-year-old Cary. Sixteen-year-old Roger expressed belief that parents got too much of the blame for their children's delinquency. "Letting a parent pay for his child's damages is not the right way," the youth asserted. He added that often the best way to handle a teen-age lawbreaker was to "find him a job and make him pay for the damages."

Several committee members at a recent meeting said that most juveniles believed that offenders put on probation actually had "gotten off." They added that court probation officers do not check often enough on cases. They cited a widespread belief among teen-agers that juveniles had "repeatedly broken" probation without penalty. Another evil mentioned was ill-advised publicity given delinquents. One member noted that "it gives glamor to the guilty ones."

Perhaps this Louisville experiment in setting up an advisory committee of youths for its juvenile court is one that would bear fruit in other communities.

Undoubtedly the courts need more money. But beyond that, they need a new philosophy, a philosophy that deals with the whole question of juvenile delinquency as one calling, not for a punitive approach, but a curative one.

The judges who are called upon to use judgment as to what to do in a particular case may not always have a ready answer. But some of them have strong opinions about who is to blame for permitting an unfavorable juvenile situation to develop. One of these is Luther Youngdahl, United States district court judge in Washington, D.C., who told the Senate subcommittee, "When I was judge of the municipal court in Minneapolis, I recall a case where a squad car was called to the northeast section of the city and the police officers found a half-barrel of moonshine whiskey in a family's basement.

"The mother was in an institution for the mentally ill. The father was a raving drunk. I had sent him to the workhouse over half a dozen times for selling liquor, having liquor in his possession for sale, manufacturing liquor, and just for plain drunkenness. He was past fifty years of age and almost beyond rehabilitation. But one of the youngsters in that family, an eight-year-old boy, had his life threatened by that drunken father.

"A five-year-old boy and a six-year-old girl were huddled together in a little doghouse," Judge Youngdahl recalled, "with tear-stained faces, arm in arm, chased out of their house by that drunken father.

"Let us take that eight-year-old boy. Suppose he continues in that environment until he is sixteen. Then he goes out in the street, with a loaded revolver. What is society saying to him today? What are some of these editorial writers demanding today? They are demanding that we incarcerate him, even for life, if you please. That boy who has never had the opportunity to learn the difference between right and wrong.

"I contend that society is partially responsible when society does not do its full job in taking up the slack where the homes are breaking down. Society stands in that courtroom, figuratively speaking, pointing its finger of scorn at these youngsters and saying that they are no good, that they are criminals and ought to be put out of the way.

"But society is partially responsible; it has not the right to say that, unless it has done its full job. By that I do not mean to say that we should pin medals on these boys and send them back out in the streets when they get into serious difficulty. That is not what I am saying at all. But I am trying to suggest that punishment is not a cure-all, that we should not glorify punishment, that it is just simply one of the factors.

"Basically at the root of all this problem of juvenile delinquency," Judge Youngdahl concluded, "are multitudinous factors—lack of housing, lack of education, lack of home life, lack of religious emphasis, and just plain lack of friendship and recognition that these boys desperately need."

In the line of battle of our war against delinquency, the juvenile courts hold a most important position. Frequently the courts are the last stopping point for a child before he turns either to a life of crime or to a useful life as your neighbor or mine. As many judges know, a misstep at a crucial point can ruin a young boy or girl for life. On the other hand, sympathetic understanding plus a definite program of treatment may open the door to rehabilitation.

It is difficult to estimate what this will mean in terms of happiness for our millions of children who come into the hands of the police, and for the 400,000 or more children who now appear in our children's courts each year. But it is easy to see that the stakes are high—for the children themselves, for the communities in which they live, for our nation.

What is needed is an immediate study of ways in which we can provide the children's courts with adequate personnel and facilities that will make them more effective and more useful to the community. When we realize that there are only three thousand juvenile courts in the country and that only about one hundred judges are assigned to these courts on a full-time basis, then we recognize the extent of the problem. When we realize further that too frequently the judge who is assigned to a juvenile court is placed there because he is the youngest member on the bench and has no alternative but to accept the assignment; or because he may feel that the work is easier than other kinds of court work; or because there were political reasons for the assignment—then we are given further cause for concern.

With regard to services, let us quote the Public Affairs pamphlet, "Children in Court," by Helen W. Puner. She states that the lack of emergency and long-term community resources to service children's court cases is not a situation that the courts themselves can do anything about directly. Public and private organizations must meet the need. However, she said that courts could make it their business, through committees of judges, to keep the public informed about what these needs are.

According to Mrs. Puner, the following are the basic needs that must be filled if the courts are to be in a position to dispose of their cases intelligently and humanely:

The expansion and improvement of temporary shelters for neglected children and of detention quarters for delinquents.

The development of more psychological testing and psychiatric diagnostic facilities to service the courts.

The expansion of public and voluntary community resources for psychiatric treatment of children.

The establishment of transitional treatment homes for teen-agers who cannot return to their homes after they have been institutionalized.

The development of skilled vocational guidance and job-placement facilities for boys and girls of school-leaving age.

Better liaison between school authorities and the courts.

Additional and better foster homes to serve many kinds of children, particularly Negroes and those of other minority groups.

Having seen young "punks" (as one judge called juvenile delin-quents) come before him and plead through their parents or their lawyer or their probation officers that they should be forgiven, "they know not what they do," a judge in a children's court may occasionally adopt a cynical attitude.

On the other hand, a judge may want to help, but recognize realistically that the available mental institutions are overcrowded and that the court and agency psychiatric workers themselves can-not keep up with the growing number of emotionally disturbed children in trouble. Seeing some of the disturbed children that come before him—children who have committed crimes that almost beggar description—seeing these youngsters let out on probation and then repeatedly violate that probation, it is not hard to sympa-thize with the judge who said, "I will not give him a treat; I will give him a treatment."

However, from a constructive point of view, we must undertake to provide both a treat and a treatment. We must recognize the importance of providing, not only a sufficient number of qualified judges, but also adequate facilities and trained personnel to enable them to do their job effectively.

The courts are an essential factor in the crusade against juvenile delinquency. But as long as we have inadequately staffed courts, incompetent or hostile attendants, poorly trained parole officers and a shocking lack of psychiatric workers, we will be unable to give the children in trouble the help and guidance that they need. This is not a general indictment against all children's courts or

judges in these institutions. I have seen some of these courts at first
hand. I have sat with the judges while they dispensed justice. And
they have been humane, understanding, sympathetic, helpful. Fortunate the unhappy boy or girl who came before them. They were
not scolded unmercifully. They were not shamed by sarcastic tirades.
They were not humiliated and embarrassed. But they were given
that bit of kindness and sympathy that is so badly needed when
one is in trouble. And it may well be that this sympathy will last
for many months.

On the other hand, I have seen courts where the disturbed children were made more disturbed. Where all sympathy and kindness
disappeared. Where the woodshed doctrine leaped forth in bitter
tones. The children's courts must be improved and strengthened.
Unless that is done, the rising rate of juvenile delinquency will
continue unchecked. The scandal and disgrace that has come over
many parents of America will continue unchallenged. That must
not happen. All who are concerned with the future of our country,
and with the needs, aspirations and desires of our youth must bend
every effort to improve our system of children's, juvenile, and youth
courts. No one task would seem to be greater at this time.

As we strengthen our children's courts, so will we move rapidly
in an approach to the solution of the problem of mounting delinquency among young people. As we are better able to accomplish
this, so will our boys and girls in trouble be assisted in developing
into adjusted individuals and useful citizens of a democratic society.

14. The Public Training Schools

"It is a work that demands the highest degree of optimism, kindliness, and self-control."

Tommy Jones was eleven when he was committed to a public training school. Tommy, the oldest of six children, knows that he was born out of wedlock. He was committed to the training school because his mother, who described him as a delinquent she could not control, filed a petition.

At the age of eight, Tommy had been placed in a foster home, and for the next three years was sent from one foster home to another. He was unable to form any meaningful attachments to his numerous foster parents.

Tommy was examined by the court psychologist and psychiatrist. The court psychiatrist reported: "Normal intelligence; is a truant, a runaway, quarrelsome, in open rebellion against his mother but offers no reason, and he doesn't wish it otherwise. Is entirely satisfied with self, must have his own way and dominate every situation. In foster homes—runs away if disciplined, and in those he likes becomes objectionable because of self-centeredness and fighting. A potential psychopath—should have long term training in appropriate institution."

During early contacts with a social work counselor, Tommy complained about his sisters, who "annoy" him. The counselor visited his mother, who complained about Tommy's behavior during weekends at home. She stated that he would not go to bed at night, left the house through the window, slept in his clothing when he finally did get in at night. The mother tearfully repeated that she couldn't control him.

During the interview, the counselor reported, the mother expressed her rejection of the boy by the following:

Feels that boy will get family into trouble with the neighbors by his practice of coming in through windows instead of front door, and letting the air out of automobile tires in the neighborhood.

States that she cannot trust him with the younger children, saying that he once took a butcher knife to them when he was in "charge."

Refused to consider working any kind of plan for the use of service such as offered by the guidance clinic, even after nature of services was explained.

Told the counselor that the father resents having to support Tommy because the boy does not "mind him."

The boy is a seriously disturbed youngster who is completely rejected by his mother, the social counselor said.

The court felt that he needed a more controlled setting than any foster home could provide, a setting where he might get specialized help for his deep-rooted emotional difficulties. He was sent to a training school.

Later the counselor asked the mother how she felt about taking Tommy home for good after his stay at the training school. She expressed her rejection as follows:

"He hits the smaller children."

"I'll take him if he behaves himself and comes in early and if he will go to school every day."

The counselor asked her how the father felt about the boy's return home. "He says I can take him back if I want to, but he says that Tommy is hard-headed and I know that." The counselor pointed out that the father in a sense was saying that he didn't want to take the risk. The mother then was told that it would be necessary for her to decide whether the boy was to remain in the training institution or go to a foster home.

In an interview with Tommy, the counselor told him that it might be best if he remain in the training institution. Tommy told the counselor that he liked the school better than his own home or his former foster home. He said he stayed out late and came in at 5 A.M. at his own home because he hated being around to hear his mother say she "cannot take" him.

"At present," the training school report on Tommy said, "counselor and supervisor are arranging a conference to discuss whether foster care will be available. It is hoped that a new placement will be infinitely more effective than previous placements because of the steps taken to prepare boy for placement at this time. Because boy is willing to remain at the training school, it was determined that he remain there for the time being. He said that he would rather stay there than go home for the next weekend. Tearfully, he said, 'I just don't like to hang around that house.' It was recommended that the adjustment committee retain the boy in the training school until the plans for placement have been followed up."

The general opinion of the teachers at the school was that the boy appeared of good mentality, though he had not worked hard in some of the school subjects. He was socially acceptable in the classrooms except for certain outbursts.

The housefather in the unit where Tommy lived made this report: "When Tommy first came in he was troublesome. During the Easter holidays when the boys went home, the mother called school and said she could not stand him and was bringing him back. He had been home two days. The custodian told her not to as he would be away until after Easter. This boy for me is a well-behaved boy. He has a detail with the housemother who reports him a little noisy but an excellent worker. The noise goes with the age group. He has a hearty laugh, even if it is on himself. I think very highly of this boy and am sure if he has half a chance he will make good."

The recommendation of the staff at the school was that Tommy be retained at the institution until acceptable placement with foster parents could be arranged.

What can be added to this case? The training school has taken this eleven-year-old boy because neither his foster parents nor his own parents could "handle" him. The training school is the only place in our society that will take him. If the training school does not recognize or cannot act on the fact that Tommy is in need of help, then we will find that society has made of Tommy an incorrigible, a potential criminal.

In former years Tommy would have been sent to a so-called reform school. A boy in trouble was considered simply a bad boy, (and that *is* what his mother considers him). Punishment was meted out to fit the crime—for children, as well as for adults.

Today, however, we are more aware of the needs of the boy in trouble. Throughout the nation we now have training schools for children who are committed to them by courts or by other agencies within the community for a period of detainment. These schools are run either by the state or by private agencies. Let us consider the public institutions first.

Historically, the public training schools developed from the idea of rehabilitating youth through training rather than through punishment. This principle was recognized as early as 1825 in the founding of the first institution in the country where juvenile delinquents were held separate from adult criminals—the New York House of Refuge.

Today some forty thousand youths are committed to training schools each year for an average stay of less than a year. A survey of typical training schools that I conducted suggests that there are numerous philosophies and policies that govern the training schools to which these forty thousand boys and girls are sent.

Tommy's case indicates the multiple responsibility that the country's public training schools must shoulder. Many times children are sent to training schools because the community fails to provide local services that would be more appropriate. A neglected child may be sent to an institution simply because a foster home is not available for him. Or a mentally defective child who does not have the ability to continue with his own age group is sent away because there is no other place for him. But even when delinquency has been obviously manifested, the training schools must still serve as a substitute for the child's home, for his school, for his community. Beyond that they have the responsibility of preparing the child to return to society better able to cope with his problems. In addition to providing for its charges' physical and mental needs, the state must also assume responsibility for meeting, insofar as possible, the emotional and spiritual needs of the child. Just as the parent must give the child love if he is to develop normally, so must the training school attempt to give love to those in its care. If the child is treated as someone who doesn't deserve any kind of help, then the old familiar pattern, the disturbed neurotic pattern that brought him to the school in the first place, will continue and probably be strengthened. And so will the rate of recidivism grow—the rate of children who are returned to the institutions for committing further offenses against society.

As psychiatrists and psychologists have reported so often, the unloved, the neglected, the rejected child is very likely to develop a demanding, aggressive personality. When he becomes delinquent, he is acting out his feelings against his parents—and the rest of society—who have denied him the warmth and sense of belonging necessary to normal growth. When he becomes hostile or aggressive or unruly, he is rebelling against authority because authority gave him a raw deal.

One of the duties of the training school is to try to change the child's attitude. To the extent that is possible, therefore, the better training schools now attempt to provide the normal life of a normal home, in an attempt to make up for some of the things the child never knew in his own home.

How can this be done?

First of all, the school's physical characteristics are important. We know that the boys and girls in training schools need informal, warm, and pleasant surroundings that most of them never experienced in their own home. We know, for example, that small cottages housing perhaps fifteen to thirty children, or even less, are better than large, cheerless dormitories. Yet the living units for these children in general are much larger than they should be. Fifty-two schools report that they have from 10 to 24 children in one unit; seventy-four report that they have 25 to 39 in a unit; thirty-four report that they have 40 to 54 in each unit; eighteen have units that house from 55 to more than 70 boys or girls.

Thirty-nine training schools reported that they had dormitories only. The dormitory type of arrangement was found chiefly in the boys' schools. Bedrooms for from one to four girls were more common in the girls' schools.

An institution cannot be a good home substitute if it looks like a jail. Nor are children inclined to feel at home if they look like prisoners. Regulations pertaining to the personal appearance of the boys and girls in the training schools should not overlook the importance of variety. In the past, despite the good intentions of many training schools, conformity in dress—as in every other way—was considered a virtue. Unfortunately, most of the children at the schools come from the type of background that makes conformity extremely difficult for them.

More important, still, is the manner in which the children are treated. Judging from all available evidence, there has been a trend in recent years away from the harsh, cruel, and inhuman punishment formerly meted out to boys and girls in these schools as a matter of course. But the use of corporal punishment is still in vogue in a number of institutions.

In one training school the superintendent said to me, "We give our children here the good old home treatment."

"And what do you mean by that?" I asked.

"Oh," he answered, "about ninety per cent of the children report that they were whipped by their parents at home. We use the same kind of disciplinary treatment here. This is the only kind that they understand."

Unfortunately, the superintendent did not see that there might be a direct correlation between the fact that 90 per cent of his boys were severely whipped or severely disciplined at home and the fact that those same boys became social problems so serious that they had to be deprived of their liberty.

A few of the cottage fathers and mothers that I have seen appear to be neurotic themselves. They are sometimes completely unfit to handle disturbed children; some are actually sadistic. When the superintendent at one public training school issued an order that there would be no more corporal punishment, no more inhuman disciplinary measures, a cottage father who had been with the institution for eighteen years, asked, "Does this mean, sir, that I will not be able to bash in the brains of these kids when they get obstreperous?"

"It means just about that," the superintendent replied.

"But how are we going to get the kids to behave?" the house-father persisted.

"We'll use the new methods of trying to be kind to them."

"I'm sorry," the other replied, in a huff, "if that is what I have to do, I shall quit." He did quit, and as he was leaving he said, "And to think I've wasted eighteen years of my life on these rats."

The superintendent turned to me and said, "I'm afraid that for the last eighteen years we have had an inefficient, and what is even worse, an entirely unwholesome influence here."

The truth of the matter is that that cottage father's attitude is an example of the attitude taken by many training school employees in the past.

The study of the federal Children's Bureau gave the following listing of disciplinary methods used in various training schools:

> 101 schools use a deprivation of privileges to discipline the children.
>
> 62 place children in security or lost privilege unit.
>
> 39 add extra or unpleasant work.
>
> 20 use the demerit system.
>
> 16 use corporal punishment.
>
> 13 place the boys on a restricted diet.
>
> 3 force the boys or girls to wear special clothing.
>
> 16 use other methods, such as confinement of the children to their own rooms, delay in date of release, or taking away from children the right to have visitors.

Any institution, to run smoothly, must have rules and regulations. And these rules are bound to be broken from time to time. The substitution of enlightened supervision, however, for rigid disciplinary measures is the most effective way to deal with the problem. According to Mr. A. Alfred Cohen, superintendent of the New York State Training School for Boys at Warwick, supervision means teaching a boy to learn new and better ways of doing things, not merely watching to see that he doesn't break a rule. Poor supervision may lead to stealing, fighting, violation of smoking regulations, sex misconduct, and so on. But if the boys are provided with interesting activities, they not only learn how to get along in groups, but they are less apt to get into trouble. Mr. Cohen maintains that prevention is the best cure for behavior problems.

"Treat all boys with equal fairness," the directive from Mr. Cohen to all employees of the Warwick school enjoins. "Very often we are attracted only to the good-looking boy with a pleasing personality and may neglect the boy to whom we are not attracted. There is something we can like in each boy and we must try to find it. It may be difficult to like the boy who is frequently in trouble, but we must be careful to treat him fairly on every occasion. If a boy is nervous or especially restless, if his actions are erratic, he needs help and attention. From experience we can generally know when a boy is heading for trouble. We should not overlook the matter or postpone looking into it, but should try to find out what the difficulty is, and try to prevent the trouble."

"We can see easily enough that a boy is getting into trouble," says Mr. Cohen. "If we can also understand why, then we are in a position to help him do something about it. For example, many boys run away, yet they have different reasons for running. That is why we must look at each boy and his individual problem rather than at only the general problems themselves."

Mr. Cohen has assembled a list of what a boy does and does not like about supervision that has a direct bearing upon the effectiveness of not only a school's disciplinary practices, but upon its program as a whole. The observations have been of value to supervisors at the New York training school, and undoubtedly could be utilized at training schools elsewhere.

WHAT A BOY DOES NOT LIKE

"Hollering." This is one of the most common complaints boys have, especially about former schoolteachers, but also about some supervisors in the training school. It makes them feel that the supervisor has poor self-control and little command of the situation. It also suggests poor manners. "I don't like him. He

is always hollering at us." There can be authority in a quiet voice.

Being ridiculed. A boy keenly resents being called crazy, jail-bird, dumb, awkward, limpy, sleeping beauty, etc. It is the sarcastic manner as well as the "public" expressions of these comments that hurt and provoke bitterness and hostility. This is increased by the fact that the boy is hurt with a weapon that he cannot himself use—he hasn't yet learned the cleverness in use of words necessary to fight back with ridicule. He merely senses that "the man don't like me" and responds with his own form of misconduct: fighting, refusal to work, cursing, perhaps under his breath, or profane and surly back talk.

Ridicule of the family. To say, "What kind of bringing-up have you had?" is reflecting particularly against the boy's mother—and children are taught to defend their mothers. The boy always has some guilty feelings about his parents, so this subject is likely to be a particularly sensitive one. Supervisors, as well as boys, have been known to suffer physical injury from having made such statements.

Having too much expected of him. We all rebel against being expected to perform far ahead of our mental, emotional, and physical capacities. Each boy's abilities should be carefully estimated and his program arranged accordingly. "He uses such big words, I never know what he is talking about."

Grudges. Leave yesterday's trials and squabbles with yesterday. Let each day have a fresh start. "Mr. ——— punishes me and then forgets it, but Mr. ——— keeps bringing it up all over again every day. It makes me mad."

Threatening. A boy quickly loses confidence in a supervisor who threatens and is unable to follow through—"gets out on a limb"—or makes idle threats without intending to follow through. A boy likes to know that the supervisor is capable of handling most situations without having to use "or else." Also, the supervisor maintains the boy's confidence in other respects as well if he is not constantly reminding him of "work gang" and "office." However, there is a place for a deserved and definite warning, not given in a provocative manner: "When he says something he means it."

"Talking all the time." Some people find a great outlet for their own tensions by rather continuous talking and explaining. A boy wants a clear-cut, simple explanation of what is expected of him at the start. This may have to be repeated every day for some boys, but he becomes irritated and restless from seemingly endless discussions. A boy feels that the adult has the advantage over him here, too, and is unable to defend himself with a like weapon so he has to resort to his more primitive means of retaliation.

Scolding a boy in front of a group. Every youngster resents being "brought down" in front of his friends. Even though he is guilty, and is rather fair-minded, he will show a very bad attitude if brought to task publicly, and pass it along to the rest of the group. This will create a very ticklish situation for the supervisor. When we scold a boy, we should take him aside. The result will be very much better. Just think how you would like to be called down by some one in authority in the presence of other supervisors. The boy feels the same way about it.

WHAT A BOY LIKES

The supervisor who is "for" him. It is more important than any other single consideration that the boy feels the supervisor is really interested in him and his welfare, likes him and will stand up for him and the other boys. "I know I'll get a square deal. Mr. —— is handling it for me."

When a boy gives a confidence it should be carefully guarded. It is easy to "double-cross" a boy without really meaning to do so. Promises should not be made without full intentions of carrying them out. And when there is a difficult matter to be taken up with the boy, he nearly always prefers man-to-man frankness to "beating around the bush." Many times it is quite a comfort to him to know just where he stands with the super-visor.

The willingness to listen. Each boy wants and deserves a chance to tell his own story—and to someone with an open mind about what has occurred. This may need to be done in private conversation. We do not generally like a public audience when we explain personal matters. "She was older, she should have let me explain." "I didn't do it, but I took the blame because I couldn't tell about it in front of the whole bunch."

Protection of his property. When a boy comes to the training school, he leaves most of his clothes, trinkets, and other belongings that have become a real part of himself, at home. It takes him a while to acquire new belongings here and they are chiefly letters from home, or articles he makes in the shops. He wants to have his personal property respected and protected. He has faith in the supervisor who has the system and interest to do this.

Trust. Within reasonable limits of the boy's capacity, he wants to be trusted. "I get along fine with Mr.———. He trusts me."

The out-going supervisor. A boy likes the supervisor who does things and tells about the places he has been. (This is proof of acceptance as fellow human beings, but can be overdone.) Such a supervisor "ain't scared to break the routine" and if a special occasion arises will allow spontaneous group activity. A supervisor who has talent or interest outside of regular work and will sponsor hobby groups in the cottage, schoolroom, or work group usually adds materially to his acceptance by the boy.

A supervisor who "isn't snooty." A boy likes a supervisor who will speak to him in a genuinely friendly and accepting fashion when he meets him in the hall or on the walk. "He is friendly. He don't go around with a sourpuss." Sometimes in group discussions the word "people" instead of "boys," "children," or "fellows" is good to use. It gives the idea of equality. "He treats us like we are real people."

Direct evidence of being liked. Appropriate souvenirs gleaned by the supervisor from a trip, a snapshot, or other incidental, inexpensive gifts to fill some special need are tangible proofs of acceptance and regard. A spontaneous verbal gift, a compliment, falls in the same category. A gift presented as a surprise occasionally is more effective than favors given because they have been earned. "He bought us a watermelon with his own money. We're not going to smoke against the rules in the cottage any more."

A supervisor who is strict. In general, a boy likes to feel that he will not be permitted to "get away with anything." He wants the feeling of strength, dependability, and fairness in his supervisor. This is what many of our boys have woefully lacked in the past, so they try out each supervisor to see if he is dependable (unless his reputation is already well established). "He is strict, but he lets you tell what happened." "Gee, we don't even *want* to be bad in his cottage."

A supervisor with a sense of humor. Boys constantly complain, "I was fooling with the man, he got mad, then I got mad" (in that order). A supervisor should not play with boys unless he can "take it."

The training school, like other schools, will be as good as its staff. This presupposes that the staff must be selected on the basis of merit. It also means a staff free of political interference. Members of the staff, if they are to have the status that professional workers require, should have tenure and opportunity for advancement. Certainly they should receive salaries equal to those paid by the community to persons doing comparable jobs.

The supervisors of a number of cottages or other units must be skilled technicians. They not only should have a background in case work and group work principles, but should have the type of personality capable of maintaining a meaningful relationship with the staffs of the individual dwelling units.

Because of the complicated nature of the supervisory process and the added duties of the supervisors, no cottage staff supervisor should have responsibility for more than five to seven cottages. An institution of twenty cottages, accordingly, should have at least three cottage staff supervisors.

As personalities, and this is generally recognized in all professional quarters, the staff members should be strong in understanding, patience, and positive leadership. Professionally they must of course have the technical skill and knowledge required in their work.

The federal Children's Bureau has set up a series of recommended standards for training schools. Among its proposals are the following:

The superintendent or director should have experience in institutional administration and should be trained in psychology, education, psychiatry, or social work.

It should be possible to develop a program to help each boy or girl who comes to a training school to make the necessary transition to institutional life.

Following the series of tests that should be given to each child after his entrance, the school should set up a definite program of treatment for any physical abnormality, defect, or disorder that may be found present.

Attempts should be made as early as possible to determine emotional psychiatric warpings the child may have, and to understand why. This may call for a definite type of individual or group therapy. It is well recognized that the testing techniques employed are important; but the atmosphere in which the tests are given is also important. Of course, this calls for trained and humane personnel to perform the tests.

Every one of these schools should have the services of a team of men and women who can develop a constructive program for each child. This team might include a psychiatrist, a psychologist, and social workers operating as a treatment unit.

There should be one full-time psychologist for every 150 children, and one social case worker for every thirty children in a training school.

Certain educational standards are also recommended. "The curriculum should be functional in nature, avoiding the teaching of subjects for their own sake in an academic fashion. Rather the curriculum should be organized so that the boys or girls gain the essentials of an ordinary course of study by working on problems and projects that relate to the desired subject matter and at the same time give free play for individual and group co-operation."

The job of the educational director at the training school is not a happy one. He must prepare a curriculum that will meet the needs of younger and older retarded pupils, pupils on both elementary and high-school levels, pupils who will return to their own schools after leaving the institutions, and pupils who will go directly to work and will have no further formal training once they leave the training school.

For that reason, many schools now provide a great variety of opportunities that may fit in with the pupil's ability and needs— while the child is at the training school and after he leaves the school. Obviously this means that the teachers at the training schools should be selected with the greatest of care.

The treatment program of a state institution that serves delinquent children must be focused on the children's feelings and attitudes, the feelings and attitudes which determine their behavior, and which got them into trouble in the first place. The program must be flexible enough to modify as necessary each child's concept of himself and of others, to the end that he can and will want to take his place as a law-abiding member of the community.

What sort of progress is now being made?

The superintendent of the New Jersey State Home for Boys, at Jamesburg, Mr. Frederic A. Fitch, gave this description of his methods and philosophy: "Here we try to help boys become mature," Mr. Fitch said. "We do everything possible to treat them as living human beings. We run on a family style. Every week or so we have a picnic in the back yard. We have a portable grill, make hamburgers, hot dogs, soda, and ice cream. Sometimes we pack the kids into a bus and go to see a double-feature movie. What we try to do is compensate children for what they lack at home. Twenty-five per cent of the kids here get no mail, packages or anything of any kind from home or elsewhere. This, of course, is as disturbing as anything that could possibly happen to them. Even if a letter comes from a Rotarian or Lion's Club—form letters—they are overjoyed.

"At Christmas we try to take care of the forgotten children," Mr. Fitch went on. "About eighty of the five hundred boys won't get a single thing at Christmas time or any other holiday. The relationship of the children to adults, whether their parents or any other adult, is extremely important, because it is important for them to know that there are adults who care whether they succeed or fail.

"Fortunate is the boy or girl who can find a person in the classroom, a teacher, a coach in the athletic field, a counselor in scouting or Y, to whom he can look up. Unhappy is the child who does not find anyone with whom he can talk things over.

"Most everybody we receive here has some emotional problem," the superintendent said. "This is a place of last resort for boys of ten to sixteen. They are questioned by teachers, by principals, by superintendents, by the policemen on the beat, by juvenile officers, by the court, by the probation officer, by the special committee. They get between fifteen and twenty interviews before they come here. Yet I rarely get a boy who says, 'I was framed.' The boys admit their guilt. After a while they get to recognize that we aren't trying to boss them or frighten them.

"The antidote of failure is success, and our job is to find an opportunity for every child to succeed at something. Our job is to find some way to give the boy recognition. Our job is to put a boy in a classroom where he can succeed. Here boys go to school half a day. They work the other half. The ninth- and tenth-grade boys have a grand time at graduation. We had three boys who were speakers who would be a credit to any high school. They stay here an average of about one year. I think that when they leave here they actually have been helped.

"It's not punishment that we seek; that won't build up success. Frustration is followed by aggression. Success is frequently followed by acceptance."

The New York State Training School for Girls at Hudson, New York, in the summer of 1954 reported that its program had been vastly improved in recent months. There were innovations in the cottage areas of the school and the addition of five cottage couples, man-and-wife teams. This is in keeping with the philosophy of Abraham G. Novick, the school's superintendent. Mr. Novick believes that girls who come to the school should have some contact with housefathers, as well as housemothers, and experience, insofar as possible, the feeling of being part of a normal family unit.

The expanded recreation program at Hudson has also enriched the girls' lives. Privileges have been increased to include off-campus trips. The addition of television sets, free off-campus movies, home vacations on a quarterly basis for girls who have been in the institution for six months, all combine to make living more normal and enjoyable.

The use of personal clothing is now allowed on and off the campus. Shapeless dresses, sewn and double-colored socks, and other unattractive features of the girls' uniform dress have been all but eliminated. Great stress has been placed on the girls' personal appearance.

The training school has organized a student council, with definite responsibilities assigned to the members of council. These officers were elected by the girls themselves under set rules and regulations which they helped to establish.

The use of restrictive measures to handle disciplinary problems was placed under close supervision and control. This helped eliminate a considerable portion of room punishment and privilege restrictions.

Mr. Novick observed that the good effects of this program were marked, and in some ways startling in view of the short period during which the changes were in operation. The results were seen graphically in these areas:

Runaways decreased markedly during the year. From April, 1952, to March, 1953, there were 724 runaways at the school. During the past fiscal year (1953-1954), there were 326 runaways—a 55 per cent reduction. After the new program was introduced, only four runaways occurred in March, 1954—the lowest number for a single month in recent history at the school.

Destruction of property and general breakage have all but disappeared as a problem. During the fiscal year from April, 1952, to March, 1953, the maintenance staff spent two thousand man-hours in overtime repairing windows, walls, and furniture, apprehending runaways, calming hysterical girls in cottages, and subduing girls who were breaking up their rooms and other sections of their cottages. From October 1st, 1953, until March, 1954, exactly two hours of overtime were spent by the maintenance department, and these two hours had nothing to do with the girls' behavior.

Turnover of the staff has been reduced to a normal percentage. During the fiscal year 1952–1953, the school had a turnover in its cottage staffs of 218 per cent. Of the 129 who served, only 11 remained for the entire twelve months. Since October, 1953, the turnover has averaged two persons per month, or 3 per cent. Even these resignations, Mr. Novick observed, are due primarily to a weeding-out process as the school increasingly evaluates the abilities of the staff members to determine whether they belong in the modernized program at Hudson.

The girls appear much happier and more relaxed. There is much greater trust of adults and some meaningful relationships are established between adults and children. Staff members are more aware of their responsibilities and, as a result, are themselves much more relaxed. A relaxed and happier staff results in relaxed and happier children.

According to Mr. Novick, the key to the successful institutional program for delinquents is effectively trained, competent personnel. This would seem doubly important in the case of cottage or house fathers and mothers. The child's relationship with the cottage parents, to be most productive of good, should be on a personal plane so that the child can express himself and develop in a constructive manner. Cottage personnel are frequently called upon to understand what lies behind a child's behavior; to recognize his idiosyncrasies and his methods of securing favors and attention.

The following report, contained in a paper by Mr. Novick, gives an accurate record of the activities of a cottage group at the State Agricultural and Industrial School at Industry, New York.

In the cottages of the school the houseparents are assisted by two staff members called supervisors, who relieve the housefather during the night. This is a record, edited by Mr. Novick, which was submitted by a housefather in charge of the activities of a cottage group from four to midnight on this particular occasion.

"I arrived at the cottage at 4 P.M. and as I entered the kitchen door the boys' cook greeted me with a hearty 'good evening' and asked me what the plans were for the evening. I asked him what he would like to do and he said, 'Work on hobbies.' I told him there was no reason why he could not do that this evening.

"The boys began coming in from their various program assignments to wash up and get ready for supper. George came in and wanted to know if he could work on his plane tonight. George knows that he can do so, but finds it necessary to ask me in order to get some attention. I answer him as usual, saying that he can do so. I find the best way to work with this boy is to give him extra attention and commend him on the good work that he is doing.

"Frank comes in and proudly shows me a drawing he made in school. I discussed this with him for a few minutes and told him that he did a good job. This boy is really talented in drawing and should be given extra instruction in this subject.

"At supper I discuss the day's activities with the daytime housefather and he informs me of the boys' behavior during the day. There was nothing unusual. After supper was over the boys washed the dishes and cleaned up a bit around the dining room and we went down to the basement where we have our workshop. The boys took out their tools and went to work on their individual projects.

"Martin is working on an elaborate birdhouse. He is a quiet boy, has made a fairly good group adjustment, but is very slow in his movements. His problem is to make the roof fit around the chimney. Every few minutes he asks if I think it will fit. I commend him on the work he is doing and give him some instructions on how to measure the chimney to make it fit. He begins telling the rest of the boys what a good job he is doing and then begins blowing on his nails and rubbing them on his shirt.

"George came in from the other part of the room with a complaint. He stated that Otto pushed him. I listened to him for a few minutes, began discussing the project he was doing, and a few minuter later all is forgotten and the two boys were friends again.

"Ten minutes later Martin again questions me, this time as to what color he is to paint his birdhouse. I encourage him to use his own judgment and state that he certainly is capable of making it look right. He goes back to his bench and looks somewhat puzzled, but begins sanding the birdhouse in preparation for coloring it. However, Robert, who is sitting next to him, begins shaking the bench and Martin can't concentrate. They exchange words, then Martin goes ahead and changes his position. He is very much satisfied with the work he has done and for the rest of the evening is a model boy.

"All the boys were busy doing things in which they were interested. I went around encouraging each boy, suggesting things here and there as was needed and trying especially to give the boys a feeling that they were doing a good job.

"Kenneth is also working on a birdhouse. He is a quiet boy. He seems to be able to adjust fairly well by himself. However, when he is teased he will fight. This evening, however, he is quite content. I have been trying to get him to participate in activities with the rest of the group and he is showing some progress.

"There were some minor arguments during the evening. These were largely started by boys who find it hard to concentrate on one thing for any length of time.

"I noticed that Bernie was becoming restless and attempting to pick on the boy next to him. I went over to him, and wondered whether he might want to do something else at this time. He declines and says he would prefer to continue on his projects.

"Charles began complaining that his neighbor Frank has taken his saw. Actually Frank had simply borrowed it to use on his own project. Frank states angrily that he just wants to saw off this board and 'What does Charles think, that he owns it? It belongs to the cottage.' I told Charles that Frank was using it on his project and that he probably would return it as soon as he finished with it. I suggested to Frank that as soon as he completed sawing the piece of wood he return it to Charles.

"Fred began working like 'a house on fire' on a pencil box. In fact he wanted to build it in one period. If he were one of the other boys, I would suggest that he tear it apart and make some repairs. However, Fred is very sensitive and needs encouragement. I feel it more important to tell him that he is doing nice work. At the same time, however, I mentioned that when he makes his next box, he can improve upon it in certain ways. This kind of thing he is able to take from me. Instead of beginning to work on another box, he begins to fix and repair the one he already made.

"I find that all the other boys are very happy and busy working on their projects. Tom is making a base for a clock; Walt is painting a birdhouse; Joe, Art, and Irv decide that they had enough of hobbies and get together to play some cards. They began shouting at each other at one point and I went over and sat down with them for a few minutes to comment about their playing. This quieted them down automatically without any need on my part to tell them to stop shouting.

"Edward is a new boy that has just been assigned to the cottage. He has very little patience and gets discouraged easily. I need to encourage him constantly and pat him on the back. Tonight he started to build a plane from a kit. A few minutes later he became discouraged and wished to make something else. This has happened a couple of times during the week. For the first few nights I allowed him to act this way. Tonight, however, I encouraged him to continue on the same project. I mentioned to him that I knew he could do a good job if he tried and even if it doesn't come out so well it will be quite all right. He began working on the plane with a little more zest and I think that he will be able to develop more patience.

"At about 8:45 I mentioned to the boys that it was time to clean up and put away their tools. They do so, although with some difficulty. The boys in this cottage are largely individualistic. It is hard for them to do this thing together. It is one thing that they need to learn while they are here. It takes time, however; after they complete their work on the individual projects, I intend to encourage them to start a group project. I don't think they are ready for that as yet.

"After they completed their cleaning, they washed, and we went upstairs to the kitchen for our evening snack. We then proceeded to the dormitory. The boys undressed, got into their pajamas, and sat around listening to the radio and talking to me. Mel asked me when he was going home. He has already been given a parole and knows it. However, an exact date has not as yet been set. He knows that he will be discussing it with Mr. W. tomorrow. I think he is a little worried about going home, and I talk with him about it.

At 9:45 I told the boys it was time for them to go to sleep, and I put the light out. Tonight all of the boys went to sleep immediately and nothing occurred until I was relieved by the night supervisor at 12 midnight. I told him what had happened during my tour of duty, and he then took over."

This record, told simply and matter-of-factly, nevertheless presents a dynamic picture of the relationship of staff member to individual boys. "It is a work that demands the highest degree of optimism, kindliness and self control," said Mr. G. F. Soelberg of the State Industrial School for Boys in Golden, Colorado. This emphasis on treatment and adjustment of the individual boy has resulted in a lessening of hostility and violence, improvement in education, manners and vocational fitness, and a reduction in the number of boys returned for parole violations. About 75 per cent of the Industrial School boys have not been returned for parole violation or for other offenses after leaving school.

The objectives of the Colorado State Industrial School are worth listing in detail:

To promote home and community activities designed for normal, wholesome living for all boys legally committed as juvenile delinquents.

To provide adequate, comfortable and cheerful housing, conducive to good morale and control.

To provide appetizing and nourishing food and attractive, comfortable clothing.

To keep before the boy standards of good behavior and to make him aware of the degree of his success in meeting them.

To determine the boy's educational level and to work with him intensively on that level.

To remedy defects and disabilities and bring him as near as possible to his normal level.

To teach constructive and profitable use of time.

To give every boy an opportunity to participate in games.

To develop good habits of personal cleanliness and hygiene.

To work with him in various ways to overcome disturbances, frustrations, inadequacies, and hostility.

To prepare him for satisfactory return to normal life of home and community.

The above examples and principles show that the knowledge of what can and should be done is growing. But one has only to visit training schools throughout the country to realize that there is still a great lag between what we know *can* be accomplished and what *is* being accomplished.

That the training schools are not doing half the job they should do is attested to by the fact that approximately 50 per cent of the boys who come to the country's training schools as juvenile delinquents still end up as adult criminals. In thirty-six state penitentiaries in the United States between 51 and 53 per cent of the inmates have previously been sent to state training schools. The Colorado State Reformatory has found that about 20 per cent of the boys who leave the institution get into further crime. The state of New Jersey found that 39 per cent of the boys in delinquency training schools are repeaters. Fifteen per cent of the delinquent children have violated parole subsequent to their first release from a correctional institution.

Recidivism is not as pronounced among the female delinquents from eight to nineteen years of age as among males of the same age group. Statistics on one group of three hundred young women and girls, aged eight to nineteen years, resident in correctional institutions, show that only seven, slightly over 2 per cent, had had earlier correctional institution commitments. The proportion who violated parole following their first release was about 25 per cent of the total number under consideration in this study. Twenty per cent of the total number, and 35 per cent among the group of girls in their late teens, became repeaters.

Why aren't the training schools doing a better job?

For one thing, most of the training schools are overcrowded. James S. Thomas, warden of the Colorado State Reformatory, pointed out that in 1954 there was an all-time high of more than 350 boys and young men at that training school. Within the past two years, total enrollment in the country's corrective schools has increased by about 30 per cent. This is a result, of course, of the increase in the delinquency rate.

We know that the population of the average training school should be kept below two hundred. Yet at the present time twenty-two training schools have from two hundred to three hundred children; another fifteen have from three hundred to four hundred; and seven have more than four hundred. It is difficult, if not impossible, to do an adequate rehabilitation job for each individual when a school has more than two hundred children who need attention and treatment.

Further, in far too many instances—as in the case of the boy who told me that one thing he had learned at his school was how to steal a car—they are thrown in with companions who often can teach them more ways to break the law than they dreamed of before they entered the school.

Paul W. Tappan, chairman of the Board of Parole of the Department of Justice, points out that this latter difficulty is one of the toughest that correctional institutions have to face. "You put a bunch of bad apples together in a barrel and expect them to improve," said Mr. Tappan. "It is the old familiar problem. It is one of the reasons why, insofar as it is possible, probation is used on those cases where it can safely be employed."

There are 129 state training schools in this country and about an equal number of training schools conducted under private auspices. Not many of the 129 public training schools have the minimum personnel necessary to do an even halfway decent job. The training schools that I visited gave evidence that they were in need of additional help in the way of psychiatrists, psychologists, social workers, housefathers or mothers, research workers, and staff in general. The influence of bad companions can hardly be counteracted when adequate adult supervision and guidance is lacking.

A study of 109 of these schools, made by the federal Children's Bureau in 1954, established beyond doubt that the great majority of schools throughout the country are inadequately staffed. For example, only 7 of the 109 were found to have full-time psychiatrists on their staff; only 35 employed full-time psychologists; only 67 had full-time social workers; 22 had full-time chaplains; 19 had full-time dentists; and 21 had full-time physicians. Virtually all of them employed teachers; schooling is compulsory in every state. Yet those who have worked in this field know that a complement of full-time psychiatrists, psychologists, and social workers is just as important—indeed, perhaps more important—to the children.

The number and type of institutions should be expanded; this expansion program will depend to some extent upon the reorganization of the commitment policy of the juvenile courts. There should be more emphasis on diagnosis at a reception center, so that treatment needs can be more accurately measured.

Since the specialized services are expensive, and since the public at this point is not ready to provide the adequate facilities and funds, the present outlook for marked improvements is not too hopeful. The best training schools in the country are restricted in the kind of job they can do. Working with limited funds, limited facilities, and decidedly limited public understanding and support, the training schools cannot be expected to perform miracles of regeneration and rehabilitation when various other state and private agencies have already failed to straighten out the children concerned.

By the time a child gets to the state training school, he has already been through a considerable emotional bath. In most cases he has been processed by various agencies, has had innumerable interviews, has possibly had some psychological treatment, has received all kinds of chances from the police, the judges, the community itself. Only as a last—or only—resort is he sent away.

Charles W. Leonard, superintendent of the Connecticut Child Study and Treatment Home, points out that in the past the state training school was used as a "social dumping ground or disposal plant." Both professional and nonprofessional workers in the field looked upon it as virtually the end of the line for delinquents, instead of a stopping place where they might be given a new lease on a better, happier, and more productive life.

The misunderstanding and misuse of training schools, according to Dr. Leonard, can be overcome only by a sound educational program, good public relations, and a clear definition of "what we can do and what we are doing."

The child committed to a training school is a child in desperate need of help. The fact that we labeled him as delinquent and punished him for his delinquent act does not in any respect change that situation. He is still maladjusted, emotionally sick, in need of treatment if he is ever to get any better. That is the basic fact we must face when we consider the role of the training school in the fight to reduce delinquency. On this level, the state must provide more clinical and diagnostic facilities, both in the schools and for parolees. The Ohio Commission on Children and Youth recommends that "the state establish small group homes with case work services for parolees from the Ohio State Reformatory who have no homes, or who cannot or should not be returned to their own homes."

It is not enough for a school to maintain high physical standards or high educational standards, and at the same time be unable because of inadequate budget or an inadequate staff to offer the boys or girls treatment that will get at the roots of their trouble. The real job of these institutions is not only to give the children some educational and vocational training and keep them from getting into trouble while in the schools; it should also be their job to function as centers where treatment can be administered.

When we consider steps for improving the situation in these schools, the greatest difficulty facing us is that of apathy and indifference. Too many citizens are too eager to forget the young boy or girl in trouble once he or she has been sent out of the community. Only when we read about the runaway youngsters who have been returned to the schools, or who have left the schools and were found in trouble again, do we realize that our responsibility does not end when we send a boy or a girl away from the community.

We are cynically writing off these children permanently if, once they are in the training schools, we deny them the chance for treatment and rehabilitation.

Surely the time has come when this great country can accept a larger degree of responsibility for the future of these children. Surely we can create within our training schools, through legislation and public support, an effective program that will help Tommy find some degree of happiness, and a place of his own as a contributing member of society.

15. The Private Training Schools

". . . therapy takes place in all the aspects of the child's life."

In addition to our 129 publicly supported training schools, we have a number of good training schools supported by private funds. These private residential treatment centers, because they are few in number, can now meet the needs of only a small minority of the children who need help. The majority must be sent to the public institutions. Though of vital importance to the individuals they can serve, the work done at the private training schools serves an even greater purpose as an example to other agencies, public and private. With this in mind, let's visit a few of these forward-looking organizations.

Probably one of the oldest and best known of these is Children's Village in Dobbs Ferry, New York. Children's Village is a nonsectarian institution operating under a charter granted by New York State. It has pioneered in the field of child care for 104 years. It was the first institution in the country to establish a child guidance clinic on its campus. It was also the first institution of comparable size to place a psychiatrist in charge of co-ordinating boys' activities.

Joseph F. Phelan, Jr., Children's Village executive director, observes that from a treatment viewpoint, the problems involved in delinquency relate primarily to the early experiences of the delinquent in the home, school, and community. All of these forces act upon the growing child. "Unfortunately," says Mr. Phelan, "we are living in an age in which a breakdown in these areas characterizes our cultural pattern. Our program at Children's Village is geared to help a boy correct his conceptions of these areas during his residence, and to help him learn to live with himself and others in the modern world."

The remedial program at Children's Village employs an orthopsychiatric approach, co-ordinated with auxiliary disciplines of education, recreation, cottage life, and religious life. The impact of these disciplines, coupled with the recognition of the individuality of the child, the Village hopes, will tend to rehabilitate the boy and make him able to live in the community.

Another of the best-known schools for the treatment of delinquent children is the Hawthorne Cedar Knolls School in Hawthorne, New York, which is run by the Jewish Board of Guardians. In this school, guidance and treatment are the paramount concerns. Ideas for its integrated program have been drawn from the fields of social work, psychiatry, and education.

Herschel Alt, the executive director of the Jewish Board of Guardians, stresses that the emphasis on treatment at the Hawthorne School represents an all-out attempt to deal with the underlying conflicts in the child. There is always the desire to understand why the boy acts the way he does, how he has been hurt, and to correct this maladjustment.

The original thesis at Hawthorne was that the delinquent child was reacting to something that he has missed in life. A delinquent, then, was defined as a deprived child who had basic needs to be filled. That theory was subsequently modified when the school realized that it was not as simple as that.

"We used to interpret deviate behavior as resulting from emotional deprivation, primarily the failure of the child to receive balanced affection from his parents," said Mr. Alt. "Yet as we have gained more experience and have seen children unable to respond to psychotherapy and a rich life experience, we have begun to be more discriminating in interpreting personality difficulties. There may be severe distortions of personality that occur for reasons other than deprivation, or because of deprivation plus other factors equally important. No one can really be certain at this point, because we do not know enough about the factors that enter into the growth of personality and the basis of mental illness. We do know, however, that the basis of many forms of disturbance lies in the parent-child relationship, and we should act on the basis of that knowledge."

When a child comes to Hawthorne he finds himself living in a homelike community atmosphere. He finds neighbors—an academic or trade school, and a farm. He will also find a clinic. He will find guidance; he will find people who stand ready to help him.

But this is an expensive job. In 1942 the average cost of care per child at Hawthorne was between $1,200 and $1,500 a year. Ten years later, in 1952, the cost per child had more than doubled. In large part, the increased cost was due to the establishment of a school and a guidance clinic. The guidance clinic, for example, within a ten-year period, grew from a staff of six full-time professional people and some part-time to a staff of fourteen full-time professionals and a proportionate increase in part-time personnel.

Each child now has at least one clinical interview a week, can talk to his cottage parents as often as he wishes, and can also discuss any special educational problems with his teachers.

Recently the Jewish Board of Guardians opened two new residential treatment projects, one for the deeply disturbed, psychoneurotic, and prepsychotic adolescent, another for a preadolescent group of youngsters between the ages of seven and eleven.

"Residential treatment at Hawthorne, as distinct from the traditional program at training schools, differs in that the entire institution becomes therapy," Jerome M. Goldsmith, director of the Hawthorne Cedar Knolls School, points out.

"Hawthorne itself has moved to its present-day status first from a training school to an institution where children lived with nonpunitive and understanding people while they received individual therapy," Mr. Goldsmith explains. "Today it is a therapeutically determined environment wherein the total living experiences of the child are planfully integrated with individual psychotherapy. The milieu so created does not stem from the buildings or geographical location; but rather is the result of the attitudes of the total staff who create an atmosphere in which therapy takes place in all the aspects of the child's life."

At Hawthorne the youngsters live in small groups with cottage parents. Cottage parents are selected on the basis of their warmth of personality, their ability to serve as parents to children, and their flexibility in accepting the wide range of the children's behavior. There are from fifteen to twenty children in a cottage. In these small cottage groups the children can receive the care that they might experience in a normal family setting. They can build close ties with the other children and with their cottage parents, who have a great impact on all the children.

The child guidance clinic plays an important role in helping the staff to appreciate the fundamental needs of the children. Staffed by psychiatrists, social workers, and a psychologist, the clinic is responsible for studying each child and helping him to understand himself. The clinic also helps teachers, cottage parents, and other staff members to understand each child as being different from any other child. In addition the clinic acts as a liaison between parents and child, interpreting the child's behavior to the parent as well as to the teacher.

The program carried on at Hawthorne, if duplicated at the training schools throughout the country, would go far toward returning delinquent, unhappy children to the community as wholesome, emotionally adjusted boys and girls. Whatever the cost, it would be well spent.

Another training school that has received national attention is the Berkshire Industrial Farm in New York. The Berkshire Farm has consistently done an excellent job in helping delinquents to develop to the point where they can return to their communities or go to new environments as rehabilitated individuals. During 1953, for example, two hundred boys benefited by the life at the Farm. At the end of the year, fifteen of them were then ready to go out on probation, and seventy-one were ready for permanent adjustment in their own homes or in foster homes which had been selected for them.

The school continues to receive a heavy proportion of rejected children, whose unhappiness bursts forth in a wide variety of serious symptoms. The clinical staff, consisting of social case workers, a psychologist, and a part-time psychiatrist, is all too inadequate. The school stresses that it is here that the program must be strengthened in the future.

Many of the boys are seriously retarded in their school work when they come to the Farm, mainly because of emotional disturbances. The Farm has a sound educational program, which includes both an academic and a vocational school. The class in printing turns out a Farm publication. There are also classes in auto-mechanics, carpentry, and vocational agriculture.

Mr. J. Donald Coldren, formerly superintendent of the Boys Industrial School at Topeka, Kansas, is now executive director at the Berkshire Industrial Farm. When he took his post, Mr. Coldren said to the boys, "Getting along together and being friends is far more important than swimming pools and fine buildings. Our job is to make friends. And to have friends you have to be a friend, and that means thinking of the other fellow. . . . At the same time no boy can afford to have a low estimate of himself or his own personal worth, because then you can't have much of an opinion of others. And this leads to delinquent behavior."

And to the staff, Mr. Coldren said, "It isn't enough to control these boys. . . . The old type of institution did that pretty well with its regulations, restrictions, and regimented regime. The boys put up a show of good behavior. But all too often they were seething inside. And then they let loose. It continues to be our problem here at Berkshire to get inside of a boy so that he will want to change himself and his conduct."

The Catholic Boys Guidance Centre of Boston is also doing excellent work. The Guidance Centre was planned as a diagnostic study house where boys presenting problems in the home, school, and community could be studied from the viewpoint of helping their emotional problems. On a residential basis or through diagnostic out-patient study, the Centre attempts to rehabilitate them. It is nonsectarian and receives boys for study and treatment without regard to race, color, or creed.

The school was started by the Right Rev. Msgr. Thomas F. McNamara. Msgr. McNamara found while doing parish work that his experience included all phases of work with boys—club organizations, Boy Scouts, athletic and debating teams, discussion clubs, youth socials—and court attendance for juvenile offenders. He felt there was a definite need, long overdue, for a place where the juvenile offenders could be studied, on a residential basis.

Through funds provided by the Catholic leaders in Boston, a residence house of ninety rooms was purchased in the city. It is near enough to social agency headquarters in the business district to be easily accessible for referrals. The building houses administrative offices for the director, two assistant priests, secretarial force, psychiatrist, psychologist, and social workers, classrooms for academic subjects, remedial reading, woodworking, and arts and crafts, a photography dark room, recreation rooms, boys' and staff dining rooms, chapel, and six double and twenty-eight single sleeping rooms, as well as accommodations for in-resident members of the staff.

This building was dedicated in 1945. Since then, services for both nonresident and resident cases, have been extended to over three thousand boys. The resident group is limited in age to the thirteen- through sixteen-year-old groups, with forty boys in residence at a time.

Msgr. McNamara believes that many of the present-day problems of youth are due to a lack of inculcation in them of a sense of responsibility, a lack of respect for authority, and a lack of realization of personal and moral values. "These factors, I feel, have much to do with a boy's antisocial expression," Msgr. McNamara observed. "The boy lacks good drives and healthy interests, and at the same time has no withholding forces, temporary or otherwise, to carry him through a situation. He can only work it out in an adverse form of behavior. Basically, according to our research project, this would seem to be dynamically important in the field of juvenile delinquency. If this is so, the problem of treatment is a serious one and must be in a supervised guidance environment where the whole warped personality can be treated. We, at the Centre, attempt this through practically a twenty-four-hour supervision of his environment, aimed at treating the whole person in the light of his individual disturbance.

"No doubt society's loss of respect for the home, and its unwillingness to sanction any expression of authority on the part of school teachers and other authoritarian figures, involving the child's subsequent loss of the intensely personal relationship of teacher and pupil, is a contributing factor. Sophisticated entertainment, thrill-exciting visual performances, lurid literature allowed impressionable adolescents, all also play their part in the general breakdown of a youth.

"The attempt to punish the child as a lawbreaker," Msgr. McNamara continued, "without a comprehensive view of his whole environmental picture and accompanying sanctions and remedies, is in great measure ineffectual. Our experience has proven that the stimulation of spiritual factors is a prime essential in treating disturbed personalities. Nonsectarian as we are, and while we utilize the best in professional, psychiatric, psychological, and educational techniques, we have always held that spiritual fortification is the most necessary of all therapies.

"Inculcation of respect for authority in the home, state, and school, omitting respect for God, the source of all authority, is a job only half done. Spiritual therapy builds personal responsibility and personal worth as does no other factor in the aggressive and the immature. It serves as a support for the fearful and the depressed."

At the Centre each boy is made responsible for the upkeep of his own room and for a particular household task, which is given a title to increase its importance. A daily marking system for room, job, co-operation in school, and ability in recreational and social activities helps encourage high standards.

An administrative staff meeting is held every week at the Boston center for the counselors, as well as a counselor-psychiatric staff meeting between the counselor and the psychiatrist. Following this a full staff meeting is held for teachers, counselors, student social workers, and priests, during which daily marks are averaged, with an appreciation of their therapeutic value. Case histories are discussed and evaluation of new referrals given. Results of the findings of the psychiatric staff are interpreted to teachers and counselors at this time. During this meeting, senior seminarians from the local seminary are in charge of the boys, and they submit each week a short résumé of their impression of the boys in their care.

The boys also have the interest of a group of male volunteer workers, the Don Michael Counselors. These men include lawyers, teachers, police officers and businessmen who spend one night a week as supportive big-brother figures interested in the boys' creative hobbies.

Psychiatric staff meetings are held every week. New referrals are screened by the staff psychiatrist and priests. Discussions of social histories, psychiatric and psychological evaluations, and personal contacts determine which boys can best be served as residents. Appropriate recommendations are made for the remainder. The parents of these boys are seen at the regular visiting periods as well as by special appointment.

"We have extended our interests to include a community educational program team of two or more of our professional staff," said Msgr. McNamara. He said that their goal was to educate the public through interested groups of people such as parent-teacher associations, Rotary Clubs, church societies, etc.

"In the past year we have been to over one hundred such educational talks and panel discussions," he pointed out.

Each boy referred to the center is given Wechsler-Bellevue, Rorschach, Thematic Apperception, or other projective tests as deemed necessary. Additional diagnostic studies are frequently used when indicated. Plans for correction of physical defects or handicaps are arranged for at the time of admission. Major problems are acne, cross-eye, hearing defects, etc.

Before a boy is accepted for residence, he is given a complete physical examination, including X rays and blood tests. The medical director of the Catholic Boys Guidance Centre is assisted by a volunteer staff of specialists in orthopedics, pediatrics, internal medicine, neurosurgery, otolaryngology, ophthalmology, dermatology, and dental hygiene. The center also has a consultant psychiatrist in addition to the staff psychiatrists.

A variety of interests is provided to stimulate drives and outlets, such as photography, woodcarving, radio repair, care and breeding of tropical fish, arts and crafts, plaster-mold making and painting. Music is used for its therapeutic value and monthly birthday parties featuring "name" orchestras are used to encourage inhibited, withdrawn boys to participate in group activities. The tape recordings of these events are fruitful occasions for interesting psychological studies. Visits to local museums, sports events, and approved entertainments are supervised by counselors. Well-known sports figures, FBI officials, etc., are invited to talk with the boys.

Four years ago the Centre's staff introduced a weekly square dance, importing chaperoned girls from a near-by community. This is an anticipated event, the staff reports, and psychologically very revealing. The boys also act as ushers, servers, etc., at various teas and social functions.

"We treat the 'whole juvenile' and reach the family when possible," Msgr. McNamara stated. "Condemnation and punishment of a boy whose history is unknown and whose conduct has not been closely observed is fruitless. I prefer to think that we are serving our boys by understanding and sympathetic support. If the emotional blockage can be penetrated and a good relationship established, discipline can be maintained. Pressure is applied or alleviated as befits the individual pattern. Our boys over fifteen years of age are allowed four cigarettes a day at designated times. This is a special privilege which may be withdrawn, as may be their nightly candy or special treat or parties, for example, the dance."

The Boston center also has a summer camp, which Msgr. McNamara says is a fertile ground for study of the individual boy under more relaxed circumstances. Here, a routine program of work, discipline, and recreation is followed under the same psychiatric direction. In fact, it was the boys themselves who did most of the work in constructing a splendid camp out of chaotic jungle in the past seven summers. Their most recent achievement has been the planning and construction of a miniature golf course.

"While we have been in existence less than nine years," Msgr. McNamara observed, "the results have been most gratifying. My youngest, and incidentally one of my best counselors, now twenty-three years of age, was one of the first boys who came to me, in December of 1945. An orphan, he came to me as Jim, a very withdrawn boy. He finished his high-school work, and became a part-time counselor. He is now known affectionately to all the boys as 'Pa.' Invariably, when I receive letters from boys in service from all over the world, the writer asks remembrance to 'Pa.'"

"Individualized work with emotionally disturbed boys is a tiring, self-sacrificing, and most often a little appreciated job," Msgr. McNamara said. The willingness of a person to spend himself for an ideal and not just a remuneration is essential for the worker, whether he be a professionally trained social worker or not. In addition to the inherent difficulties, sometimes the work is further complicated by a lack of co-operation and ineffective or unintelligent reactions of many so-called "responsible" outside individuals.

The creed of the Starr Commonwealth for Boys in Albion, Michigan, notes that each boy merits confidence and trust, and that the secret of the development of honor in a boy lies in appealing to his inherent goodness.

The Starr Commonwealth was founded in 1913. Boys are referred by courts, by private and public social agencies, schools, parents or guardians. The individual boy is helped to a better understanding of himself and of the world in which he lives by the combined efforts of trained social workers, interested housemothers, specialized teachers, and carefully selected work supervisors. A full-time psychologist is on the staff, and the school also has the part-time help of two consulting psychiatrists, the head of the Adult Division and the head of the Children's Division of the Neuropsychiatric Institute of the University of Michigan.

The goal of the Starr Commonwealth is to teach boys to accept responsibility, to make wise choices, and to become happy, useful citizens. In the spring of 1955, 150 boys were enrolled on the Albion campus. Thirty advanced boys lived in near-by Jackson in Starr-owned cottages and attended the public school. Twenty Ohio boys were in residence at the first out-of-state branch of Starr Commonwealth at Van Wert and were students in the public township school.

The school operates its own academic institution. There is a teacher for every thirteen boys and a housemother for every ten. A manual arts department offers training in many skills, including woodworking and auto repair and maintenance. There is a Boy Scout troop, and many other educational and recreational activities are available.

Mr. Floyd Starr, the Commonwealth's founder and director, has found, as have others, that the delinquent boy who has suffered continuous rejection feels himself outside society and hence not bound by its laws and customs. The best way to handle such children, Mr. Starr believes, is through love and affection. To a greater or lesser degree, most of the boys who come to the Commonwealth have had experiences that left them emotionally shaken.

"Take the case of the boy whose mother killed his pet kitten before his eyes and broke his ball bat as punishment for some misdemeanor," Mr. Starr said. "What could he have known of human love, tenderness or sympathy? The lad whose mother had been married four times and was about to take another husband and whose father had chosen his third wife could hardly have known he had either parents or a home. Certainly there was little stability in his life and less selfless affection.

"Some boys are unwanted. Some have been shocked by disagreeable experiences. Some have been thwarted in whatever ambitions they may have had. Psychiatrists tell us that a child who is completely rejected till he is two is an 'empty child,' unable to receive or give affection. He doesn't know how. A pretty thorough handicap I would say. There are times when the word 'parents' is bitter in my mouth.

"We enrolled a boy at the Commonwealth who had an apparent intelligence quotient far below our entrance requirement of 90. But we were pretty sure from his case history that when existing emotional blocks were removed, he would measure far above that figure. Within a matter of months he was earning B's in school, and losing some of the tension that had characterized him. Today he is relaxed and happy, expressing his abilities through good performance.

"We have had boys whose parents side-step having them at home for even one vacation a year," Mr. Starr went on. "They will make one flimsy excuse after another to avoid taking that bit of responsibility for their sons. Can you imagine what that means to a teen-ager who asks his social worker, again and again, if his ticket has come yet. It is a common saying among social workers that parents may give up a child but a child never gives up a parent. The child carries within him a desperate and undying longing for the love denied him by his own father or mother."

In a study made of the boys at Starr Commonwealth it was found that 75 per cent of the boys came from disrupted families. Of 157 boys, only 40 came from homes where both parents were living together.

The boys stay from six months to two and one half years at the institution. The average stay is one year and five months. A study over a five-year period showed that just about 90 per cent of the boys were helped to make a successful social adjustment. They did not become recidivists. Twenty-seven Commonwealth "graduates" received various citations, medals and awards in World War II.

These training schools, and more, have been able to take emotionally disturbed children and help them develop into competent citizens. How much better that is than to wait until boys become thrill-killers, or otherwise dangerous personalities. As Senator William Langer, recently a member of the Senate subcommittee investigating juvenile delinquency, warns, "Fifty per cent of our adult criminals—think of it, one half of our hardened criminals—began their lawless careers as juvenile offenders." A high percentage of them would undoubtedly have been deflected from their antisocial course if they received the type of treatment that is offered at Hawthorne or Berkshire or the Centre or Children's Village, or some of the other top privately supported training schools. Schools of the type referred to in this chapter are important for what they accomplish. But, as we have noted, they are even more important to the nation at large because of the example they set, the proof they offer us that a better job *can* be done by other schools—public and private.

I recently attended the annual reunion of graduates of an orphan asylum, which could also serve as a model for our state schools. To most people the words "orphan asylum" bring to the imagination pictures of gray squalor; perhaps a memory of Cruikshank's famous illustration of Dickens's *Oliver Twist* with the boy Oliver holding out his empty soup bowl, asking for "More, please"; or images of iron fences, bleak buildings, dormitories with rows of cots, grim matrons and half-starved youngsters. The connotation is still justified by the conditions at many institutions for homeless children. The Graham School is a happy exception. This institution, founded in 1806 as the Orphan Asylum Society in the City of New York, was renamed the Graham School in 1929, partly in an attempt to avoid the unpleasant stigma attached to the word "orphan," partly because "orphan asylum" was no longer an accurate designation.

A few days before my visit to the school I had lunch with its executive director, Allen M. Thomas. He informed me that of the two hundred children at Graham School, one half come from homes broken up by divorce, separation, or desertion. One fourth are half-orphans. Five per cent are full orphans, and 10 per cent have parents who are mentally or physically ill. Another 10 per cent are the result of court cases of neglect. Clearly, all of these children, like those judged delinquent, have emotional problems.

As I drove through the rolling countryside of Westchester to Hastings-on-Hudson, I came upon the school quite suddenly. Its buildings were handsome, the campus green, tree-studded and neatly kept. The thought came to me that this was a beautiful place to raise children. I hoped that the institution lived up to its director's claims. I was determined to talk to the children themselves, to the "graduates" and to some of the supervisory personnel—and to do this by myself. I wanted to avoid being deluded by superficial appearances or prejudiced opinions.

There is no wall or fence around the Graham School. It has the ·

outward aspect of a preparatory school for wealthy children—at least from what I could see driving through the grounds. Later, when Mr. Thomas took me through the administration building, I paused before we entered to comment on this impression. He looked concerned rather than pleased.

"Oh, no," he said. "All of our buildings date from 1902 to 1903. Many major repairs are needed which we cannot afford to make on our present income from investments and gifts." He went on to explain that Graham School was not what he called a "plant-oriented institution." There are many institutions for children throughout the country where the main interest of the directors is in buildings and grounds upon which much money is lavished. There are other institutions which are psychiatrics-oriented. The emphasis at Graham School, the director assured me, is to create a homelike atmosphere—as far as that is possible in an institution. What I found and saw and learned in my talks with children, graduates and cottage parents convinced me that this is true.

At Mr. Thomas' suggestion, I wandered around the grounds by myself. One of the cottage mothers took me through the building in which she had charge of twenty girls. All the rooms were pleasantly furnished in a homelike manner. There were comfortable chairs, bookcases, writing tables, growing plants, cut flowers in vases, a canary in a cage, a television set. A friendly dog that followed us on our tour was introduced as the house pet. Each of the nine cottages has a dog. In the large airy kitchen I met the cottage mother's assistant who, with the help of four or five of the girls, was preparing that cottage's contribution to the picnic spread which was served on the lawns when the reunion got under way. When I met the girls, they were cordial and pleasant. They were outgoing and talkative and poised. There was none of the shyness or bashfulness which I had come to expect from institutionalized children. As we went through the house, many of the graduates were also going through the common rooms, visiting the small dormitories where they had once slept, greeting the cottage mother with unmistakable affection.

"For many of these girls," she said, "Graham is the only home they ever had; and I'm the only mother they ever had."

Little by little the evidence began to accumulate that "home-like atmosphere" was not merely a catch phrase nor even a lofty ideal which the school administration aimed for but did not attain. I found that there was no regimentation at this school. In this respect (as in others) it was superior to many fashionable private schools. The children wear no uniform. Although blue jeans predominate among the boys, shirts were of many colors and styles. Most of the girls wore dresses; though some I noted also wore blue jeans and shirts. In both girls' and boys' cottages, there are children of all ages living under the understanding supervision of highly trained cottage parents. The older children are taught to take care of the younger ones the way they would in a normal home. The cottage mother and her assistant are helped in the daily routine by the children, but on a participation, not a chore, basis.

On Saturdays and in after-school hours children of all ages have an opportunity to earn money—this they are free to spend or save as they see fit—on the home grounds *or in the village*. The school is not a little island unto itself. The children are to a definite degree integrated with the community of Hastings-on-Hudson. For their schooling, classrooms are provided for the first six grades in the administration building, but only because past insecurity and interrupted schooling make special help necessary. Above the sixth grade, the children attend public and vocational schools in the community. The children themselves choose and direct their own amusements and intramural sports, under supervision. They belong to scout troops. They have parties, movies and television, and are often joined by their friends from the community. They participate freely in community affairs and attend athletic events and parties. They may attend dances in nearby Yonkers. The girls may choose fluffy formals from the school clothes closet which is kept up to fashion by the director's wife.

At one point in my tour of the first cottage, I managed to get the cottage mother quite alone and asked her in confidence whether there was anything about the Graham School that was open to criticism. She thought carefully. "There is nothing that I would criticize about the school or the way it is run. I will say this. We should receive higher salaries, but I know the school cannot afford them. We should have more people to do the work, but it is very difficult to attract good people, people who are so dedicated to this kind of work that they are willing to take less money than they could get in New York." In different words, these same points were later made to me by the director and his wife.

As I left the cottage I tried to think what else had impressed me as different from the traditional orphanage. I remembered the dining room so cheerfully furnished—small tables seating four or six; and in the kitchen cabinets, restaurant-grade china, none of the metal bowls and plates commonly found in institutions. When I joined Mr. Thomas and his wife and friends who were sitting on the lawn in front of their house, I was introduced to a young man in his middle twenties who offered to take me through one of the boys' cottages. It was somewhat more sparsely and ruggedly furnished than the one I had been through, but it was still very homelike. The young man spoke with the ease and assurance of a junior executive (which he was). He was a graduate of the school. "How do you feel personally about the Graham School?" I asked him. He looked at me strangely.

"The Graham School," he said, "is the first good thing that ever happened in my life." I did not press further. Later the director told me that this man's father had deserted the home, that his mother was a psychotic who had murdered two of her children. Among the other graduates with whom I talked was a young woman who had come to the Graham School at the age of eight after she had been chained in a garret. She remembers nothing of her life before the Graham School. It was not possible to question the graduates nor the children currently attending the school in the same way that I had questioned children at other institutions. These people were not delinquent, though they might have become so. To ask them about their home backgrounds would merely have awakened ugly memories. I had to confine my questions to their opinions of the school, ask them what the school meant to them, what it had done for them.

I talked to Loretta, a former student. Her mother was in a mental institution when Loretta came to the school at the age of four. Loretta was part Negro but did not become aware of her racial background until she attended the public school in Hastings-on-Hudson. The wise guidance of the director and his staff helped her to adjust to this circumstance so that her social life and her school work continued on a satisfactory basis. Loretta is now making an excellent record at a junior college. How is this paid for? She told me about the Graham School's Dun Fund. This is a fund from which the children may borrow to finance higher education, paying back the loan gradually when they ultimately find employment.

Mr. Thomas showed me many letters of appreciation from school alumni. Among the case histories was Joe. Joe holds a very responsible position in a local shop. He is especially proud of his own stable family life and the companionship which he and his wife have with their six-year-old son. Joe wrote to Mr. Thomas: "My father was a dipsomaniac. He left home during the great depression and my mother was not able to find sufficient work adequately to support a family of three. Graham School welcomed me, fed me, clothed me—kept me out of the ranks of the juvenile delinquents and gave me companions that have remained such down through the years. It gave me the opportunity to attend the finest schools in the country when my elementary education was completed. I will be forever grateful to Graham School for all that it has done for me."

Miss J —— was deeply troubled about her sixteen-year-old niece, Lynn. One of three children whose parents had separated because one was alcoholic, Lynn had been her father's favorite. She was antagonistic to one of her sisters. When her father married again, she was sent to live with him. But Lynn couldn't get along with the stepmother and again she was moved—this time for a very short period—to live with her grandmother. Then her father committed suicide, using a shotgun he had once given his favorite daughter for her birthday. At Graham, it was discovered Lynn's IQ is high, but her school accomplishment extremely low. Through guidance and attention, even in a short time, Lynn has made definite progress. She is working an hour a week outside the school, in exchange for violin lessons. Not long ago she visited her aunt, who wrote to Mr. Thomas: "I want to tell you how pleased we are with Lynn's improvement. It was not only that she didn't do and say the things she used to either. There was a kind of positive sweetness that we had never seen before. There seemed to be at last a readiness to love and be loved."

I was particularly interested in the evaluation that one young man made of Graham School. He wrote, "First, Graham School gave me a home which was clean—food that was plentiful and dietetically balanced, and clothing that was adequate. I think these things might be overlooked or taken for granted. The significance of these three benefits to a child cannot, in my opinion, be over-emphasized. If a child is free from worry about these basic needs, his mind and personality are more free to absorb all kinds of training leading to good citizenship. Good, clean air in a country atmosphere helped raise my objectives to a level above what they probably would have been had I to live in a tenement section in New York City. Certainly this environment is conducive to good health, which is important to one's over-all personality. Living together with other children under a self-government plan provides opportunity for leadership development; and only as an example of this thought I cite that I personally attribute to that my own success in various enterprises I have engaged in."

I talked to many of the children, both boys and girls, of various ages. Without exception they were vocal and enthusiastic. Nobody said, "Oh, it's all right." The general sentiment seemed to be, "This is wonderful, and I'm glad I'm here." I noticed that although the children were energetic, there was no boisterousness, rowdiness, or shouting. There were no quarrels. No one came to the director to complain of the behavior of some other child. The children seemed to be kinder to one another than the children of "normal" backgrounds. At first I thought that this was almost too good to be true—no aggressiveness, no competitiveness. After talking with many of the children I realized that these youngsters were happy having known unhappiness, that they had security having experienced profound insecurity. For them the Graham School was a kind of paradise. They were determined not to do or say anything that would jeopardize their place in it.

The Graham School has been impressively successful in raising children. It has salvaged potentially delinquent children with a high per cent of success. If its methods were imitated by other institutions for children, institutions of every kind, fewer predelinquent children would become delinquent, fewer delinquent children would become criminal.

Not all private training schools are in the Graham School category, nor that of the others described in this chapter. I have deliberately chosen only the better schools. These have set the standards for the others to follow. Unfortunately, there are too many poor private training schools, just as there are too many poor public institutions for delinquent children. Many private schools have been set up on a proprietary basis, to make money for the owners. A number are operated under an entirely unsound philosophy, with the emphasis on fear rather than affection. But in the main the private training schools are doing commendable work. Many, of course, still have a long way to go to meet the high standards that we know can be reached. They lack an adequate psychiatric staff. They are overcrowded and undermanned. There is not enough supervision or follow-up programs. It is the same story heard throughout my study—"We need more money." "We need more teachers." "We need more clinical psychologists." "We need more attendants." Significantly enough no one said, "We need more boys and girls." Almost every institution is filled beyond capacity. The delinquency rate is rising everywhere—and the training schools find themselves jammed to the rafters. That these schools are attempting to work out a good program is a healthy omen for the future.

16. What of the Future?

"These are the children who will one day become our Nation's leaders."

The number of different electrical circuits required for the unified operation of a single telephone exchange is so large that the mind of no single man can encompass all of them. Yet we have a world-wide telephonic communications system that works with great efficiency. It does so because the specialized knowledge, research, time, and effort of many thousands of people were applied to its development.

Like the six blind men who felt six different parts of an elephant, and—came up with six different impressions of what it was that they touched—we find six professional people coming up with six different emphases when they discuss the solution to the problem of delinquency. Their approach depends somewhat upon whether they are educators, psychiatrists, public housing experts, recreational directors, judges, police officers, physicians and so forth. But we know today—and every thinking professional agrees—that delinquency is a multiple problem demanding a multiple answer.

It is, therefore, the conviction of most social scientists that delinquency must be studied in several frames of reference. That is, it must be considered simultaneously from the viewpoint of medicine, psychiatry, anthropology, sociology, economics, etc. This approach is called the holistic attitude. It insists that the child be considered from the point of view of his physical condition, his relations with his parents and with other children in the family, his relationship to his school—the first social organization outside the family which is important in his life—his reaction to the social conditions of his neighborhood, his relations with other children

339

in that neighborhood, his relations to the community at large.

Delinquency will not be prevented by merely railing against the increase in the number of young criminals. We know that it is a social and economic problem as well as a parental one, and we must approach it in that light. We know too that for the first time we are confronted with young delinquents from "the right side of the railroad tracks." It may come as a shock to many to find that there is a sharp increase in delinquency rates among groups where ostensibly the child has every advantage.

As the intricacies pile up and compound themselves, parents may be appalled by the thought, "How can we bring up our children so that they will not become delinquent?" On the basis of the tremendous number of studies and surveys that have been made I would like to re-emphasize the ten areas in which we must concentrate our efforts to prevent and to correct juvenile delinquency.

1. The Home

The home is the key to any program to prevent or correct juvenile delinquency. We don't have to make every parent into an amateur psychologist. But we can get the parent-teacher association, the citizens' committees for better education, and the service groups to sponsor classes for parents. In addition, every high school and college should have realistic courses in marriage for all students. These should not consist of superficial lectures on sex education or practical lessons on how to bake a custard pie. Rather, the courses should give serious study to the basic issues involved in marriage, parenthood, child raising and interfamily relationships.

We know that a child soon becomes emotionally disturbed if he does not have a normal home life. And that means, for the boy or girl, the love, affection, and understanding that comes from a cohesive family. The child not only wants, but needs, a mother who can show him love, a father who can become his idol, and siblings with whom he can grow and develop. Without mother-love, the young child simply doesn't have a chance to grow his emotional wings. Without an adequate father-image, the child is handicapped.

The divorce rate growing at a rapid rate, causing so many broken homes, is part of the delinquency story. There is a direct correlation between broken homes and juvenile delinquency. At the same time, the child suffers just as grievously when the home is broken emotionally, when the family ties are kept together only on a superficial basis. Where tension and hatred and spite and ugliness enter the home, we find unhappy, maladjusted, neurotic children, ready for the delinquency trail. I cannot overemphasize the importance of sound parent education. The schooling should not end with parents—rather, it should begin with high-school students—with all children, in fact.

2. The School

The school serves as the eyes and ears of every community. We know that a wide-awake, alert, and integrated school program can help solve the problem of delinquency. All schools can and should establish the machinery for detecting children who need help while they are still young.

Teachers should be trained to recognize the child in need as early as the first grade or even in kindergarten or nursery schools. In this connection, every teachers' training institution in the country could well consider introducing in its curriculum courses that would help the young teacher recognize the signs of serious emotional disturbance in their pupils.

It follows that greater emphasis should be placed upon the importance of the teacher of the elementary grades. Too often the elementary teacher, particularly in the first, second, and third grades, is considered not quite on a par with the high-school teacher. Indeed, some communities still persist in the double salary scale whereby the high-school teacher receives more money than the elementary-school teacher because she is required to have more training, and on the assumption that the job is more important on the upper level. We know now, from all the evidence, that for developing healthy personalities the job is far more important on the elementary level. By the time a boy reaches high school, his ways are pretty much set. It doesn't take an expert high-school teacher to recognize a delinquent boy or girl. But it takes a considerable amount of sympathetic, patient, humane understanding for a first-grade teacher to discover a predelinquent.

This presupposes smaller classes of course. And this is a matter of raising money to provide more classrooms and teachers, a community affair and an expense which would soon pay for itself as a means of crime prevention.

Beyond the well-trained teacher, each school system should have a trained psychiatrist, a trained social worker, and a trained psychologist on its staff. Of course, some of the smaller school systems could not afford this service, nor would they need a full-time team of this type. But just as we have eliminated many of the little one-room schoolhouses and brought the children together in a centralized school where greater activities and greater opportunities are available, so can we on a regional basis provide an adequate clinical staff.

The public mind must grasp that the components of "school" no longer include only "classroom" and "teachers." Every educational board should include a division of child guidance, and there should be an increase in the extent of activity in remedial education, community centers, community education, and agencies for the early detection of abnormalities in youngsters. Psychology courses for teachers, psychological testing procedures, a complete machinery to discover the potential factor in the predelinquent, should be provided in public, private, and sectarian schools.

3. The Church

Religion can play an important part in guiding the life of the child along the right paths. A child who attends Sunday school regularly will be less likely, as all evidence indicates, to get into trouble than the child who has no regular religious training.

It is true that from time to time we hear of children who have gone wrong who have attended church. Many of the boys and girls whom I interviewed in the course of this study told me that they had gone to church, some of them regularly. There is more to it than merely "going to church." Families that go to church together, that attend Friday night services or Sunday services as a unit demonstrate that they have some of the cohesiveness that is so essential for a child's normal growth.

Above all, going to church should mean that the child is learning under the highest of auspices the concept of morality and unselfishness.

On the community front, the church can take a dynamic role in helping to eliminate those conditions within the community that lead toward juvenile delinquency. Young people should be encouraged more by religious institutions to participate in service activities such as helping the sick, aiding the handicapped, promoting citizenship, inspecting their own localities, making reports on health, housing, playgrounds, and assuming some responsibility in promoting the welfare of those younger than themselves.

A primary factor in juvenile delinquency is the broken home, whether physically broken or emotionally so, and religious institutions must seek ways of trying to lower the rate of this breakage, or ways to meet the resulting needs of the child.

The churches and temples must find more ways to enhance the moral tone of the adult community, must increase or create in the child a respect for spiritual standards that will be accepted and that will be lasting.

There should be greater co-operation between the churches and synagogues and all other social institutions that are working against delinquency. Directly co-ordinated with this is the need for religious institutions to make a greater effort to attract persons released from penal institutions or training schools, to show a sincere interest in making the individual feel wanted, and to encourage them in developing and maintaining a participating interest in the church's valuable activities.

4. The Community

As already observed, good housing and adequate recreational facilities are strong deterrents to delinquency. Every community should have as part of its antidelinquency program a sound program for providing these for all its people.

It is essential too that the resources of the entire community be effectively co-ordinated if the over-all program is to be successful. All states and communities, therefore, should have what some states and some cities have already set up—Youth Commissions to co-ordinate all antidelinquency activities.

A step in the right direction was made in November, 1954, when officials of national organizations and federal agencies concerned with efforts to combat juvenile delinquency met with the Senate Subcommittee to Investigate Juvenile Delinquency in Washington, D.C. Senator Robert C. Hendrickson, chairman of the subcommittee, asked, "What is to be done to round out and co-ordinate the leadership and know-how about the prevention and treatment of juvenile delinquency?" This was the first time that representatives of all these groups had gotten together, and it was the consensus that a co-ordinating mechanism be established to work on specific programs.

5. Moral Standards

Our youth see too much corruption in high places, on the national, state, and local scenes. Whenever we read about crime or corruption involving our officials, we must remember the effect that their lack of morality has on our children. "So what?" one young thief remarked to me. "I stole a hundred and fifty dollars from a gas station. But how much did Hoffman steal from the people of New Jersey?"

To prevent this kind of reasoning in our children we must work to raise the moral standard of living at every single level. We should ban horror comics, pornographic literature, or other crime-provoking books. Although comic books by themselves will not create delinquency, repetitive dunning into the child's mind of ways to commit crime, of glorifying crime, as horror books do now, can well create an attitude within the child that makes him more susceptible to delinquency than he might otherwise be.

We should get rid of the danger spots in the community. Every community has some recognizable sore spot. This may be a "gin mill" where undesirables gather. It may be a corner poolroom where dope is sold or pushed. It may be an old, abandoned warehouse that is used for illicit purposes by adolescents. Whatever it may be, these sore spots are temptation zones.

We must make our democracy more effective, more efficient, and more in keeping with the high traditions and ideals of our founding fathers.

These, then, could be some of the areas to be strengthened in an all-out preventive program. But what about the corrective measures? We must live with our present generation, and deal with the delinquent who is with us today and will be with us tomorrow. That calls for another series of measures to be considered as part of an antidelinquency program.

6. The Police Departments

As has been seen, juvenile delinquency bureaus have been set up by police departments in many parts of the country. But more are needed. Every community should have a well-trained juvenile police staff.

Many of the cities that I reached in my survey of the juvenile police program indicate that they are hamstrung by lack of funds and by lack of trained personnel. A child's first contact with the police is most important. It can mean a turning point for better or for worse. Accordingly, we must develop throughout the country a network of the best juvenile police officers that the world has ever seen. These officers can and should implement a new philosophy in their dealings with delinquent youth, a philosophy that does not use the night stick to "break" a young offender, but rather the clinic to help remake him.

The entire community should come to the help of police juvenile officers, instead of expecting an undersized staff to handle the cases. The officers themselves should receive the best psychological training, should be chosen with as much care as a teacher or social worker, and should have those qualities that a child will like, and which will make the child desire to emulate, not despise, him.

7. The Psychiatric Clinics

Throughout the country today we recognize the need for more psychiatric help. We simply do not have enough mental hygiene services for our children, or for our adults, to be used both for the prevention and the early treatment of delinquency. The psychiatrist, the psychologist, and the guidance worker can help correct the social and emotional problems remaining after the child has passed through the various earlier preventive programs that have been set up.

These professionals must work directly in some communities. The remedial help that a predelinquent or delinquent school child can receive in the clinic may be far more important and is obviously far less expensive than the treatment that he may be expected to get once he reaches training school or prison.

Every community should co-ordinate its efforts to create better psychiatric and psychological help for those in need. With the vast tensions and strain confronting us today—ranging all the way from the cold war, the hydrogen bomb, and the every-day pressures of a technological age—the importance of mental health looms larger than ever before. Not only children, but adults too, should receive the help, guidance, and attention that can be given by psychiatric clinics. The need for these clinics, in the battle against juvenile delinquency and adult crime, has never been more urgent. We must no longer remain indifferent to the importance of the mental health approach in our every-day lives.

8. The Juvenile Courts

There is too great a lag between what we know about the penal service of children and adolescents and what we are doing to put our knowledge into practice. We must provide a greater opportunity for our courts to do a better job. At the present time the majority of communities do not even have juvenile courts. Those juvenile courts that do exist are all too often too ill-equipped to function effectively. Even in some of the better supported courts, like those in New York, the courts are not doing the job that they should. The children's courts are not adequately staffed, either with probation officers or judges.

If we are to help rehabilitate our boys and girls in trouble, the courts must receive greater attention and consideration from the community.

The Temporary State Commission on the Courts of New York approved a plan, in December, 1954, to establish uniform courts for youthful offenders between the ages of sixteen and twenty-one throughout the state. It was pointed out that long waits in prison with hardened criminals could be avoided if youthful offenders waived their rights before grand juries, and that young people are spending too much time in jails waiting for grand jury action.

Competent judges are handicapped by overcrowded calendars. A judge who has to preside over fifty to sixty cases in a single day, as happened during a day when I observed one of New York City's children's courts in action, cannot be expected to do a constructive job. Often the best he can do is blindly accept the recommendation of the probation officer and continue on to the next case.

This situation is worsened by the fact that we rely upon probation officers who are not adequately trained themselves. Statistics show that only about 10 per cent of the probation officers of the country actually meet the standards set by the experts.

We must also work to bring about on the part of many judges in our juvenile courts the attitude that their job is to help young boys or girls along the road to rehabilitation—not to lecture, not to moralize, not merely to punish them for their misdeeds.

The community can act to provide adequate personnel, adequate funds, and adequate philosophy to the courts, as well as to the schools, the clinics, and other centers dealing with our children.

9. The Foster Homes and Detention Places

It is sometimes entirely necessary to remove a child from his home temporarily or permanently, either because of delinquency or because he is seriously neglected or mistreated. Our entire system of temporary detention places—often these are jails shared by adult criminals —and of foster homes is in dire need of overhauling. The community must therefore evaluate the important role played by these places in the lives of scores of thousands of delinquent and potentially delinquent children, and take active measures to raise their standards. Improved foster home placement and improved temporary detention homes, coupled with increased treatment facilities in the local communities, can drastically reduce the future population of the training schools.

10. The Training Schools

The change of the name "reform school" to "training school" has not yet transformed these institutions into effective rehabilitation centers for the delinquent children committed to them. We must strengthen these schools by providing them with better equipment, sufficient and trained staffs, and greatly enlarged social work, psychiatric, and psychological services. No corrective program of the future can be based on the meager facilities of the training school of the past, or even of the present.

There should be an increase in the number of correctional institutions (not maximum security prisons). Every community should then have a central agency to diagnose emotional and physical problems to aid the correctional institutions. The training of staff members should be constantly dynamic and advanced.

The aim of parole procedures should be to lessen the period of time of parole. These procedures should be examined and evaluated frequently. The local parole boards should co-operate with all other agencies by imparting the knowledge and facts they have about individual cases.

Vocational training in correctional institutions should be improved as much as possible, and industrial leaders should be asked to co-operate in the training by advising what their companies' future needs will be, and by taking an interest in possible potential employment of the parolee. Religious groups should also participate in training school activities and maintain deeper contact with the child after his release.

The entire system of probation should be examined, then strengthened.

The colleges and schools of social service should emphasize the need for workers in the training schools, and stimulate an increase in the number of pupils studying for this as a career.

To implement these recommendations, it will be essential that we work on every possible level—on the local level, on the state or regional level, and on the national level.

The splendid antidelinquency work now being done by the federal Children's Bureau indicates the direction in which we must go. The control must come from the local community, although the support and the guidance should, in most cases, come from state and federal governments.

The principles formulated at the Berkshire International Forum in 1951 merit study. The forum brought together fifty authorities in the field of delinquency, including representatives from the bench, psychiatry, education, institutional and agency administration, as well as delegates from the United Nations Secretariat. They met to set up standards for the treatment of delinquent persons. This is the statement of policy and principles to which the forum subscribed:

"We believe that society has the obligation as well as the need to provide for those children who become delinquent the services and situations needed by them to achieve constructive social living. The roots of delinquent behavior lie in part in the defects of society itself, and we all share responsibility for them. A realization of the ideals of a democratic society is inconceivable without common effort to redirect toward constructive citizenship those children who have not learned how to relate themselves to others acceptably, or who persist for whatever reason in a destructive way of life.

"We conceive nothing to be of so great importance in the readjustment of delinquent children as a readiness to recognize their individual dignity and worth as human beings, and the capacity to extend to them that human understanding of their desires, aspirations, and feelings which all men crave and need. We recognize further that the effective readjustment of delinquent children generally requires, and is promoted by, that human understanding and aid made possible through the development of professional specialties such as general medicine including psychiatry, clinical psychology, social case work and group work, special education, and related professions.

"We recognize the place of, and need for, institutions for the treatment of delinquent children who cannot be effectively treated in the community, or who can be better treated in resident institutions than in the community. Such treatment institutions should effectively represent one essential phase in an integrated program of preventive and treatment services for the social adjustment of children.

"In instances in which parents or guardians neglect the welfare of children or in which delinquent actions of children cannot be controlled, we recognize the right and obligation of the community to intervene through legal actions if other measures fail, preferably by way of a specialized children's court.

"We unanimously condemn any philosophy of taking social vengeance upon delinquent children, or any reliance upon a philosophy of punishment. Specifically we condemn the use of any corporal punishment, or any humiliating devices in discipline of the child.

"We hold that it is the primary function of institutions for delinquent juveniles, whether public or private, to become centers of constructive training and treatment, to the end that the children may return to their communities prepared to make adequate adjustment to the requirements of family and community living.

"Treatment measures, however, are effective only as they are related to the nature and needs of the child. We believe, therefore, that treatment should relate to the causal factors of delinquency in the individual child. Individualized study of the delinquent should form a basis for seeking to meet his needs. Professionally skilled diagnostic study by trained people is necessary, and such personnel should be available to aid the general staff of the training school in working with the children constructively, and to give specially skilled therapy to those children needing such treatment.

"Program planning within the institution should be based upon continued study of the individual and his development at the institution as well as by the social and diagnostic information provided from the community.

"We believe it is essential that there be careful selection of children for placement in institutions for delinquents so that only those will be referred who (1) may profit from the specific advantages of the social experience that an effective institution can provide, (2) cannot remain in their own homes or foster homes in the community, or (3) must be removed from the community because of the serious nature of their behavior.

"Placement at a particular institution should be based upon careful study of the individual: social investigations through an appropriate social agency and, wherever possible and necessary, study and observation in a diagnostic clinic or reception center before disposition."

As this statement emphasizes, every child is an individual. How can we make reliable and useful generalizations about people in general, about children in general? The psychiatrist in T. S. Eliot's *The Cocktail Party* said, "All cases are unique and very similar to others." Nevertheless, we must constantly be aware that with human beings it is the unique individual that is our chief concern—in the Quaker sense of "concern"—and that any generalizations we may make about people, however interesting they may be, are of primary social importance only insofar as they provide us with procedures that will help us to better our relations with *individuals*.

With a rapidly mounting rate of delinquency and crime, we do not have time to consider the total validity of theories about the nature of human beings. It is easy to become distracted; consequently we must be ever ready to make the proper distinctions.

However intimately connected the research and curative endeavors may be for the analyst—for the purposes of our particular problem, juvenile delinquency, we must recognize the *difference* between research and cure. Our entire interest at the moment is children. Moreover, we must guard against the tendency of the analyst, the legal mind, the social reformer, to concentrate only on a particular aspect of an individual. The divided attention of the specialist may result in programs that lead us down narrow paths away from the holistic attitude that alone can help each single delinquent. For example, there are schools for disturbed children and for children from broken homes that are so oriented psychoanalytically that they neglect the child's need for a homelike atmosphere.

Juvenile delinquency is a negative phenomenon. Positively, what interests us is that we have happy, healthy children. If there is some *doubt* as to whether or not a particular line of action, (for example, slum clearance), will substantially decrease the rate of juvenile delinquency, and no doubt that it can do harm, we have nothing to lose in taking it. In a broad, all-out program for improving the lot of our children, we can, I believe, achieve a condition in which delinquency is diminished to a fraction of its present incidence. We may never be sure in detail that what we did was *right*.

It is possible first to prevent a boy or girl from becoming delinquent and then to help that boy or girl develop as a normal individual. It is also possible, when once a child does become a delinquent, to correct, or at least mitigate his emotional disturbance, and bring about a transformation that will make him into a constructive citizen.

No task, to my mind, can be more important to us today, when we are fighting an ideological war, a war for men's minds. The warped, unwholesome minds of delinquents will not help the cause of democracy. Contrariwise, every child who is saved from becoming delinquent, or who is rehabilitated, adds to the inherent strength of our country.

Let us make childhood a happy experience for all of our children, not for just a part of them. Statistically, only from 2 to 5 per cent of our youth become delinquent. The other 95 to 98 per cent are not overtly troublesome. Yet, surely the 2 to 5 per cent are worth saving. In a democracy, each individual is important; it is worth while to save *one* child, and we now know how to save a high proportion of delinquents. Working within the democratic concept, it is possible for us within our generation to wipe out a growing menace.

Herman Rikelman, director of community and personal services for the Jewish Board of Guardians, made the following point: we now have the knowledge to cut delinquency by 75 per cent, without new panaceas, or atomic discoveries in psychology. Applying that knowledge, he stated, is merely a matter of dollars and cents.

And, on January 26, 1955, Governor Averell Harriman of New

York State called for an all-out frontal attack on the causes of juvenile delinquency. He presented a program to the legislature designed to destroy "the forces which distort the behavior of our children and cause untold personal suffering and human ills."

Governor Harriman warned that child crime is a type of infection which if allowed to spread would seriously sap the strength of our society. The governor suggested a program of slum clearance, more recreational facilities, better schools, more police, additional psychiatric guidance, more court and probation officers, and better detention facilities.

As the governor said, it is necessary "to reduce the terrifying human loss resulting from juvenile delinquency." And he concluded: "We must find the means to assure that as few as possible of our children become lost to society, and to achieve the speediest restoration of those who do get into trouble.

"If we succeed, the gain in happiness for thousands of our families will be of a value beyond our ability to measure."

This program will cost money.

Society unfortunately does not always recognize the importance of spending the money necessary to prevent youngsters from becoming confirmed delinquents. Ironically, almost tragically, it was brought out that the capital of the United States paid more for taking care of the monkeys in the Washington zoo than it appropriated for taking care of children in the city's detention homes. We are practicing false economy when we provide our young offenders with inadequate rehabilitation facilities. One estimate shows that not more than two hundred million dollars ($200,000,-000) is now spent annually in this country by the police, courts, detention facilities, and institutions for juveniles. The current cost of all crime in America is estimated by the FBI at fifteen *billion* dollars ($15,000,000,000). If we spent more to rehabilitate our juvenile offenders, we would substantially reduce this staggering crime bill. This would be a true saving, not only of money but of children.

We are practicing false economy, too, when we let the courts, police, and institutions bear the brunt of the juvenile delinquency problem. Just as it is less, much less, expensive to rehabilitate unhappy children and prevent them from becoming adult criminals, so we will save a tremendous amount by giving them guidance in their early years and preventing them from needing such rehabilitation.

The Senate subcommittee commented:

"In the fight against juvenile delinquency this Nation can be said to be fiddling while Rome burns. We devote much attention, energy, and resources—and rightly so—to the fight against communism, both at home and abroad. We are waging that fight to keep this Nation free. To what avail is that fight if the moral fiber of more and more of our children is being undermined? These are the children who will one day become our Nation's leaders. It is for them that we are fighting to keep America free.

"We devote untold millions to the protection of our national resources through reforestation, prevention of soil erosion, and the like. But we are neglecting our biggest national resource—our children and youth."

We can view the future optimistically if we set out with firm determination to reach our goal. Our goal is to reduce, if not eliminate completely, those factors and forces that contribute to making a child emotionally disturbed, mentally sick, and potentially, or actually, delinquent.

That is the job that confronts us. A country that was able to enlist all its human and material resources within two generations to win gigantic wars against aggression should not find it too difficult to mass its energies, facilities, knowledge and funds to win our domestic war against juvenile delinquency.

In that way we will strengthen our own democratic nation. In that way we will strengthen our communities. In that way we will strengthen our families.

There is no finer crusade for us to follow.

A Comparison of the Experiences
of Boys and Girls AT THE NEW JERSEY STATE
HOME FOR BOYS IN JAMESBURG IN 1937 AND IN
1954 AND AT THE NEW YORK STATE TRAINING
SCHOOL FOR GIRLS IN HUDSON IN 1954

NOTE: *In questions where total number of children exceeds base figure used and total percentage exceeds 100 per cent, some children have checked more than one answer.*

A. QUESTIONS ABOUT SCHOOL

	Jamesburg, 1937 Total: 500 Boys	Jamesburg, 1954 Total: 208 Boys		Hudson, 1954 Total: 208 Girls	
	Percentage	Percentage	Number	Percentage	Number
1. How did you get along in your school work?					
Generally good	40.0	27.4	57	30.8	64
Good in most subjects, not so good in others	44.0	44.7	93	43.3	90
Fair		13.9	29	11.1	23
Poor in most subjects, better in others	16.0	7.7	16	8.7	18
Generally poor		6.3	13	8.2	17
2. When you were poor in your school work, was it because you didn't try?					
Yes	48.6	66.3	138	61.5	128
No	32.8	31.3	65	38.5	80
No answer	18.6	2.4	5	—	—
2a. If you didn't try, what made you feel that you didn't want to?	[Base fig.: 243]	[Base fig. : 138]		[Base fig. : 208]	
Disliked school	43.9	17.4	24	25.9	54
Disliked subject		27.5	38	27.4	57
Other interests	22.0	27.5	38	18.8	39
Didn't care	7.8	9.4	13	1.4	3
Lack of help	10.2	4.3	6	12.5	26
Laziness	16.1	15.2	21	8.7	18
No answer	—	0.7	1	5.3	11

	Jamesburg, 1937 Total: 500 Boys	Jamesburg, 1954 Total: 208 Boys		Hudson, 1954 Total: 208 Girls	
	Percentage	Percentage	Number	Percentage	Number
3. Did you have any trouble with teachers?					
Most teachers		12.5	26	8.2	17
Some teachers	54.0	19.2	40	17.3	36
A few teachers		21.6	45	19.2	40
One teacher especially		18.8	39	19.7	41
No	46.0	27.4	57	31.7	66
No answer	—	0.5	1	8.7	18
4. What school grade were you enrolled in when you came here?					
Grade 1	0.2	—	—	—	—
2	1.0	—	—	—	—
3	3.3	1.4	3	—	—
4	8.2	1.0	2	—	—
5	19.0	5.3	11	1.0	2
6	25.0	10.6	22	3.8	8
7	23.0	24.1	50	18.8	39
8	14.3	23.5	49	22.1	46
9	4.3	23.5	49	27.4	57
10	1.3	5.8	12	13.9	29
11	—	2.4	5	5.3	11
12	—	0.5	1	0.5	1
Other	0.4	1.9	4	2.9	6
No answer	—	—	—	4.3	9
5. What was your last school?					
An elementary school		23.1	48	12.5	26
A junior high school		50.4	105	63.9	133
A senior high school		14.9	31	14.4	30
A vocational school		11.1	23	8.7	18
No answer		0.5	1	0.5	1
6. How did you like school?					
Enjoyed it		23.6	49	38.0	79
Something I had to do		29.3	61	24.0	50
Indifferent		15.4	32	7.7	16
Disliked it		29.8	62	30.3	63
No answer		1.9	4	—	—

	Jamesburg, 1937 Total: 500 Boys	Jamesburg, 1954 Total: 208 Boys		Hudson, 1954 Total: 208 Girls	
	Percentage	Percentage	Number	Percentage	Number
7. How many grades did you repeat?					
None	25.0	28.8	60	55.2	115
One		38.0	79	26.0	54
Two	75.0	22.1	46	8.2	17
Three or more		11.1	23	8.7	18
No answer	—	—	—	1.9	4
8. What subject did you like most?					
Reading		19.2	40	12.0	25
Arithmetic and other mathematics		26.0	54	27.9	58
Spelling		23.1	48	23.1	48
Writing		3.4	7	4.3	9
Social studies [including history and geography]		7.2	15	5.3	11
English		1.4	3	3.4	7
Science [including biology and chemistry]		4.8	10	8.6	18
Arts and crafts		6.3	13	1.4	3
Physical Education, health		1.9	4	—	—
Miscellaneous		0.5	1	10.6	22*
No answer		7.7	16	3.4	7
9. What subject did you dislike most?					
Reading		3.8	8	3.8	8
Arithmetic and other mathematics		35.1	73	45.2	94
Spelling		17.3	36	15.9	33
Writing		4.3	9	2.4	5
Social studies [including history and geography]		8.2	17	10.1	21
English		13.9	29	6.7	14

* Includes: 5—typing; 3—none; 2—all subjects, citizen education, dressmaking; 1—all commercial subjects, bookkeeping, business, cooking, music, nursing, record keeping, Spanish.

	Jamesburg, 1937 Total: 500 Boys	Jamesburg, 1954 Total: 208 Boys		Hudson, 1954 Total: 208 Girls	
	Percentage	Percentage	Number	Percentage	Number
Science [including biology and chemistry]		1.0	2	4.3	9
Arts and crafts		0.5	1	—	—
Physical education, health		0.5	1	0.5	1
Miscellaneous		—	—	10.1	21*
No answer		15.4	32	1.0	2
10. Did you play truant?					
Often	69.2	40.8	85	40.4	84
Sometimes	30.0	45.7	95	38.9	81
No	0.8	13.5	28	18.8	39
No answer	—	—	—	1.9	4
11. How were you treated by attendance officers?					
Fairly	33.6	60.5	126	74.0	154
Unfairly	5.4	15.0	31	8.2	17
Otherwise	} 61.0	8.6	18	7.2	15
No answer		15.9	33	10.6	22
12. Were you ever taken to court for truancy?					
Yes	37.0	34.6	72	45.2	94
No, but my parents were	59.4	1.9	4	4.8	10
No	} 3.6	49.1	102	48.1	100
No answer		14.4	30	1.9	4

* Includes: 11—none; 4—all of them; 1—guidance, grammar, homemaking, Latin, music shorthand.

B. QUESTIONS ABOUT LEISURE-TIME ACTIVITIES

	Jamesburg, 1937 Total: 500 Boys	Jamesburg, 1954 Total: 208 Boys		Hudson, 1954 Total: 208 Girls	
	Percentage	Percentage	Number	Percentage	Number
1. How did you spend your time outside of school? (Check what you did mostly.)					
Sports or play	30.0	25.0	52	19.2	40
Working	23.0	14.9	31	12.5	26
Part work and play	11.0	37.5	78	25.5	53
Running in the streets, loitering	7.0	33.2	69	26.0	54
Gambling, hanging around gamblers	14.0	15.9	33	3.8	8
Reading, hobbies	4.0	11.1	23	6.3	13
Radio, television	Not asked	22.1	46	22.6	47
Paid entertainment	10.0	11.5	24	12.5	26
Other	1.0	9.1	19	38.9	81*
No answer	—	1.0	2	—	—
2. What organizations did you belong to?					
YMCA/YWCA		39.9	83	20.2	42
Boys Club		22.1	46	—	—
Boy Scouts/Girl Scouts		27.4	57	16.8	35
Church group		15.4	32	26.4	55
Other [including PAL, community centers, gangs]		16.8	35	37.0	77
No answer		26.0	54	—	—
3. Were there playgrounds near your home?					
Yes	82.0	82.7	172	85.1	177
No	18.0	17.3	36	12.0	25
No answer	—	—	—	2.9	6
4. Did you use them much?					
Yes	65.0	37.0	77	45.7	95
No	35.0	58.7	122	50.5	105
No answer	—	4.3	9	3.8	8

* Includes: 69—hanging around boys; 2—gang fights, stayed home; 1—at sister's home, dancing, drinking and smoking, taking care of sister's baby.

	Jamesburg, 1937 Total: 500 Boys	Jamesburg, 1954 Total: 208 Boys		Hudson, 1954 Total: 208 Girls	
	Percentage	Percentage	Number	Percentage	Number
5. What kind of gang did you go with (boys or girls in trouble or not in trouble)?					
Good, none in trouble	24.0	17.8	37	26.4	55
Mixed, some in trouble, some not	19.0	56.2	117	56.7	118
Bad, most in trouble	49.0	26.0	54	20.2	42
No answer	8.0	—	—	—	—
6. Did you go around with boys or girls who had been sent to places like this?					
Yes	38.0	45.7	95	34.2	71
No	62.0	53.8	112	64.4	134
No answer	—	0.5	1	1.4	3
7. Did you take part in breaking the law with boys or girls who had been sent to places like this?					
Yes	63.0	37.0	77	19.7	41
Sometimes	Not asked	45.2	94	37.5	78
No	37.0	17.8	37	41.8	87
No answer	—	—	—	1.0	2
8. Did they lead you into your first trouble with the police?					
Yes	56.0	34.6	72	27.9	58
Maybe	Not asked	28.8	60	16.8	35
No	44.0	35.6	74	55.3	115
No answer	—	1.0	2	—	—

C. QUESTIONS ABOUT YOUR FAMILY

	Jamesburg, 1937 Total: 500 Boys	Jamesburg, 1954 Total: 208 Boys		Hudson, 1954 Total: 208 Girls	
	Percentage	Percentage	Number	Percentage	Number
1. With whom were you living when you came here?					
Both parents	72.0	39.4	82	22.1	46
Mother and stepfather		13.9	29	10.1	21
Mother only		21.2	42	27.9	58
Father and stepmother		6.7	14	5.3	11
Father only	28.0	4.8	10	3.8	8
Other relatives		6.3	13	18.3	38
Foster home		6.7	14	3.4	7
Institution		2.4	5	9.1	19
1a. If you were not with both parents, why weren't you?		[Base fig. : 126]		[Base fig. : 162]	
Both parents dead		4.0	5	2.5	4
Father dead		19.8	25	19.1	31
Mother dead		8.7	11	14.2	23
Parents parted		52.4	66	38.8	63
Other		5.6	7	19.8	32*
No answer		9.5	12	5.6	9
2. Did your family (or relatives) try to keep you out of trouble?					
Yes	98.8	94.3	196	95.7	199
No	.2	4.3	9	4.3	9
No answer	1.0	1.4	3	—	—
3. Did they ever help you or ask you to break the law?					
Yes	1.6	3.4	7	3.4	7
No	94.6	94.7	197	95.2	198
No answer	3.8	1.9	4	1.4	3

*Includes: "Do not know parents"; "Neglect"; "I was sent away"; "They were not married"; "Institution."

	Jamesburg, 1937 Total: 500 Boys	Jamesburg, 1954 Total: 208 Boys		Hudson, 1954 Total: 208 Girls	
	Percentage	Percentage	Number	Percentage	Number
4. How many brothers and sisters have you?					
None		—	—	3.4	7
One		12.5	26	20.2	42
Two		19.7	41	13.0	27
Three		16.9	35	20.2	42
Four		9.6	20	5.8	12
Five		11.5	24	9.6	20
Six or more		20.7	43	21.5	45
No answer		9.1	19	6.3	13
5. Were you—					
Oldest child in family?		36.1	75	29.3	61
Youngest child in family?		16.8	35	24.5	51
In the middle?		42.8	89	40.4	84
No answer		4.3	9	5.8	12
6. Do you feel that your parents loved you?					
Yes, loved all children	82.6	79.7	166	77.4	161
Liked me better than others	6.2	3.4	7	2.4	5
Liked me less than others	7.2	8.2	17	9.6	20
Did not care much for their children	—	2.4	5	4.3	9
Other (write in)	—	2.9	6	6.3	13*
No answer	4.0	3.4	7	—	—
7. How did your parents (or stepparents) get along with each other?					
Fine, rarely quarreled		41.3	86	46.1	96
Usually well, sometimes quarreled		35.6	74	27.9	58
Quarreled most of time		13.5	28	14.9	31
No answer		9.6	20	11.1	23

*Includes: "I was her only baby"; "Didn't bother to care for me or give me love"; "Mother, yes—Father, no"; "Stepfather didn't like me"; "I don't know but I think so."

C. QUESTIONS ABOUT YOUR FAMILY (Cont.)

	Jamesburg, 1937 Total: 500 Boys	Jamesburg, 1954 Total: 208 Boys		Hudson, 1954 Total: 208 Girls	
	Percentage	Percentage	Number	Percentage	Number
8. What kind of a house did you live in when you came here?					
One-family		45.2	94	31.7	66
Two-family		17.8	37	17.8	37
With three or more families		33.2	69	29.8	62
Other		1.4	3	18.8	39
No answer		2.4	5	1.9	4
9. How long had you lived there?					
Less than six months		12.0	25	16.4	34
Six months to one year		11.5	24	8.2	17
One year		8.7	18	13.9	29
Two years		13.0	27	12.0	25
Three or more years		38.0	79	31.7	66
All your life		14.9	31	17.3	36
No answer		1.9	4	0.5	1
10. How many times have you moved in last five years?					
None		38.0	79	30.8	64
One		21.2	44	18.3	38
Two		12.5	26	14.4	30
Three		9.6	20	11.5	24
Four		4.3	9	5.8	12
Five or more		11.5	24	14.4	30
No answer		2.9	6	4.8	10

D. QUESTIONS ABOUT HOW YOU CAME HERE

	Jamesburg, 1937 Total: 500 Boys	Jamesburg, 1954 Total: 208 Boys		Hudson, 1954 Total: 208 Girls	
	Percentage	Percentage	Number	Percentage	Number
1. How old were you when you started doing things against the law?					
Under 8	19.9	16.8	35	6.7	14
9	10.8	9.1	19	5.8	12
10	12.6	7.7	16	5.8	12
11	12.2	5.8	12	12.5	26
12	20.2	15.4	32	15.9	33
13	12.6	12.5	26	20.6	43
14	7.6	13.5	28	15.9	33
15	3.7	4.3	9	9.6	20
16	0.4	—	—	0.5	1
Don't remember	—	14.9	31	3.8	8
No answer	—	—	—	2.9	6
2. When you first got into trouble, what did you do?					
Stealing	51.0	44.7	93	11.1	23
Burglary, unlawful entry	13.0	17.8	37	3.8	8
Auto theft	1.0	11.5	24	—	—
Damage to property	6.0	13.9	29	1.9	4
Ungovernable	3.0	4.3	9	8.7	18
Truancy	12.0	16.4	34	32.2	67
Sex	1.0	11.5	24	17.8	37
Running away	9.0	14.9	31	43.8	91
Injury to person	4.0	7.2	15	3.8	8
Other	—	1.9	4	8.2	17
No answer	—	0.5	1	—	—
3. Why do you think you first got into trouble?					
Bad companions	38.0	38.5	80	31.3	65
Wanted excitement	3.0	19.2	40	18.8	39
Wanted luxuries	11.0	13.0	27	5.8	12
Bad habits	4.0	4.8	10	3.4	7
Dislike of school	19.0	15.4	32	15.4	32
Having fun	6.0	15.4	32	21.6	45
Lack of necessities	16.0	Not asked		Not asked	
Don't know	Not asked	12.5	26	11.5	24
Other	3.0	3.8	8	10.6	22*
No answer	—	0.5	1	—	—

* Includes: 3—family troubles; "Love boys"; "My mother never let me out to play"; "Running away with boy friend"; "I thought I was a big shot"; "Because of moving all the time"; "I wanted independence. I did not have it, fought with mother."

	Jamesburg, 1937 Total: 500 Boys	Jamesburg, 1954 Total: 208 Boys		Hudson, 1954 Total: 208 Girls	
	Percentage	Percentage	Number	Percentage	Number
4. How did you learn how to do these things?					
Older boys or girls	44.0	40.3	84	40.9	85
Grownups	12.0	3.4	7	6.3	13
Boys or girls of own age	58.0	37.5	78	26.9	56
Relatives	2.0	2.9	6	1.0	2
Newspapers	9.0	2.9	6	3.4	7
Movies	38.0	6.7	14	2.9	6
Radio	} 8.0	2.4	5	1.4	3
Television		4.8	10	2.4	5
Comic books	} not asked	4.8	10	3.4	7
Magazines		2.4	5	4.3	9
Other	—	5.3	11	16.4	34*
No answer	—	7.2	15	—	—
5. When you first started getting into trouble, did you think about getting caught?					
Didn't think about it	72.0	38.5	80	38.0	79
Was scared of it	23.0	13.0	27	12.0	25
Took a chance	2.0	48.0	100	43.3	90
Didn't care	—	—	—	4.8	10
Other	3.0	—	—	—	—
No answer	—	0.5	1	1.9	4
6. How many times were you in trouble with the police before you went to court?					
Never	—	—		13.5	28
One	26.0	54		34.1	71
Two	16.8	35		10.6	22
Three	10.1	21		8.7	18
Four	9.1	19		2.9	6
Five	4.3	9		1.9	4
Six or more	26.5	55		11.5	24
No answer	7.2	15		16.8	35

* Includes: 19—"myself"; 3—"Don't know"; 2—"my big sister."

	Jamesburg, 1937 Total: 500 Boys	Jamesburg, 1954 Total: 208 Boys		Hudson, 1954 Total: 208 Girls	
	Percentage	Percentage	Number	Percentage	Number
7. Were you given a fair break by the police?					
Yes	80.0	48.6	101	50.0	104
Usually	Not asked	6.7	14	3.8	8
Sometimes	Not asked	16.4	34	6.7	14
No	20.0	24.0	50	21.7	45
No answer	—	7.2	15	17.8	37
7a. Do you feel you have been sent here [Hudson] unfairly?					
Yes				43.3	90
No				54.3	113
Don't know				1.0	2
No answer				1.4	3
8. How many times were you in court before you came here?					
Never		—	—	1.0	2
One		26.9	56	21.6	45
Two		22.1	46	19.7	41
Three		16.9	35	14.9	31
Four		10.1	21	11.1	23
Five		5.3	11	7.2	15
Six or more		14.9	31	19.2	40
No answer		3.8	8	5.3	11
9. Did you go to a child guidance clinic before you came here (not the Diagnostic Center in Menlo Park, N. J.)?					
Yes		32.7	68	44.2	92
No		65.4	136	52.0	108
No answer		1.9	4	3.8	8

	Jamesburg, 1937 Total: 500 Boys	Jamesburg, 1954 Total: 208 Boys		Hudson, 1954 Total: 208 Girls	
	Percentage	Percentage	Number	Percentage	Number
10. Did you go the Menlo Park Diagnostic Center?					
Before coming to Jamesburg		20.2	42		
After coming to Jamesburg		4.8	10		
No		73.1	152		
No answer		1.9	4		
11. Were you put on probation before coming here?					
Yes	67.0	75.0	156	58.7	122
No	33.0	25.0	52	37.5	78
No answer	—	—	—	3.8	8
12. Have you been out on parole since you came here?					
Yes		23.1	48	6.3	13
No		76.9	160	85.5	178
No answer		—	—	8.2	17
13. Whose fault is it that you are here [Hudson]?					
Police				1.9	4
Court				9.6	20
My own				73.6	153
School				6.3	13
Parents				13.0	27

	Jamesburg, 1937 Total: 500 Boys	Jamesburg, 1954 Total: 208 Boys		Hudson, 1954 Total: 208 Girls	
	Percentage	Percentage	Number	Percentage	Number
1. How old are you now?					
10 and under	1.7	—	—	—	—
11	3.0	1.0	2	—	—
12	7.0	1.0	2	4.3	9
13	13.0	6.7	14	7.2	15
14	17.0	19.7	41	22.6	47
15	33.1	40.4	84	31.2	65
16	19.0	26.9	56	27.9	58
17	5.0	3.8	8	5.8	12
18 or over	1.2	0.5	1	—	—
No answer	—	—	—	1.0	2
2. Do you think you will be able to get along all right after leaving here?					
Yes	96.6	79.3	165	90.8	189
Uncertain	—	18.8	39	6.3	13
No	1.2	1.9	4	1.0	2
No answer	2.2	—	—	1.9	4
3. Do you think you have learned more good or bad here [Jamesburg]?					
Mostly good	90.0	42.8	89		
Some of both	1.0	40.4	84		
Mostly bad	9.0	15.4	32		
No answer	—	1.4	3		
3a. Have you learned anything from being here [Hudson]?					
A lot				74.0	154
Some				13.0	27
A little				5.8	12
Nothing				5.3	11
No answer				1.9	4

	Jamesburg, 1937 Total: 500 Boys	Jamesburg, 1954 Total: 208 Boys		Hudson, 1954 Total: 208 Girls	
	Percentage	Percentage	Number	Percentage	Number
4. Do you plan to keep on going to school when you leave here?					
Yes		50.5	105	61.0	127
Don't know		18.8	39	15.4	32
No		29.3	61	18.8	39
No answer		1.4	3	4.8	10
5. Do you think you have learned anything here which will help you get and keep a job?					
Yes		87.0	181	89.4	186
No		12.0	25	10.6	22
No answer		1.0	2	—	—
6. What kind of work do you think you might do best? [Hudson.]					
Office				21.2	44
Store				10.6	22
Factory				19.7	41
Beautician				13.5	28
Cook				5.8	12
Waitress				14.4	30
Armed forces				13.5	28
Housekeeping				20.2	42
Other				14.9	31*
6a. What kind of work do you think you can do best after leaving here [Jamesburg]?					
Professional	12.0	13.0	27		
Clerical, business	8.0	15.9	33		
Industrial [skilled and semiskilled]	45.0	71.2	148		
Unskilled	27.0	10.1	21		
Miscellaneous [includes athletics]	—	2.9	6		
Armed forces	—	23.1	48		
No choice	8.0	—	—		

* Includes: 14—Nursing.

	Jamesburg, 1937 Total: 500 Boys	Jamesburg, 1954 Total: 208 Boys		Hudson, 1954 Total: 208 Girls	
	Percentage	Percentage	Number	Percentage	Number
7. What do you want to do when you get out? (*Note*: This question was asked only at Hudson, where the girls wrote in their answers, paraphrased here.)					
Go back to school				14.0	29
Go to work				12.0	25
Go to school and work				7.7	16
Get married				3.8	8
Singing and dancing				3.4	7
Nursing				2.9	6
Beautician				2.4	5
Sewing, tailoring				1.9	4
Telephone operator				1.4	3
Work in a store				1.4	3
Waitress				1.4	3
Miscellaneous				47.7	99*

* Includes: 2—baby sitter, factory work, housekeeping, be a better girl, cook in a cafe.

COMMENTS

In connection with this survey of children in institutions, we were fortunate enough to have the counsel and guidance of Douglas H. MacNeil, Chief of the Bureau of Community Services in the State Department of Institutions and Agencies in New Jersey. Mr. Mac-Neil has been closely associated with the correctional work of New Jersey, particularly as it deals with juveniles, since 1938. The Bureau of Community Services was established in 1945 at about the same time as the New York State Youth Commission was established. An average of 5,000 children annually, or a total of 80,000 children in trouble, have come within his purview. Mr. MacNeil is, therefore, excellently qualified to interpret some of the facts brought out by our study, and to recommend courses of action that will reduce delinquency.

Here are some of Mr. MacNeil's observations:

The significance of this kind of study is not so much in the contribution it makes to literature, as it is in the contribution it makes in aiding community leaders to get at the roots of delinquency in the community in which the children live and in which they have difficulties.

In reviewing the Jamesburg questionnaires, I am struck by the note of optimism expressed by the children in answering the question "How did you get along in your school work?" A surprising number of them—more than half—claimed that they were "generally good," or "good in most subjects." I doubt very much that examination of their school records would support this claim.

Correlation of the questions about retardation tells us that some of the same children who happily said that they were "generally good" in school repeated two to three school years. Many boys at Jamesburg have severe reading handicaps. The educational program at the institution, therefore, is basically a remedial program. Inability to read, or difficulty in reading, has long been recognized as constituting a major block in educational progress. The nonreader or the slow reader is himself very often among those who are most unhappy about their lack of progress.

Of course, we frequently find that the reading difficulties require psychiatric rather than educational remedies. However, it is significant that the retardation rate among the children who claim to be generally good in school work is less pronounced than those who admit their inadequacy.

We compiled some cross correlations of the questions concerning attitudes toward school in order to find out primarily whether or not the children were consistent in their replies.

One correlation dealt with the question "If you didn't try, what made you feel that you didn't want to?" as against the question "How did you like school?" The boys at Jamesburg were consistent in this respect. Only one boy answered the former question by saying that he disliked school and answered the latter one by saying that he enjoyed it.

On the other hand, when we correlated the responses to the questions "How did you like school?" and "Did you play truant?" even those who said that they enjoyed school replied that they sometimes played truant, and about 80 per cent of both boys and girls said that they played truant often or sometimes. However, the largest number of those who said that they played truant often were those who said that they disliked school.

When we were trying to evaluate which findings were most significant in this study, we explored a number of topics about which divergence of professional opinion has been expressed. One of these subjects hinged on the question of whether or not there is likely to be more educational retardation among children from normal homes—normal in the sense that the children were living with both of their own parents—than among those who came from broken homes. We did not find any marked difference in this respect. Relatively speaking, there were more mildly retarded children from broken homes and more severely retarded children from normal homes.

There was no appreciable difference between children from broken homes and children from normal homes with respect to their attitude toward school.

There was also no marked difference between the two categories when it came to belonging to such organizations as the YMCA, boys' clubs, Boy Scouts, and church groups, and belonging to no organization at all.

We did see some significant differences when we analyzed the types of gangs the children belonged to—whether or not the gangs were made up of boys and girls who had been in trouble. Surprisingly enough, we found relatively fewer of the children from broken homes had associated with children who were in trouble.

In this connection, we wonder whether or not the practices of the modern juvenile courts may account for this unexpected correlation. The modern juvenile court commits a child to an institution, not so much because of what he has done specifically—that is, because he has violated the law—as in consideration of his personality and need for training and direction, and the likelihood—or lack of it—that such guidance and direction can be provided in the child's own home and community. This suggests to us the possibility that the children from nonbroken, or normal, homes who are institutionalized rather than being treated in their own homes and communities may be more severely disorganized and in need of intensive correctional treatment and of a controlled environment than are many children who come from broken homes. However, this theory is purely conjectural.

We do find that children from broken homes are more likely to be very young when they start to violate the law. Only 30 per cent of the children from normal homes started their delinquencies when they were less than twelve years of age, as compared with 45 per cent of those who came from broken homes. Among the children from broken homes, 21 per cent claimed that they had started their delinquencies before they were nine years old, as compared with 11 per cent among the children from normal homes.

However, there does not seem to be much of a difference between the two groups with regard to the number of times they had been in trouble with the police before they went to court, or with regard to the number of times they had been in court before they were institutionalized. This finding may be inconsistent with the hypothesis expressed earlier that courts tend to consider broken homes less competent to deal with problems of delinquency than normal homes, resulting in the tendency to commit such children to institutions at a relatively early age.

Another item in our series of comparisons is of interest. The child from a broken home evinces a sense of insecurity concerning the future more often than does the child from a normal home.

In answering the question "Do you think you will be able to get along all right after leaving here?" nearly 90 per cent of the children from normal homes answered yes. Only 70 per cent of the children from broken homes said yes. In other words, more than a quarter of the children from broken homes indicated an uncertainty as to whether or not they would be able to get along after they left the institutions, as compared with 10 per cent of the children who were to return to normal homes. In both categories only a very small minority were quite sure that they would not be able to get along after they were to return to their communities.

The responses to the question "Why do you think you first got into trouble?" are also illuminating. It is interesting to compare the replies given by the girls at Hudson with those given by the boys at Jamesburg. Identical proportions among the two groups answered that dislike of school was what they thought had first caused their trouble. It is also interesting that between 36 per cent of the boys and 40 per cent of the girls stated that they got into trouble because they had been seeking excitement and fun.

In 1937 only 3 per cent of the Jamesburg boys wanted excitement and only 6 per cent said they got into trouble through seeking fun, or a total of 9 per cent.

Speculation about the reasons for this can be continued indefinitely. Does it reflect the temper of the times?—the present being one of tension in which excitement and thrills represent the acme of pleasure as against the more relaxed atmosphere prevailing in 1937. This study, of course, cannot hope to answer these questions, but it may stimulate professional research.

One surprising difference between boys and girls is shown by the fact that 13 per cent of the Jamesburg boys in 1954, 11 in 1937, said that they got into trouble because they wanted luxuries; and that despite popular opinion that girls are more luxury-loving than boys, less than 6 per cent of the girls said that they got into trouble for that reason.

The findings on the question of where the delinquent children get their ideas about how to do the things that cause them to end up in training schools are pretty consistent over the years, with two important exceptions. The percentage of children who got into trouble by learning from older boys or girls has remained about the same; but there has been a marked drop in the proportion who say they learn these things from their contemporaries. There has also been a drop in the number who say they learned them from adults.

The declining significance of the movies in contemporary life is indicated by the fact that in 1937, 38 per cent of the delinquent children said that they got their ideas from movies, as against 6.7 per cent of the Jamesburg boys in 1954 and only 2.9 per cent of the girls at Hudson. Radio, television, newspapers, magazines, comics, etc. are mentioned by relatively small numbers of delinquent boys and girls as important influences.

In summary, Mr. MacNeil makes these observations and recommendations:

We believe that the facts which this study brings out about the disorganization in the family, in the school, and in the community, as far as these children in the training schools are concerned, can be utilized preventively. An average of two out of three of the children studied in 1954 come from broken homes, the majority of which are not broken by death, or yet by divorce. They are homes which are broken by desertion; they are the homes, perhaps, of parents who have never gone through the formality of marriage.

Does not the costliness to society, as well as the tragic experiences which these children have undergone, justify the demand to expand

and strengthen community services which will help keep families together?

Very few of the children questioned in this study had undergone treatment, or even diagnosis, at the hands of a child guidance clinic before they came to the attention of the court. Community clinics in this field are needed in far greater number than is, to date, furnished by any state or locality. This kind of research can help to explain that need to the community, to make people see at least the possibility of doing a better job in redirecting attitudes, and solving emotional problems that prevent so many children from living and growing as normal members of the community. The findings also indicate the desperate need for strengthening our recreation resources.

In short, studies of this kind lend the support of fact to community ventures in areas in which too many decisions in the past have been made on the basis of emotional reactions to specific crises.

Our task now is to insure that the facilities and skills, that we already know can help to develop healthy personalities, be made available promptly and effectively for the many children who now fail to receive this guidance.

Teamwork among community agencies is an essential, and we believe that this teamwork needs to be applied at two different levels, which might be termed policy and practice levels. First, we need sound community planning, bringing the school, the government, the charitable facilities of the community, and its health, welfare, recreation, and mental hygiene forces together in some form of a community council. This is what some of our New Jersey legislation—such as the enabling act on Municipal Youth Guidance Councils—is designed to promote. Through planning at the policy level, we can make sure that everything possible is done to create a favorable climate for dealing with our children.

Secondly, for children who begin to manifest indications of disordered behavior, we also need a somewhat different kind of coordination. We need an interdisciplinary committee or council which will meet regularly and exchange information and ideas about children in the early stages of delinquency or, for that matter, emotional disability manifested in other ways. On this level of action, the principal, the school psychologist, the school social worker—if there is one—the policeman who handles delinquency problems, the case worker from the community family society or child welfare agency, should actually work out what each agency can do as a member of the community team.

It has always seemed to me that the more people understand about what kind of children become delinquents, what kind of homes they come from, what kind of difficulties they have had in school, what kind of opportunities they have had for associating with their peers and for participating in community affairs in general, the more understanding can be applied to community planning of a constructive nature. Concomitantly, the more easily will the need for diversified facilities to care for the atypical child gain acceptance.

About the Author

BENJAMIN FINE, Education Editor of *The New York Times,* has always been actively concerned with the welfare of America's youth. A series of his articles on the teaching of American history in our public schools won the *Times* the Pulitzer Prize in 1944 "for meritorious public service." Dr. Fine has been a member of the *Times* staff since 1937, serving first as education reporter for four years. In 1941 he was made Education Editor. That same year he received his doctorate in education at Columbia University. Dr. Fine has received many other degrees, as well as awards and citations, among them The Education Writers Association award for national reporting, the George Polk Memorial Award "for outstanding reporting in the field of education," and the Medal of Merit, Pi Delta Epsilon, for distinguished service to the fields of education and journalism.

In addition to serving on the *Times* staff, Dr. Fine teaches and lectures at various colleges and schools, and has written a total of eight books on education.